A Big Picture of Heaven and Hell

.

A Big Picture of Heaven and Hell

Near Death Experiencers and Christian Mystics

Andrew S. Park
Foreword by Howard Storm

Unless otherwise noted, Scripture quotations are from New Revised Standard Version of the Bible, 1989 by the Division of Christian Education of the National Council of the Churches of Christ in the U.S.A. are used by permission.

CreateSpace Independent Publishing Platform
North Charleston, South Carolina
ISBN 13: 9781984378101
ISBN: 1984378104

Dedication

I dedicate this book to my adored spouse Sunok Jane Myong who is my best friend and my true partner in every aspect of my life. She heartily supported this project with her prayers, encouragements, and technical assistance.

Table of Contents

Acknowledgement

I TRULY THANK God for making the publication of this book possible. It is my earnest desire that God will be understood better and honored by the publication of this book.

My sincere gratitude goes to Howard Storm who read the manuscript and pointed out several significant aspects of the writing with his own experiences and even wrote the foreword of this book. I would like to convey my heartfelt gratitude to Dr. Randy Clark for reading a draft and giving me invaluable suggestions and writing a strong endorsement. I would like to express my grateful heart to Dr. Jeffrey Long for his generous heart, helpful words, and for his kind endorsement. I sincerely thank Dr. Rolland Baker of Mozambique who suggested writing on heaven and hell to me. My deep gratitude also goes to Rev. Lynn Labs who volunteered to read the manuscript and edited it with superb comments and sharp insights. I truly thank Mr. Barry Gannon who attentively edited this work for me with good and helpful suggestions. I sincerely appreciate my former students who helped the writing of this project at United Theological Seminary; Rev. Chad Clark read the entire manuscript with his excellent editing and formatting skills. Rev. Lucretia Campbell, Rev. Gregg Heminger, and Rev. Daniel Mershon have done their wonderful research work for the project.

I also thank God for our great sons Amos and Thomas Park who supported and helped me to write this book by cheerfully listening to my stories of near-death experiences and heaven and hell.

Foreword

ANDREW PARK IS both a theologian and a pastor that is the basis for this book. He is a Doctor of Theology, Professor at a major Methodist Seminary, and Pastor of churches. His experience has been global, academic, and in the front line trenches of the church. There is a sea change taking place in Christianity today which is disturbing the complacency of the universal Christian church. All serious Christians are seeking ways to regain the hearts and minds of the great "unsaved masses" that were once members of the church and supported the moral and theological assumptions that were heralded as Christian doctrine. The trend for distrust for authority is one major factor but there may be a deficiency in the way the truth and message of Jesus Christ are being presented has lost the Spirit that wins souls. This book is presenting a path to recapture the Spirit of Christ as revealed in the Gospels and as Christ is revealing Himself to us today. Andrew Park has breathed light and love into a world that has suffocated on doctrinal legalisms. These obstructions to the Spirit are bases on a tradition of intellectual authoritarianism that sought to enlighten and save the illiterate masses for two millennia. Such an effort might have worked in the past but does not speak to a population that has access to the entire body of knowledge and information at their fingertips through the World Wide Web.

The church is in a precipitous decline in the world where the materialism of the economic development and the skepticism of scientism have convinced the majority of the people of the irrelevance of the church. In the still de-veloping parts of the world, the church is growing at a surprising rate. The apparent difference is in the developing world the church addresses the needs of the people directly. This openness and use of charismatic gifts and per-sonal testimony have become powerful tools of evangelism. These tools of healing, miracles, and testimonies were the very same tools of evangelism Jesus used in the Gospels. In the dying churches in the developed world healings, miracles, and testimonies are often viewed as an embarrassment to the educated church members. Andrew Park does not tell us how we should do church in this book. What is professed is an openness to the Spirit of Christ as it is being revealed in our time within and beyond the institu-tion of the church. If we are wedded to a rigid set of dogmas this book will be threatening. If we want to reclaim the Spirit of Christ Jesus before the church ossified the Spirit this book will be living waters.

There is no doubt in my mind that Andrew Park is preparing the way for a revival in the church and He speaks to the world today knowledgeable but unencumbered by the weight of our beautiful tradition. He is a Holy Spirit-filled theologian. He is a radical believer in Jesus Christ and has the ability to articulate the truth as it has been revealed to him.

Reverend Howard Storm, former atheistic professor and the author of *My Descent to Death*

Introduction

My BELOVED FATHER-IN-LAW was a faithful elder in a Presbyterian church (USA) in the Orange County, CA. Influenced by several skeptical authors, this former university professor denied the existence of heaven,hell, and angels and strongly argued against my writing of this book. In 2015, he had strokes. As he approached his near death, he met his deceased brother and other relatives in his dreams. More surprisingly, an angel appeared to him, told him about heaven and hell, and encouraged him to sing hymns. After these supernatural experiences, he enjoyed daily singing hymns with the family with his silent motions and in tears, accepted the existence of heaven and hell, and passed into the next life in the joy of hymn singing.

During my college freshman year, I had an out-of-body experience and was confused by it. After that, I was fascinated by out-of-body and near-death experiences. The following year I had a spiritual experience of the Holy Spirit. That was a turning point in my life. Since then, I have read books written by mystics such as Thomas á Kempis, Sundar Singh, and Emanuel Swedenborg. So near-death experiencers' and mystics' understanding of heaven and hell have naturally converged at my thought and teaching.

In 2010, after reading Rob Bell's *Love Wins,* my friend Dr. Rolland Baker of Mozambique suggested that I should write on heaven and hell. Since then, I have been working on the issues of near-death experience and heaven and hell. This book is the fruit of his suggestion.

Every life on earth is precious. No one lives forever on earth. We are going to expire. Do we really know what is waiting for us after death? Nowadays near-death experiencers (NDErs) briefly undergo their transitory lives after death and tell us about their own experiences. Also, Christian mystics have told us what would happen after life. This book intends to draw a holistic picture of heaven and hell, integrating resources from the Bible, near-death experiences (NDEs), and

Christian mystics. Exploring the reality of heaven and hell, however, does not mean escaping from the reality of this life, but rather signifies to engage in this life with more energy to live out our true meaning of this life.

Agnostics and atheists usually deny the existence of heaven and hell. Brilliant scientists such as Stephen Hawkin and Richard Dawkins have publicly defended their atheistic beliefs and the conviction of no next life. Since Dr. Raymond Moody published his first near-death experience book, *Life After Life* in 1975, most near-death experiencers (NDErs) have told their stories of the glimpse of the next life.

On the one hand, many of these NDErs experienced God's incredibly unconditional love and the wonderful heaven so that they might be unable to think of such loving God creating hell and discard the idea of the reality of hell. Some religious people reject the existence of hell on the same ground.

On the other hand, other NDERs, most Christians, and Christian mystics uphold the existence of both heaven and hell. Regarding the reasons for the existence of hell, most Christians and Christian mystics diverge from each other. We will unfold this matter in detail later.

This book covers the following:

Chapter 1: Are there any scientific evidence of the existence of the next life?

After engaging with the ideas of prominent atheists such as Stephen Hawking and Richard Dawkins, this chapter presents scientific research for the existence of the life after life, God, and the existence of our consciousness independent of the mind (brain) and the body. It includes such shared near-death experiences of the dying and their intimate folks, near-death experiences of a woman born blind, Carl Jung, and an aneurism patient with no blood in the body. Their NDEs are scientifically verifiable.

Chapter 2: Is there any empirical evidence of the existence of heaven?

In this chapter, we look into extraordinary NDEs of orthopedic surgeon Mary Neal, Brain surgeon Eben Alexander, businessman Jeff Olson, and skeptical scientist Nancy Reynes. Their testimonies empirically authenticate the existence of heaven. After their NDEs, their worldviews and priorities of life have drastically been shifted.

Chapter 3: How can our loving God send some people to hell?

In this chapter, we will examine whether God sends God's children to hell. In reality, people choose their own destinies and God allows the most comfortable space for rebellious children after this life (e.g. the prodigal son). Consequently, hell exists because of God's love for God's defiant children.

Chapter 4: Is there any empirical evidence of Hell?

This chapter recounts the experiences of hell of diverse NDErs. Hell's torments were super-real to them. Most NDErs of hell have shared their sharp torments in it. After receiving their second chances to live, they have drastically changed their lifestyles and have borne noticeable fruits of their near-death experiences.

Chapter 5: Children's Near–Death and Mystical Experiences

This chapter presents children's near-death experiences and their significance, including those of Todd Burpo, Abraham Lincoln, Albert Einstein, and Akiane Kramarik. Their stories reveal amazing aspects of NDEs adult NDEs cannot.

Chapter 6: What Would Happen to Suicides?

Near-death experiencers of suicide share their different experiences of heaven or hell. In this chapter, we will unravel the destinies of the five types of suicides and the reasons for their returns to this life.

Chapter 7: What a Big Picture of Heaven and Hell Does Emanuel Swedenborg Draw?

This chapter explores mystic Emanuel Swedenborg's understanding of the next life. His picture of the next life is far-reaching, enlightening, and profound. As far as I know, no one has ever described heaven, hell, and the intermediary world of spirits more clearly and extensively than Swedenborg. Along with the insights of NDErs, we will deal with his breathtaking understanding of the life after life.

Chapter 8: What a big Picture of the Afterlife Does Sundar Singh Depict?

Based on his profound personal encounters with Jesus, Sundar Singh portrayed heaven and hell with his amazing stories. This Christ-like missionary to Tibet shares his version of heaven, hell, and the world of spirits with his extraordinary, astonishing, and insightful stories.

Conclusion

Christian eschatology (death or the end of the world) is not about the end of life or the end of this world but is about the beginning of the new life and the new world. A much more beautiful and love-filled world is waiting for us. God loves even those who refuse God and opt out of their lives in heaven and allows rooms for them.

Once started, our life never ends. Each of us needs first to live through this valley of the shadow of sorrows, tears, suffering, and death. We are here on earth only to learn how to love others with the unconditional love of God and how to grow in the wisdom and understanding of God.

The more we love God, the wiser we become. The more intimately we walk with God, the more loving we become. The more fully we surrender to God, the more joy-filled we become.

Appendix 1 delves into what the Bible says about heaven, hell, and universal salvation. Will God save all human beings or annihilate some in the end? I will share different views and my own view.

Appendix 2 examines why more people experience heaven than hell during their NDEs. The estimated incidence of negative or hellish NDEs has ranged from 1% to 15% of all NDEs. One of the four reasons is that many NDErs mistake the intermediate world of spirits for heaven. Another is due to the seduction of evil spirits. The spiritual world is much more vast and complex than this world.

CHAPTER 1

Is There Any Scientific Evidence of the Next Life?

ALTHOUGH HE BELIEVES that our scientific mind is able to do a lot of things, world-renowned physicist Steven Hawking thinks that we are simply mechanical parts of the grand computer of the universe. He says: "There is no heaven or afterlife for broken-down computers; that is a fairy story for people afraid of the dark."[1] He contends that like a computer, the human brain is will stop working when its parts crash. Hawking gives a tantalizing answer regarding our survival after physical death. "I think the brain is like a program in the mind, which is like a computer. So it's theoretically possible to copy the brain onto a computer, and so provide a form of life after death."[2] However, just when we imagine Hawking may share a theory of how this could be done, he leaves our hopes dashed, explaining that such a possibility is way beyond our present capabilities. Hawking claimed in his book *The Grand Design* that God is *unnecessary* to create the universe given the existence of physical laws such as gravity.[3] He argued further in *Curiosity* that God had made no universe because no time existed before the big bang. Consequently, he is certain that there is no god since there is no need for god's creation of the universe.[4]

> When people ask me if a god created the universe, I tell them that the question itself makes no sense. Time didn't exist before the big bang, so there is no time for god to make the universe in. It's like asking directions to the edge of the earth; The Earth is a sphere; it doesn't have an edge; so looking for it is a futile exercise. We are each free to believe what we want, and it's my view that the simplest

explanation is; there is no god. No one created our universe, and no one directs our fate. This leads me to a profound realization; there is probably no heaven, and no afterlife either. We have this one life to appreciate the grand design of the universe, and for that I am extremely grateful.[5]

During Richard Dawkins' appearance on Jon Stewart's Daily Show, Stewart asked the prominent Oxford biologist about life after death. Dawkins answered, "I don't *know* what happens to us but I know that our consciousness is wrapped up in our brains and I know that our brains rot."[6] Our survival beyond our deaths is similar to magical thinking to him. Dawkins reasoned that there is "something beyond us; there are many things we don't understand, but the particular thing of surviving our own death (is) palpable wishful thinking that goes against everything we understand about how the nervous system works . . . we are apes, we are African apes."[7] Toward the end of the interview, Dawkins restated that although he was not 100 percent certain, he was pretty sure that there is "nothing" after death.[8]

Dr. Susan Blackmore is a freelance writer, lecturer, and broadcaster, and a Visiting Professor at the University of Plymouth. She identifies herself as an "ally of Naturalism" and "a Distinguished Supporter of Atheism.[9] She is one of the most articulate naturalists who oppose the idea of near-death experiences (NDEs) and a next life. In her book *Dying to Live*, Blackmore lays down several major points of her "dying brain" hypothesis.[10] Here are three of them. First, natural means such as drugs, dreams, and oxygen deficiency can generate each of the elements of the NDE. Second, since the feeling of peace and joy may be produced by natural opiates generated by the body during extreme stress, the dying brain hypothesis suggests ways that each element of an NDE might occur naturalistically during a near-death event. Third, if our unconscious brain can see events happening in the operating room, such evidence, she admits, will confirm the spiritual hypothesis, debunking her dying brain hypothesis. She states that no such compelling evidence, however, has been provided during NDEs.[11]

Another denier of NDEs and the next life is Dr. Nelson, a professor of neurology at the University of Kentucky with more than three decades of experience examining spiritual sensation. Using the research of Dr. Thomas Lempert's team on fainting and the NDE, Nelson comes to his conclusion that fainting and NDE are not much different: "Lempert's team compared the experience of their subjects to Moody's descriptions of the near-death experience. Surprisingly, they found *no real difference* between the two types of experience. To these investigations, fainting in the laboratory and a near-death experience in crisis looked about the same."[12] The differences, however, exist. For instance, a third of the fainters "heard sounds, such as rushing, roaring (a typical aspect of near-death experiences), screaming, and human voices."[13] Dr. Raymond Moody, however, says clearly that NDErs did not hear audible sounds.[14]

Facing these deniers of NDEs and the next life, there are those physicians who scientifically and empirically endeavor to corroborate the existence of a consciousness independent of the brain and of the next life. Let us examine their claims. Before we do that, though, we need to define the meaning of science. Science means "Knowledge or understanding acquired by study; acquaintance with or mastery of any branch of learning"[15] or "the systematic study of the structure and behavior of the natural and physical world, or knowledge obtained about the world by watching it carefully and experimenting".[16] So, when using the term *science*, I mean mainly medical science. Thus, medical science denotes medical knowledge attained by careful medical observations and repeated medical experiments.

Dr. Raymond Moody (author of *Life After Life*), Dr. Michael Sabom (faculty of Emory University Medical School), and Dr. Pim van Lommel (a world-renowned Dutch cardiologist) are primary NDE researchers who seriously considered naturalistic and rationalistic explanations but eventually found them inadequate. All of them have used scientific methods to examine NDEs. Dr. Moody proved the reality of life after life through shared NDEs.[17] Dr. van Lommel embarked on a twenty- year scientific study of near-death experiences. With several other scientific NDE researchers,[18] they have validated that there is the next life beyond this life. Dr. Sabom has scientifically documented the existence of the spirit through the experiences of NDErs.[19] Let us check what scientific data they have collected.

Raymond Moody

Moody grew up in a non-religious home where his atheist father held the idea of an afterlife in contempt. His father was a surgeon and would be agitated at the simple discussion of religion, considering it "institutionalized superstition or worse."[20] Even to Moody, an afterlife didn't look like "a live option" at that time.[21] But while studying philosophy at the University of Virginia, he went to hear Dr. George Richie, a respected psychiatry professor, who had been pronounced dead and later come back to life, telling of an incredible experience on the other side of death.[22] This was the lecture that turned Moody to his NDE research.

His first book *Life After Life* initiated the study of so-called "near death experience," the term he coined. In the book, he says that lots of readers "will find the claims made in this book incredible and whose first reaction will be to dismiss them out of hand."[23] He comments further that he himself would have done the same only a few years ago.[24] Nevertheless, his interviews with the subjects both challenged and changed him.

As we have already seen, critics of NDEs believe that an NDE is caused by the lack of oxygen in an individual's brain. Here Moody tries to dispute that hypothesis by providing NDE cases that are not individual but shared.

SHARED NDE

Since the publications of *Life After Life* and *Reflection on Life After Life*, numerous people have contacted Dr. Moody each year to share the unexpected things they underwent when they were near-death or when someone dear to them passed on. *Glimpses of Eternity* reports a common experience of family members and friends when their beloved has passed on. They have drifted into the first transitional moments of their loved ones' otherworldly journey. Dr. Moody named such a common experience as "shared death experience."[25] Some reported that they accompanied their departing ones halfway to heaven. A whole family gathered around their loved one and witnessed a bright light from an unknown origin. A woman disclosed her participation in the review of her husband's life including events unknown to her. *Glimpses of Eternity* is the first book to report on the spiritual interconnectedness of different people in certain NDEs. This shared experience of death tells us that NDE is not just a phenomenon happening due to an oxygen-deprived person's hallucination.[26] It confirms that NDE can happen to a normal person due to their empathy and sympathy with the dying. Such a phenomenon cannot be easily dismissed as a hallucination since two or more people independently experienced the same thing. Here are some incidents of shared NDE.

JAMIESON

After publishing *Life After Life,* Dr. Moody received a lot of comments and inquiries about NDEs. One day he was standing at the school's magazine stand, reading an article. Then a sophisticated woman approached him and shook hands with him, saying "Raymond, I'm Dr. Jamieson."[27] She was an esteemed member of the faculty and wanted to talk about her extraordinary experience with her mother's passing. Two years ago, her mother had a cardiac arrest at home and she happened to be visiting her mother at that very time. She had to perform CPR on her mother in spite of her own uncomfortable feeling. About thirty minutes later, she stopped performing the futile CPR because her mother was dead. While resting, suddenly she had an out- of- body experience, in which she watched her mother's body and her own body from above. More surprisingly she realized her mother was hovering with her in spirit form. She calmly bid goodbye to her mother, who was smiling and truly happy. Dr. Jamieson witnessed something more surprising when she looked in the corner of the room; a breach in the universe filled with outpouring light in which she saw people she had known for years, deceased friends of her mother, and other unknown people. As she was watching, her mother glided into the light in a very joyful reunion with all of her friends.[28] After this, "the tube closed down in an almost spiral fashion, like a camera lens, and the light was gone."[29] This was the first shared near-death experience Dr. Moody had heard of.

THE ANDERSON FAMILY

In metropolitan Atlanta, a mother was dying after an extended illness and her three children and a daughter-in-law were at their mother's bedside. "Suddenly, a bright light appeared in the room," a daughter recalled. The lights were extraordinary and unlike "any kind of light on this earth. I nudged my sister to see if she saw it too, and when I looked at her, her eyes were as big as saucers . . . . I saw my brother literally gasp. Everyone saw it together and for a little while we were frightened."[30] Before their eyes, lights formed themselves into an entranceway. Then their mother passed. They saw their mother "lift up out of her body and go through that entranceway."[31] Coming out of her body, their mother departed through the passage in a feeling of ecstatic joy. "Being by the entranceway, incidentally, was a feeling of complete joy. My brother called it a chorus of joyful feelings, and my sister heard beautiful music, although none of the rest of us did."[32] All four children concurred that the entranceway looked like the Natural Bridge in the Shenandoah Valley.[33]

KARL SKALA

A vivid story of a shared NDE by renowned German poet Karl Skala during World War II is told in the book *Parting Visions* written by Dr. Melvin Morse. "He and his best friend were huddled together in a foxhole during an artillery bombardment. The shells hit closer and closer until one finally hit close to Skala's friend and killed him. Karl felt his friend slump forward into his arms and go limp with death."[34] Then an inexplicable thing happened to Skala. He said that he felt himself being drawn up with his friend, above their bodies and then above the battlefield. Skala could look down and see himself holding his friend. Then he looked up and saw a bright light and felt himself going toward it with his friend. Then he stopped and returned to his body. He was uninjured except for a hearing loss that resulted from the artillery blast.[35]

SUSAN'S SON

Of all the recurring aspects of the shared NDEs, the joint review of the life of the beloved is the most surprising. Susan (an alias) told Dr. Moody the sad yet extraordinary story of her adult son's death from cancer.[36] As her son died and went up to a cloud, she was taken up there with him and reviewed various scenes from his life. They were familiar scenes to her, particularly from his childhood to teenage years. Some other scenes were unknown to her, "like those from what she called 'his private years.'"[37] Although she avoided elaborating on those scenes, she stated clearly, "I wasn't embarrassed in the least by anything I saw."[38] Dr. Moody was stunned by Susan's shared NDE due to the fact that her new information was so specific and accurate for her to be able to verify it. When she checked everything out, she could identify the unknown friends and visit the places of the shared scenes.[39]

CARL JUNG

While his contemporary psychologist Sigmund Freud asserted that the need to commune with God is neurotic, Carl Jung believed that such a need was completely natural and not neurotic.[40] He underwent an NDE in 1944 and had an opportunity to examine his own beliefs and the meaning of his existence. He shared his experience and inner thoughts in his autobiography, *Memories, Dreams, and Reflection*. The NDE must have been a turning point in his life, an occasion of soul-searching:

> At the beginning of 1944 I broke my foot, and this misadventure was followed by a heart attack. In a state of unconsciousness I experienced deliriums and visions which must have begun when I hung on the edge of death and was being given oxygen and camphor injections. The images were so tremendous that I myself concluded that I was close to death. My nurse afterward told me, "It was as if you were surrounded by a bright glow" That was a phenomenon she had sometimes observed in the dying, she added. I had reached the outermost limit, and do not know whether I was in a dream or an ecstasy. At any rate, extremely strange things began to happen to me . . . This experience gave me a feeling of extreme poverty, but at the same time of great fullness. There was no longer anything I wanted or desired. I existed in an objective form; I was what I had

been and lived. At first the sense of annihilation predominated, of having been stripped or pillaged; but suddenly that became of no consequence.

Everything seemed to be past; what remained was a fait accompli, without any reference back to what had been. There was no longer any regret that something had dropped away or been taken away. On the contrary: I had everything that I was, and that was everything.

In reality, a good three weeks were still to pass before I could truly make up my mind to live again. I could not eat because all food repelled me . . . . And now I should have to convince myself all over again that this was important! Life and the whole world struck me as a prison, and it bothered me beyond measure that I should again be finding all that quite in order. I had been so glad to shed it all, and now it had come about that I—along with everyone else—would again be hung up in a box by a thread.[41]

After the NDE, Jung became a devout believer. The NDE gave him an empty feeling regarding worldly matters and offered him the feeling of enrichment toward the purpose of his existence. He became "a great observer and certainly a believer in our ability to communicate with the other side."[42] This inconceivable experience caused him to say that it was wholly normal to think of life after life and not irrational and neurotic at all. Instead, to him, those who try to push thoughts of the afterlife and God out of their minds are neurotic.[43] Furthermore, just around the time that Jung had a shared death experience with one of his wife's cousins, he said, "The unconscious psyche believes in life after death."[44]

I dreamed that my wife's bed was a deep pit with stonewalls. It was a grave, and somehow had a suggestion of classical antiquity about it. Then I heard a deep sigh, as if someone were giving up the ghost. A figure that resembled my wife sat up in the pit and floated upward. It wore a white gown into which curious black symbols were woven.

I awoke, roused my wife, and checked the time. It was three o'clock in the morning. The dream was so curious that I thought at once that it might signify a death. At seven o'clock came the news that a cousin of my wife had died at three o'clock in the morning."[45]

It was very normal to Jung that we have the ability to communicate with God.[46] Jung stated in his essay "that at least part of the psyche is not subject to the laws of space and time."[47] A complete view of the world would require another dimension, he wrote; then and only then could life be given a "unified explanation."[48] Jung pointed out the limit of the rationalists who push everything into the confined categories of time and space: "Hence it is that the rationalists insist to this day that parapsychological experiences do not really exist; for their world-view stands or falls by this question. If such phenomena occur at all, the rationalistic picture of the universe is invalid, because incomplete . . . we must face the fact that our world, with its time, space, and causality, relates to another order of things lying behind or beneath it, in which neither 'here and there' nor 'earlier and later' are of importance." Pointing to "a relativity of space and time," he released our consciousness from narrow worldviews of the rationalists.[49]

These shared NDEs point to the reality that the NDE is not caused by lack of oxygen since healthy sympathizers experienced the NDE. Because of repeated shared experiences, they are not isolated incidents and can be considered to be scientifically verifiable. As far as I know, no atheist or skeptic has attempted to debunk the supernatural events of shared NDEs.

Kenneth Ring and Sharon Cooper

Kenneth Ring and Sharon Cooper[50] published a groundbreaking article "Near-Death and Out-of-Body Experiences in the Blind: A Study of Apparent Eyeless Vision" in the Journal of Near-Death Studies about the blind.[51] They reported the outcomes of an investigation into near-death and out-of-body experiences in thirty-one blind respondents in the article. They raised three main questions to them: (1) whether they had NDEs and, if they did, whether their experiences and those of sighted persons were the same or different; (2) whether they ever claimed that they were able to see during NDEs and out-of-body experiences (OBEs); and (3) if such claims were affirmed, whether they could ever be substantiated by reference to objective evidence.[52]

Vicki Noratuk

One of the blind NDErs is Vicky Noratuk. Her previous name was Vicky Umipeg.

Vicky Noratuk was born in Pasadena, California in December 1950. She became blind shortly after birth, for her optic nerve was completely destroyed due to an excess of oxygen she received in the incubator. She had never seen light, shadows, or anything at all. So she has no visual images when she dreams. She underwent two NDEs, one at the age of twelve and the other at the age of twenty-two. The first NDE was caused by appendicitis. During that time, she *saw* Jesus who told her to go back home because her mother was crying for her.[53]

During her second NDE, Vicki could see more clearly than during her first NDE without her physical eyes. Vicki told Dr. Ring, who interviewed her with Sharon Cooper,[54] that she found herself floating above her body in the emergency room of a hospital after an automobile accident. From her elevated position near the ceiling, she *saw* a male doctor and a female nurse working on her body. She knew that the body below her was hers because she was not in her own body.[55] She was able to identify some of her own physical features proving that the body she was watching was surely her own: "I think I was wearing the plain gold band on my right ring finger and my father's wedding ring next to it. But my wedding ring I definitely saw . . . . That was the one I noticed the most because it's most unusual. It has orange blossoms on the corners of it."[56] As her testimony implies, there is something remarkable and astounding about Vicki's recollection of these visual impressions, for this NDE was the only time she could ever relate to seeing and to what light was like through her experience.

During her out-of-body experience, Vicki found herself ascending through the ceilings of the hospital until she reached above the roof of the building where she could *see* a brief panoramic view of her surroundings. And then she was sucked into a dark tube, moving toward the light. When she arrived at the opening of the tube, she "rolled out" onto the grass while listening to music that changed into hymns. Surrounded by trees and flowers and a vast number of people, Vicki recognized specific acquaintances who welcomed her to the place. They were Diane and Debbie, Vicki's blind schoolmates who had died at ages six and eleven, respectively. Whereas they had both been severely physically impeded as well as being blind and being hurt by classmates, there they emerged bright and beautiful, healthy, loving, and very much alive "in their prime" instead of remaining as children. Next, Vicki met Mr. and Mrs. Zilk. Mrs. Zilk was an elderly next-door neighbor who babysat her when her grandmother had to work. She was a really sweet person. Lastly, Vicki encountered her grandmother who had virtually raised Vicki and who had died two years before this incident. While meeting these precious persons, Vicki used no actual words but had feelings of welcome and love.[57] Later, Jesus visited her and gently asked her to go back to learn and teach others to love and to forgive more and so she reluctantly came back to this life.[58]

Since that experience, Vicki suffered an attack by a stranger. The stranger tried to murder her. She asked for Jesus' help. Jesus said, "Pray out aloud." So she prayed out aloud, "God, bless this man. Help him realize this is not the way he'd treat people." And he couldn't handle it and said, "Why don't you fight with me? Then I can put you asleep pretty easily." It was an attempted rape and strangulation. She replied, "I hate what you've done to me, but I love you as a child of God." "Stop it, Stop! You remind me of my momma taking me to Sunday school. May be there you belong." Then he wept, wept, and wept. I am sorry, Oh God! What I've done. I am sorry." Then he let her go.[59]

Ring and Cooper examined other cases of the blind seeing during their NDEs.

Their findings disclosed that the blind share typical elements of NDEs with the sighted: that most of the blind confirm that they can see during their NDEs and OBEs; and that sometimes claims of visually-based knowledge that could not have been acquired by the usual means can be independently verified. Through these presentations and evaluations they arrived at an interpretation based on the concept of transcendental consciousness beyond physical consciousness.[60]

The reality of life after life may be scientifically upheld by the fact that those who are blind from birth can have full visual near-death experiences, not fragmented visual experiences. Furthermore, Dr. Jeffrey Long's massive quantity of qualitative data and careful analyses support the scientific evidence of the authenticity of NDEs.[61]

Michael Sabom

Dr. Michael Sabom is a cardiologist, who once despised non-scientific explanations for any paranormal phenomena, including near-death experiences. In the first part of his book, he stated: "Unscientific—that I would never be."[62] One Sunday morning, at the adult Sunday school class of his local Methodist church, psychiatric social worker Sarah Kruetziger presented on Dr. Raymond Moody's book, *Life After Life*. Being the only physician in the class, he was asked for his opinion at the end of the class. The kindest thing he could say at that time was "I don't believe it."[63]

Being skeptical of Moody's claims, Sabom decided to investigate them by doing his own scientific research. The way he conducted his research has advanced the field of NDE reports:

- He interviewed the subjects as soon as possible after the event, often in the hospital.
- He checked patient records and personally interviewed patients to rule out psychiatric problems.
- He verified claims of veridical perception with a control group, medical records, family, and attending doctors and nurses.
- He considered possible ulterior motives for sharing their experiences. Are they a bit too eager to share? Are they searching for attention?[64]

Dr. Sabom remains an innate skeptic and devotee of science. He avows to be scientific thoroughly and straightforwardly and would not believe anything without ~~sold~~ solid scientific facts.[65] He is an impeccable type of researcher of near-death experiences. His concluding remarks tell where his heart is: "My personal reaction to these events is not so much a 'scientifically weighted' response as it is a keenly felt identification with the tears of joy and sorrow that have accompanied the unfolding of many of these stories."[66] He realized after all that science does not mean a detached objective truth apart from our experiences of life. Using Einstein, he includes the Spirit in his understanding of scientific equations: "In short, my involvement in the lives and deaths of the people in this book has made me humble to the ways of the universe, much like Albert Einstein, who once wrote: "Everyone who is seriously involved in the pursuit of science becomes convinced that a Spirit is manifest in the Laws of the Universe—a Spirit vastly superior to that of man, and one in the face of which we, with our modest powers, must feel humble.'"[67] This Spirit is the ultimate key to our quest for the ineffable truth of NDEs.

In 1994, Sabom founded the Atlanta Study to launch the first comprehensive investigation of its kind on NDEs. It aimed at documenting life-and-death NDE dramas, which unfolded in hospital rooms, operating rooms, and simultaneous happenings, which were invisible to medical personnel but recounted with amazing clarity ~~lucidity~~ by almost fifty NDErs. From both medical and personal standpoints, he discloses the captivating stories of people from all walks of life and religious affiliations. He studies the clinical effect of the NDE on survival and healing and unveils surprising findings. He presents the impact of NDEs upon their experiencers. Sabom probes the clinical effect of the NDE on survival and shares surprising findings in the Atlanta Study in his latest book *Light and Death*.[68] He reexamines some common conclusions about NDEs. And in light of the Bible, he reflects and delves into the significance of near-death experiences.

On the one hand, he is concerned about certain NDE researchers such as Dr. Raymond Moody and Dr. Kenneth Ring who seem to be moving toward a direction that mixes NDE experiences with New Age beliefs. On the other, he reproves Dr. Maurice Rawlings who once bent the results of his research to support his conservative Christian beliefs.[69] Dr. Sabom upholds that NDEs are scientifically verifiable and confirm life after life, but that they must be viewed with discretion.

PAM REYNOLDS

Thirty-five-year-old Pam Reynolds was being operated on for a giant basilar artery aneurysm. A weakness in the wall of the large artery at the base of her brain had caused it to balloon out much like a bubble on the side of a defective automobile tire. Rupture of an aneurysm would be immediately fatal. The size and location of an aneurysm, however, precluded its safe removal using the standard neurosurgical techniques available to Pam in her hometown of Atlanta. She had been referred to Dr. Robert Spetzler, Director of Barrow Neurological Institute in Phoenix, Arizona. Spetzler had pioneered a daring surgical procedure known as hypothermic cardiac arrest, which would allow Pam's aneurysm to be excised with a reasonable chance of success. This operation, nicknamed "standstill" by the doctors who perform it, would require that her body temperature be lowered to sixty degrees, her heartbeat and breathing stopped, her brain waves flattened, and the blood drained from her head.[70] A nurse handed Spetzler the pneumatically powered Midas Rex. With the cutting tool, Spetzler began to carve out a sizable section of Pam's skull.[71] At this time, Pam began to undergo an NDE. She retold the story with extraordinary detail:

> The next thing I recall was the sound: It was a natural D. As I listened to the sound, I felt it was pulling me out of the top of my head. The further out of my body I got, the more clear the tone became. I had the impression it was like a road, a frequency that you go on . . . . I remember seeing several things in the operating room when I was looking down. It was the most aware that I think that I have ever been in my entire life . . . . I was metaphorically sitting on Dr. Spetzler's shoulder. It was not like normal vision. It was brighter and more focused and clearer than normal vision.[72]

She saw many instruments and people in the operating room that she could not recognize.[73] She thought the way they had her head shaved was very odd. She expected them to shave all of the hair, but they did not:

> The saw thing that I hated the sound of looked like an electric tooth-brush and it had a dent in it, a groove at the top where the saw appeared to go into the handle, but it didn't . . . . And the saw had interchangeable blades, too, but these blades were in what looked like a socket wrench case . . . . I heard the saw crank up. I didn't see them use it on my head, but I think I heard it being used on something. It was humming at a relatively high pitch and then all of a sudden it went Brrrrrrrrrr! like that.[74]

Dr. Robert Spetzler detached the bone flap from Pam's skull, revealing the outermost membrane of her brain, and opened the tough, fibrous covering with special scissors.[75] While Spetzler was opening Pam's head, a female cardiac surgeon found the femoral artery and vein in Pam's right groin. These vessels, however, ended up too small to handle the large flow of blood needed to feed the cardiopulmonary bypass machine. Thus, the left femoral artery and vein had to be prepared for this purpose. Pam later recollected this point in the surgery:[76] "Someone said something about my veins and arteries being very small. I believe it was a female voice and that it was Dr. Murray, but I'm not sure. She was the cardiologist [sic]."[77]

At 11:00 a.m. her core body temperature dropped twenty-five degrees Fahrenheit. A steady warning tone indicating cardiac malfunction interrupted the regular intermittent beeping of the cardiac monitor.[78] After twenty minutes, her core body temperature dropped another thirteen degrees to a tomblike sixty degrees Fahrenheit. The clicks from her ear speakers prompted no response. It was a total brain shutdown.[79]

At 11:25 a.m., the head of the operating table was tilted up, the cardiopulmonary bypass machine was switched off, and the blood was drained from Pam's body like the oil drain of a car.[80] Meantime Pam's NDE proceeded: "There was a sensation like being pulled, but not against your will. I was going on my own accord because I wanted to go . . . It was like the Wizard of Oz—being taken up in a tornado vortex, only you're not spinning around like you've got vertigo . . . It was like a tunnel but it wasn't a tunnel."[81] In the tunnel vortex she became ~~cognizant~~ aware of her grandmother calling her. But she didn't hear it with her ears. It was a clearer hearing without her ears. She trusted that sense more than that of her own ears. The feeling was that her grandmother wanted her to come to her, ~~so~~ so she continued going down the shaft without fear. It was a dark shaft that she passed through and at the end there was a tiny pinpoint of light that grew bigger and bigger: "The light was incredibly bright, like sitting in the middle of a light bulb. It was so bright that I put my hands in front of my face fully expecting to see them and I could not. But I knew they were there. Not from a sense of touch."[82]

She started to discern different figures in the light and they were all permeated and wrapped with light. They were light. They were her grandmother, Uncle Gene, great-great-Aunt Maggie, and her grandfather on Papa's side. They were taking care of her and looking after her in particular.[83] These people would not allow her to go further: "If I went all the way into the light something would happen to me physically. They would be unable to put this me back into the body me, like I had gone too far and they couldn't reconnect. So they wouldn't let me go anywhere or do anything. I wanted to go into the light, but I also wanted to come back. I had children to be reared."[84]

Her aneurysm sac with no blood was flattened like a balloon with no air. After clipping the neck of an aneurysm at its point of attachment to the basilar artery, Spetzler removed the empty sac. The cardiopulmonary bypass machine was switched back on and warm blood began to be refilled into Pam's empty body.[85]

Shortly after the warming had started, Pam's body appeared to be waking up, perhaps at a time during her near-death experience when she was being strengthened.[86] Her deceased relatives were feeding her. Doing this not through her mouth, but they were nourishing her with something sparkly: "I definitely recall the sensation of being nurtured and being fed and being made strong. I know it sounds funny because obviously it wasn't a physical thing, but inside the experience I felt physically strong, ready for whatever."[87]

Then, at noon, a serious problem occurred. The first silent heart monitor began to register the jumbled electrical activity of ventricular fibrillation. Efforts to correct this lethal cardiac rhythm with additional warming were unsuccessful. If uncorrected, this problem would kill Pam on the table within minutes. The cardiac surgeon quickly fixed this problem.[88] Pam began her "return" from her near-death experience:

> My grandmother didn't take me back through the tunnel, or even send me back or ask me to go. She just looked up at me. I expected to go with her, but it was communicated to me that she just didn't think she would do that. My uncle said he would do it. He's the one who took me back through the end of the tunnel. Everything was fine. I did want to go.[89]

When she regained her consciousness, she was still on the respirator. Spetzler's surgical report shows that at 2:10 p.m. the "patient was taken to the recovery room still incubated but in stable condition."[90]

In the world of academic debate, three clinical tests normally conclude brain death. First, a standard electroencephalogram (EEG) gauges brain-wave activity. A "flat" EEG signifies non-function of the cerebral cortex. Second, auditory evoked potentials gauge brain-stem viability. The absence of these potentials denotes non-function of the brain stem. Third, documentation of no blood flow to the brain exhibits a generalized absence of brain function. During "standstill," Pam's brain was found to be "dead" by all three clinical tests: the silence of her electroencephalogram, the absence of her brain-stem response, and no blood flow in her brain.[91]

Sabom's findings confirm four things about the NDE: "(1) it occurs in the realm of the spirit or soul and not in the physical realm; (2) it is essentially religious in nature and pertains to the things of religion that transcend the material world; (3) it is not amenable to scientific quantification—no instruments have ever detected and diagnosed an NDE; and (4) it is real, not imaginary or the product of a hallucination—experiencers strongly insist that NDEs are not just another dream."[92]

Pam's case in the Atlanta Study is extraordinary scientific evidence of NDE independent of the brain death. Her case is one of the strongest examples of verified substantiation in NDE research because of her ability to describe the unique surgical instruments, the surgical procedures used on her, and her ability to describe in detail these events while she was clinically brain dead.

Pim van Lommel

Dr. Pim van Lommel is a prominent Dutch cardiologist. He was a naturalist who denied any life beyond death. Being reared in a strictly academic environment, he could not accept any spiritual explanation of events and he believed that everything could be explained with reductionist and materialist answers.[93] Although he had not forgotten an unusual story told by a successfully resuscitated patient during his cardiac arrest in 1969, he had done nothing with it until he read George Ritchie's *Return from Tomorrow* in 1986. After having been "dead" for longer than nine minutes, Ritchie regained consciousness.[94] In addition, Raymond Moody published *Life After Life*. From 1986 van Lommel started systematically asking all of the patients at his outpatient clinic who had undergone so-called "near death experiences."[95] He had collected twelve cases from just over fifty cardiac arrest survivors for two years. Since then he had not heard any other reports because he had not been open to his patients. After all, he reasoned, it is impossible to experience consciousness when the heart stops beating.[96] ~~However, empirical~~ Scientific studies on NDEs, however, show phenomena that are not consistent with present scientific theories. Thus, for van Lommel, we must approach them with better ways of studying consciousness rather than denying, suppressing, or ridiculing the new facts.[97] While observing that clinically dead patients in a hospital cardiac wing who had been resuscitated tell about the other side, he started to reconsider his naturalistic assumptions. He learned from NDErs about their feeling that during their NDEs they experienced shaking off their bodies like old clothes, retaining their own identities, and feeling with their clear consciousness. It is important for doctors, nurses, and family members that we scientifically verify the out-of-body experience in order to recognize that it is real.[98] Here is the report of a nurse of a Coronary Care Unit Dr. van Lommel attained:

> During night shift an ambulance brings in a 44-year old cyanotic, comatose man into the coronary care unit. He was found in coma about 30 minutes before in a meadow. When we go to intubate the patient, he turns out to have dentures in his mouth. I remove these upper dentures and put them onto the "crash cart." After about an hour and a half the patient has sufficient heart rhythm and blood pressure, but he is still ventilated and intubated, and he is still coma-tose. He is transferred to the intensive care unit to continue the nec-essary artificial respiration. Only after more than a week do I meet again with the patient, who is by now back on the cardiac ward. The moment he sees me he says: "O, that nurse knows where my den-tures are." I am very surprised. Then he elucidates: "You were there when I was brought into hospital and you took my dentures out of my mouth and put them onto that cart, it had all these bottles on it and there was this sliding drawer underneath, and there you put my teeth." I was especially amazed because I remembered this happen-ing while the man was in deep coma and in the process of CPR. It appeared that the man had seen himself lying in bed, that he had per-ceived from above how nurses and doctors had been busy with the CPR. He was also able to describe correctly and in detail the small room in which he had been resuscitated as well as the appearance of those present like myself. He is deeply impressed by his experience and says he is no longer afraid of death.[99]

He knows that during the cardiac arrest the functioning of the brain and of other cells in the body halts because of an absence of oxygen, that the electromagnetic fields of our neurons and other cells depart, and that the possibility of resonance, the interface between consciousness and physical body, is disturbed.[100]

A number of NDErs have come back to life without damaging the quality of their consciousness. Consequently, Dr. van Lommel thinks that without a functioning brain, our consciousness would continue to function after this life, even though research on NDEs cannot offer us the unassailable scientific proof for such a conclusion because people with NDEs have not completely passed into the next life.[101] For him, such a conclusion of the continuity of consciousness independent of brain function "might well induce a huge change in the scientific paradigm in Western medicine, and could have practical implications in actual medical and ethical problems such as the care for comatose or dying patients, euthanasia, abortion, and the removal of organs for transplantation from somebody in the dying process with a beating heart in a warm body but a diagnosis of brain death."[102]

According to Dr. Peter Fenwick, concurrent recording of heart rate and brain output confirms that as the heart stops, the brainwaves go flat within eleven seconds. The flat electroencephalogram (EEG) signifies no brain activity during cardiac arrest and the high rate of brain damage afterward. They indicate that the unconsciousness in cardiac arrest is complete. No one can argue that there are fragments' of the brain that are working; there are not. The NDErs testify that their NDEs transpire during unconsciousness; the present medical science, however, upholds that this is impossible.[103] Our conclusion must be that either all NDErs are wrong or that our present medical science is limited in this field.

CHAPTER 2

Is There Any Experiential Evidence of Heaven?

Has anyone experienced heaven during a near-death experience? Many people have done so, some of them well-educated medical professionals. Their experiences give us an idea of what the afterlife may be like.

Mary Neal

Dr. Mary Neal is an orthopedic spine surgeon who drowned while kayaking on a river in Chile and had an NDE.[104] She was born and grew up in Michigan and graduated from the University of Kentucky before attending the UCLA medical school. With a love of outdoor adventure, Mary and her husband Bill had gone to Chile for a white-water kayaking vacation.[105] Their veteran guides were their good friends, Tom and Debbi Long, along with their sons.

One morning Bill experienced some back pain and decided to take the day off. He drove them to the put-in, found a nice place to read, and planned to meet them at the takeout after their kayaking.[106] The group paddled downriver, stopping at the eddy above the falls. There was a narrow channel to the right and a larger main channel to the left. The first boater paddled down the narrow channel on the right and got lodged between two rocks. Consequently, Mary had to go the main channel on the left that was treacherous. She took a deep breath and plunged 15 - 20 feet down the falls. Her kayak dove straight down. The force of the crushing water ripped the paddle from her hands. She smashed into some underwater rocks. Still upright, she was pinned and trapped underwater. Her kayak turned into her coffin.

Thinking of her family, she prayed: "God, I know you love me and have a plan for me. Thy will be done."[107] For the first time she sincerely gave up trying to control the outcome in her Lord's Prayer. At that very moment of surrender to God's will, something shifted in her, like a spiritual jolt. A great calm and peace took her over.[108] At once the rough current grabbed her and jerked her out of her kayak. As her knees folded back under her, she diagnosed herself: "Your knee bones just broke... You just tore your ligaments..."[109] And then the strangest thing happened. Her soul was peeling off from her body.

She shot above the river into another realm. About fifteen to twenty spirits rushed forward to welcome her. They hugged, danced, and rejoiced in their reunion.[110] They began to glide along a path. Her companions could hardly contain their joy. A feeling of absolute love overwhelmed her. They were bathed in a light brighter than she had ever seen. They traveled toward a great dome, whose central arch was formed with shimmering gold blocks. She felt drawn toward its entrance by its ever-present radiance. "There were many spirits inside," she says, "and when I arrived, they were overjoyed and welcoming me and greeting me, and really joyful at my arrival."[111] In that irresistible eternal home, Jesus was holding her. There she went through a portion of her life-review. The review was looking at the unseen ripple effects of her life events, how they had impact on not just one or two degrees removed but sixteen, twenty, twenty-five degrees removed.[112] This review was another profound part of the experience that helped her truly understand the significance of every action, every decision, every choice, and every interaction.[113] When they approached the archway with the golden bricks, the spirits suddenly turned to her and said, "Not yet." "It's not your time to enter. You have more to do on earth."[114] As powerful as the great joy, sorrow filled her, knowing she had to go back to earthly life.

Below her she could see her own body on the riverbank. Beside her body, Tom and his sons screamed, "Breathe, Mary, breathe," while giving her CPR.[115] When she opened her eyes to see the faces of the Longs staring at her, they were relieved, amazed, and excited to see her conscious again. She couldn't move her legs and presumed she had broken her back. She was submerged for 12 minutes and went for 24 minutes without oxygen.[116] The Longs arranged a kayak to be her lift and secured her body to the top. The rocky river bank bordered with an extremely thick bamboo forest. The incline of the steep hillside appeared impossible.[117] Suddenly local young men appeared and carried her out of the bamboo jungle.[118] Then they saw an ambulance parked on the side of the road. It was inconceivable they find an ambulance in such a remote and unlikely place.[119] During her resuscitation, one woman ran away from the scene and miraculously ran to the exact spot where Bill was reading. In search of the group, Bill and the woman found it just as Neal was being loaded into the ambulance.[120] The young local men disappeared after their help. No villagers knew who they were.[121]

In an interview, Neal says the spiritual beings forewarned her of a tragic event: "They did tell me about the future death of my oldest son," she said. "They didn't tell me the date or the time, but it was very clear that would be happening." [122] She had always been very close to her oldest son Willie through a sense of deep spiritual connection. When he was four or five, she chatted with him before bed. When she said something about, "When you are eighteen ...," Willie looked startled and said, "But I'm not going to be eighteen."[123] She responded, "What did you say?" with a somewhat lighthearted tone. Looking back at her with serious intensity, curiosity, and disbelief, he said, "You know. I'm never going to be eighteen. That's the plan. You know that."[124] He said it as if she must be kidding with him. The exchange pierced her heart like a sword. After that conversation, she cherished each day with him, wondering which day would be his last.[125] Not wanting to burden others with these thoughts, however, she did not tell anyone.

The day she finished her memoir, Willie was in an accident during his cross-country skiing. Willie was skiing with his friend Hilary in New England. Eighteen-year old Erik was just driving around. Distracted by his cell phone, Erik sped and hit Willie from behind and killed him instantly, missing Hilary by only a few inches.[126] "I woke up every day hoping the plan for my son's life would change," Neal says.[127] Before his death, Willie wrote a letter about how grateful he was for his family, his friends, his God, and for his faith. That letter was a precious gift to her.[128]

Dr. Neal's NDE has transformed her life for good so that she could have a deeper appreciation of God's love, her intimate relationship with Jesus, her understanding of natural and supernatural connections, and the fresh realization of her purpose of life. She underwent the ecstatic experience of the love of heaven, her deep sadness about her return to this life, her miraculous rescue, her mission in life, and the foretelling of the tragic death of her son Willie. The series of these events confirms the actuality of life after life and its close connection to her earthly life. By sharing her story, this orthopedic spine surgeon risked her reputation and her career, moving beyond her medical practice and telling people about the ultimate meaning of life in the love of God through Jesus Christ.

Eben Alexander

Another physician who experienced heaven through an NDE is Dr. Eben Alexander III, a neurosurgeon with outstanding medical training. Before his NDE, he had rejected near-death revelations of God and heaven based on his training in the hard wiring of the human brain. Dr. Alexander *served on the faculty of Harvard Medical School for almost fifteen years and reached the rank of associate professor by 1994. He has contributed to promoting the development of stereotactic radiosurgery, intraoperative MR imaging, and MRI-guided focused ultrasound surgery in neurosurgery.*[129] Because he was tired of "medical politics," he left Harvard in 2001 and moved to Lynchburg, Va.[130] In 2006, he was engaged in research on less intrusive forms of brain surgery through focused X-rays and digital scanners. Then in 2008, he contracted E. coli meningitis, and his life was entirely changed.

On November 10, 2008, Alexander had a progressively severe headache and back pain that intensified into massive seizures, sending him into a coma. He had inexplicably contracted a very rare bacterial meningitis-encephalitis. "Cases of bacterial meningitis are uniformly fatal if untreated."[131] Because no one in the emergency room knew that he had E. coli meningitis, he stayed in the coma for seven days.[132] According to Alexander, "seven days is an enormously long time to be in coma with bacterial meningitis . . . It was time to let my body die."[133]

During those days, he was in heaven. He discovered himself in a place of darkness which, as he later realized, was an escorted trip to heaven. He experienced flying over the earth surrounded by millions of butterflies. He noticed "a beautiful girl with high cheekbones and deep blue eyes" next to him on the wing of a butterfly.[134] She looked at him with a love higher than friendship love or romantic love, and communicated three things to him: "You are loved and cherished, dearly, forever." "You have nothing to fear." "There is nothing you can do wrong."[135] Of all that Alexander experienced, one of the most astonishing parts was the way that communication took place. When he raised a question in thought such as "who am I?" and "why am I here?" she answered instantly in an explosion of light, love, color, and beauty blowing through him like a rolling wave.[136] He learned a great deal through his questions and their answers. His guide told him in advance that he would have to go back although many things would be revealed to him. When his time in heaven was up, he came back to earth and found himself in a hospital room. His messages to those who deal with dying are a relief. "Our spirit is not dependent on the brain or body," he said. "It is eternal, and no one has one sentence worth of hard evidence that it isn't."[137]

Why his mind was alive and active during his coma cannot be explained scientifically.

> While the neurons of my cortex were stunned to complete inactivity by the bacteria that had attacked them, my brain-free consciousness journeyed to another, larger dimension of the universe: a dimension I'd never dreamed existed and which the old, pre-coma me would have been more than happy to explain was a simple impossibility.[138]

He said that the larger dimension of the universe exists where we learn and grow, where we are bigger than our brains and bodies, where death is never the end of consciousness but opens a positive and vast new journey. His coma and NDE case is unique because few people (perhaps none) have entered this dimension while the brain cortex was entirely shut down and the body was under careful medical observation for the full seven days of the coma.

Many of his peers believe that the brain is necessary for consciousness and that the universe is empty of any kind of emotion, not to mention the unconditional love of God. Alexander himself believed this before his NDE.[139] What happened to him disproved such a theory. He has committed himself to investigating what we are; in particular the nature of a consciousness that is greater than our physical brains. The plain truth is that the materialist understanding of the brain and the body as the manufacturers of human consciousness is indefensible. Reality is, in fact, beyond our full comprehension. In this multi-dimensional universe, God cares for each of us even more profoundly and ardently than our own parents.[140] As a doctor and a person of science, he makes the following confessional statement: "But on a deep level I'm very different from the person I was before, because I've caught a glimpse of this emerging picture of reality. And you can believe me when I tell you that it will be worth every bit of the work it will take us, and those who come after us, to get it right."[141]

Alexander wondered about the lovely young woman who guided him on the butterfly wing in the Gateway of heaven. His parents had adopted him at the age of four months.[142] In 2007, after several efforts, he finally met his biological parents who had married later after giving him up for adoption and had his other siblings, Kathy and David. With him, they shared their deep wound of losing his youngest sister, Betsy, in 1998.[143] Alexander received his birth sister Betsy's photo only four months after his coma. The photo showed Betsy in her long brown hair, deep blue eyes, and a beautiful smile of love and kindness. She looked hauntingly familiar. The next morning, while reading On Life After Death written by Elisabeth Kübler-Ross, he came to a story about a twelve-year-old girl who met her unknown brother during her NDE. Hearing this story, her tearful father told her that she indeed had a brother who had died just three months before her birth.[144] Inspired by the young girl's story, Alexander scrutinized the photo of Betsy carefully, she who is standing "without the powder blue and indigo dress, without the heavenly light of the Gateway around her as she sat on the beautiful butterfly wing" and then concluded, "Now there was no mistaking her, no mistaking the loving smile, the confident and infinitely comforting look, the sparkling blue eyes. It was she."[145]

One of the few places where his stories were unexpectedly well received was church. After his coma, he entered a church for the first time and saw everything with fresh eyes. The colors of the stained-glass windows with clouds and angels recalled to him the celestial beauty of the Gateway. A painting of Jesus breaking bread with his disciples reminded him of the communion of the Core, which is the deepest Holy of Holies of God and a deep dazzling darkness.[146]

He learned a number of things through his coma. Above all, near-death experiences and other connected mystical states of awareness disclose significant truths about the nature of existence. The reductive materialism of conventional science that reduces everything to what we can perceive with our senses is fundamentally faulty, for it deliberately disregards the nature of consciousness that is the foundation of all existence. While scientists who hold to the conventional model affirm that the material universe is the sole foundation of existence and reality, Alexander believes that the essence of the mystery of the universe is consciousness based on quantum processes. He specifies an excellent resource "Irreducible Mind: Toward a Psychology for the 21st Century" as the proof of such reality for all manner of extended consciousness.[147] He believes that our consciousness descends from God who is the creator of our consciousness. During Alexander's NDE, his brain was entirely shut down in a deep coma and was thus not functioning. The only viable explanation for his experience is that his spirit, being separated from his body, traveled to another world and met his sister, angels, and God.

In his new book, The Map of Heaven, Dr. Alexander elegantly describes the actuality of heaven, pointing out how we have forgotten and explaining how we can recollect our origins and destiny. He holds that we have hidden memories of a heavenly realm, and that we will go back to our heavenly plane for our further growing into tranquility, love, and goodness. Quoting quantum physicist Max Planck on consciousness, "I regard consciousness as fundamental. I regard matter as derivative from consciousness," Alexander holds that consciousness has produced this material world.[148] As a result of his NDE, he has begun to realize that quantum mechanical experiments and spirituality have converged at consciousness as the core of our existence. On earth, we are supposed to learn the virtues of unconditional love, forgiveness, acceptance, and compassion.[149] To this cheerful and optimistic mystic, these heavenly gifts only come when we open ourselves to the single greatest truth of a larger world after this one.[150]

Before his NDE, this renowned academic neurosurgeon had researched the brain for over thirty years and thought he knew about our brain and consciousness. After his NDE, he realized our consciousness exists independent of the brain and changed his previous understanding of its origin. Since his NDE, he has spent his energy integrating his NDE with quantum physics and has discovered that his spiritual experience concurs with the cutting-edge scientific research. His spiritual experience has challenged the present state of medicine's materialistic view of the mind.

Jeff Olsen

It was Easter weekend in 1997 when Jeff Olsen and his wife and two sons were traveling home to Bountiful, Utah. Olsen believes that he momentarily fell asleep at the wheel, and then overcorrected when his eyes blinked open. The following rollover accident instantly killed his 31-year-old wife and 14-month-old son. Olsen was badly injured, but his 7-year-old son survived.[151]

Right after the accident, Jeff was gone. From the nightmare of the crash, he slipped into "the quietness of pure nothing."[152] He was encircled with a bright-white light that appeared to be energized by unconditional love. The almost tangible light infused peace and calmness into him. As if waking up from a dream, his chest pain disappeared. Then he felt a familiar touch. He opened his eyes and found Tamara right next to him. She was very real.[153] "You can't stay here," she said. "You have to go back. You can't be here," she was crying.[154] "You can't come. You cannot stay here." He wondered what did she mean I couldn't stay? He believed that he belonged there, but she insisted, "You have to go!"[155] But he wanted to go nowhere. So he pulled Tamara to him tightly. She was solid and tangible. He even felt her wet tears on his skin. He kissed her. That was real. He smelled her hair with senses that seemed to be tenfold what he had experienced on earth. "You can't be here. You have to go," she sobbed.[156] He looked into Tamara's sky-blue eyes. Everything in the universe was calling him back to Spencer, but he wanted to stay with her. And he wondered where Griffin was. He felt a warm tear roll down his face and fall from his upper lip. "I have to go." "I know."[157] He leaned forward, putting his forehead onto hers. Another tear fell from his eye and onto her eyelashes. He watched as it rolled down over her collarbone. "I love you." "I know."[158] He had experienced no judgment and no life review. It had only been a brief peek into something profound.[159] And as he drifted away, there was only one overwhelming question, not asked by a voice, but with energy that echoed into every cell of his own being. The question was simply, "To what degree have you learned to love?"[160]

Their little son crying in the back seat helped Olsen survive the painful return to reality and recovery. "I had no sense of time," he said. "It could have been two hours or two minutes. It was like a download of information that was personal to me. It was like here's some insights to your life, to your being."[161] When he came back to his body, his back was broken, his rib cage crushed, and the seat belt had cut through his abdomen and ruptured his internal organs. Both his legs were crushed, and eventually his left leg was amputated above the knee. He spent six months in the hospital fighting for his life and enduring 18 surgeries to put him back together: "I had one foot in this world and one in the next," he said.[162]

> When I came back I found myself wandering on the hospital and in encountering people at the hospital I knew them. I mean they were strangers in this realm and I never met them before but out of the body I knew everything about them. I mean I knew their love, their hate, their Joy, their motivations of the choices that are made, and why. I had this overwhelming sense of love. I love them. I wanted to embrace them. It didn't matter if they were the heroin addict or the saintly grandma. I wanted to embrace them and I felt this connection, this oneness with them and that was really the big shift and I'm paraphrasing but that was the big shift as I realize we really are

connected. I also realized I spent so much of my life in judgment, in comparison that they're good they're bad this is better that's best. In seeing things in different eyes, I call it the way God sees it, I realize that we really are connected and we really are on our perfect path, and so letting go of that judgment and letting go of that comparison and embracing people and honoring where they are in their journey and what they're learning without judging; it completely changed a lot.[163]

When Jeff was judging his own son's unhealthy path, it was almost like God was laughing at him and wondering "When he is going to finally get this." We just get to love people and stop judging people and even love ourselves and recognize that it's all in perfect order.[164] After the accident, he eventually resumed his job at an advertising agency, remarried, and adopted two more sons.[165] Jeff's NDE delivered him from his comparative living and judgmental life and led him to unconditional love, teaching him how to respect the positions of diverse people in their own journeys. He felt the warmth of the tears of Tamara with his spiritual body. His NDE was as tangible as his experience of her tears and as real as his love for people from all walks of life. No one can assert that his experience was a hallucination because his transformed life argues otherwise.

Nancy Rynes

Nancy Rynes' life was turned upside down when she was run over while riding her bike. In her book, Awakenings from the Light, Nancy tells us about the traumatic story of her crash and the deep spiritual awakening she had during her near death experience.[166] She began as a skeptical, agnostic scientist, and wound up an awakened writer, artist, and speaker with a joyous view on life.[167]

While her time in the next life was brief in terms of earthly time, she felt as if weeks or months passed when she was there. She perceived an amazing amount in just a couple of human hours at most.[168] The first wonderful thing that she experienced was the beauty of heaven, both visually and feelingly. When she arrived there, a landscape of gentle hills surrounded her. Flower-filled verdant meadows spread out on the hills around her; and huge, broad-leaved trees in full leaf, trees larger and grander than any here on Earth, surrounded the pastures. A barest sense of a light mist, as if it were a moist summer morning, clung to the tops of the trees. The sky displayed a very light blue, similar to what you might see at the ocean's shore, with translucent clouds and a very bright but somewhat dispersed golden light.[169]

That was what she saw. But there is more to Heaven than what she could see with her five senses. Beneath the outward visuals was a well of feeling operated by love, peace, and an abiding Presence that she calls "Spirit or God."[170] Through the landscape around her, she experienced a profound sensation of peace, "rightness," goodness, and love. The beauty there was Beauty. Beyond the Beauty just pleasing to the eye, there was something deeper to it, more harmonious more welcoming, and more influential. "Everything felt tied together by love and peace, and the beauty of the scenes around me were the product of this unconditional love."[171] While the beauty of Heaven impressed her profoundly, the Presence of love completely captured her so that she yearned to stay there forever. She felt a deep sense of that love flow through all things around her: the air, the land below her feet, the trees, the clouds, and herself. That love was curving around her, running through her, and eventually netting her by the heart. She felt held by such a loving Presence so prevailing, yet so gentle, that she cried again. She had never felt such unconditional love and acceptance in all of her years on the planet.[172] It felt as if this place were built from love and harmony on a colossal cosmic scale.

Later her Guide told her that love formed the foundations of Heaven. Although each spirit might perceive the "landscape" differently, all recognized and understood that the love formed the basis for everything in the place. That love and peace seemed to play as glimmering of light beneath the surface, blinking in and out of visual sight. It had colors, vivacity, and texture. It seemed to take the form of what she saw such trees and a meadow, but it was also simultaneously detached from the forms themselves.[173]

Her Guide welcomed and greeted her with an energy-embrace of pure love. Love sprang from her Guide and encircled her. Her Guide didn't touch her with her hands or hug her but simply sent Rynes waves of loving energy as a welcome.[174]

In time, as Rynes grew more relaxed in the presence of the Guide, she began telling Rynes more about this place. In fact, Rynes wasn't in Heaven per se, just in a place to prepare her for what was to come. She calls it "a slice of Heaven."[175] It is the "world of spirits" according to Christian mystics. If we could equate Heaven to a cathedral, she was in the vestibule as we come in the exterior doors, but before we enter the main doors into the nave (the main worship area).[176]

If this was the waiting area, heaven's equivalent of TV's green room, she cannot imagine how amazing the full experience of Heaven would be! A glow of hope sparked in her heart.[177] It is amazing that Rynes' guide differentiated heaven from its green room. Many NDErs visited this area and considered their NDEs as a visit to heaven. Regarding the clarification of heaven and heaven's waiting area, Rynes' NDE is significant to our understanding of NDE.

This agnostic scientist underwent the overwhelming Presence of the loving Spirit and was so moved by the incident that she wrote a book on her undisputable experience of the greenroom of heaven. Nowadays she goes talks about the heaven that is constructed on pure love. Her NDE has drastically changed her outlook on life and has made a substantial impact on others because of its authenticity.

CHAPTER 3

How Can Our Loving God Send Some People to Hell?

THE NEAR-DEATH EXPERIENCES of the previous chapter are uniformly positive. Each person felt overwhelming love and acceptance. But there is another side to what we call the afterlife: the concept of hell, a place of punishment for those who, for whatever reason, are not accepted into heaven. How can we reconcile the existence of a loving God with a place of eternal punishment? Charles Darwin, for example, rejected the doctrine of hell. Even though he grew up and was baptized in the Church of England, Darwin gradually rejected Christianity. In his autobiography, he confessed that the doctrine of hell was one of the main reasons for his abandonment of the Christian faith:

> Thus disbelief crept over me at a very slow rate, but was at last complete. The rate was so slow that I felt no distress, and have never since doubted even for a single second that my conclusion was correct. I can indeed hardly see how anyone ought to wish Christianity to be true; for if so the plain language of the text seems to show that the men who do not believe, and this would include my Father, Brother and almost all my best friends, will be everlastingly punished. And this is a damnable doctrine.[178]

It is very clear that Darwin rejected the doctrine of hell because it is a place of punishment and damnation. Like Darwin, Bertrand Russell criticizes the idea of hell-fire as the promoter of cruel torture:

He repeats that again and again also. I must say that I think all this doctrine, that hell-fire is a punishment for sin, is a doctrine of cruelty. It is a doctrine that put cruelty into the world and gave the world generations of cruel torture; and the Christ of the Gospels, if you could take Him as His chroniclers represent Him, would certainly have to be considered partly responsible for that.[179]

Russell partially blames Jesus for the cruelty of hell. Is it true that God punishes sinners in hell? In this chapter we will examine whether God or Jesus is responsible for hell and its cruelty.

Augustine asserted that the wicked undergo the horror of everlasting torment on the basis of Isaiah's statement: "So then what God by His prophet has said of the everlasting punishment of the damned shall come to pass—shall without fail come to pass—their worm shall not die, neither shall their fire be quenched (66:24)."[180] For Augustine, their suffering is neither for purification nor a deterrence, but punishment. They will be burned in anguish, "repenting too late and fruitlessly."[181] They suffer eternally without being consumed.[182]

Recently, Rob Bell rejected the idea of hell. He pointed out that Jesus referred to hell as "Gehenna," and that Gehenna was Jerusalem's city dump in Jesus's day. He explained that in Gehenna, the fire never stopped burning, and the threatening noise of the gnashing teeth of hungry wild animals could be heard.[183] Thus, Jesus' reference to Gehenna was nothing more than a metaphor. He noted that for many in the modern world, the notion of hell is "a holdover from primitive, mythic religion that uses fear and punishment to control people for all sorts of devious reasons."[184] He also has difficulty "believing that somewhere down below the earth's crust is a really crafty figure in red tights holding a three-pointed spear . . ."[185] For Bell, the traditional idea of hell goes against Jesus' very teaching:

A staggering number of people have been taught that a select few Christians will spend forever in a peaceful, joyous place called heaven, while the rest of humanity spends forever in torment and punishment in hell with no chance for anything better.... This is misguided and toxic and ultimately subverts the contagious spread of Jesus" message of love, peace, forgiveness, and joy that our world desperately needs to hear.[186]

He firmly believes that Jesus' core message contradicts the traditional idea of the eternal punishment of hell.

In response to Rob Bell, Francis Chan and Preston Sprinkle were very clear about the fact that Jesus warns us about the reality of hell if we reject God. In their book, Erasing Hell, Francis Chan wished there were no hell because of the death of his unsaved grandmother, but he was unable to deny the biblical statements of the existence of hell.

I don't know what your life is like or what hardships you've faced. I don't know what your thoughts on hell are or whether or not you've been attacked or manipulated with threats of hell in the past. All I know is that from my best understanding of Scripture, hell is a real place for those who choose to reject God. Yet God is not licking His chops looking for any poor soul that He can send to hell. In fact, the opposite is true: "have I any pleasure in the death of the wicked, declares the Lord God, and not rather that he should turn from his way and live?" (Ezek. 18:23, cf. 33:11).187

God is love, but God's love is not incompatible with the reality of hell. To Chan, God's standards of love include the existence of hell for the wicked.

The Existence of Hell by God's Mercy

A number of NDErs have reported that there is no hell, and many Christians deny the reality of hell because of it is the very opposite of God's love. God's goodness and love, however, are threatened if there is no hell. Thousands of NDErs have reported that they met God or were approached by light. If there were only the heaven of light or God, what would happen to those who do not want to go to the heaven of light or to God? Millions of people prefer darkness to light. For instance, would Satan worshippers want to go to heaven after this life? Many Christians and non-Christians raise the question of how a good God could create hell and send God's own children there. The answer is that God neither created hell nor sends people there. Instead, God allows hell to exist.

Was Hell Created by God?

Genesis 1:1 declares, "In the beginning when God created the heavens and the earth." It does not say that God created the heavens, the hells, and the earth. In the parable of the judgment (Matt. 25:31-46), Jesus says, "Then he will say to those at his left hand, 'You that are accursed, depart from me into the eternal fire prepared for the devil and his angels'" (v. 41). The original word "prepared" in Greek is *hetoimazó* denoting "prepare, provide, make ready."[188] The eternal fire was prepared or provided but not created. God does not want us to commit sins but allows us to do sin if we choose. Our sin separates us from God, and that separation is tolerated by God's grace. The space created by this separation is hell in this life and the next. Sin has created the remoteness between God and us, and that split has produced the area that is called "hell."

God's Grace as the Guarantee of the Continuation of Hell

In the parable of the lost son (Luke 15:11-32), when the younger son asks his father to give him the share of the estate, the father does so. Later, the son gathers everything together and goes on a journey into a distant country, which the father allows. Similarly, in our own lives, God allows us to go away from God and does not deprive us of our free choices. If this were not so, those who want to escape God would be bound by God's order, unable to move away from God. Such a place where we would be unable to walk away from God would be much worse than hell because there would be no freedom to refuse God. As seen in the parable of the lost son, however, God is gracious and merciful and permits the withdrawal of those who want to escape from God. Those who withdraw from God gather together in hell. If God were not gracious, God would not allow people to move away from Godself and would annihilate them instead. Such a god would not be gracious and merciful, but a tyrant. If that were the case, the whole universe would turn into a prison. If we experienced an afterlife where we could not hide from God, we would be hostages, and God would be our tormenter. Living eternally under such a tyrannical god in the afterlife would truly be more hellish than hell.

As strange as it appears to be, hell exists because God is compassionate, merciful, and graceful; and it is necessary in order to preserve God's grace, mercy, and tolerance. The interior walls of hell have been made of peoples' denial and disdain of God, while its exterior wall consists of God's patience. If God allows our freedom on earth, why would not God allow it in the next life? If we are allowed to choose or reject God or reject in this life, we will be permitted to do in the next. Hell and heaven exist together in order to preserve our free will.

Does God Torment Those Living in Hell?

God loves everyone and yearns to live eternally with everyone. Our love, however, is far shallower than the love of God. Our own selfish love desires our well-being over that of others. Deep inside, self-love does not care for the church, community, nation, and world except in the interest of our own reputation, status, well-being, and glory. Many people only love the people who accommodate their own needs because of that selfish love.[189] Their own needs and desires guarantee that they live a hellish life in this world; and because they have never learned to love anyone outside themselves, they will continue a hellish life after this life is over. They will associate with people like themselves, building and reinforcing a hellish community there. The punishments that they endure in associating with people like themselves are built into hell itself. The evil within them builds the hell that they experience.[190] Although they will be brutally tortured in the next life, that torment is not from God. The torture derives from the evil itself; evil and its punishment are so closely interwoven that it is very difficult to separate them.[191]

In the world of spirits, evil spirits are punished severely to prevent them from doing evil things. Although this seems to come from the Lord, the punishment is not from God. It actually originates in the evil itself, since an evil thing and its consequences are so closely united that they are inseparable. As a matter of fact, the hellish mob has no greater craving than to inflict harm, to punish, and to torture anyone who is unprotected by the Lord. So when something evil is being done from an evil heart, it prevents any safeguard by the Lord, and evil spirits rush into the evildoer and afflict them.[192]

A Wicked Man Permitted to Enter Heaven

As a proof of God's love for sinners even in the next life, Sundar Singh (see ch. 7) shares his witness to an event in which a wicked man was permitted to enter heaven but refused. On one occasion in Singh's presence, a wicked person entered into the world of spirits. When the angel and saints showed their willingness to help him, he immediately cursed and scorned them, saying, "God is altogether unjust. He has prepared heaven for such flattering slaves as you are, and casts the rest of mankind into the dark. Yet you call Him Love!"[193] The angels responded, "God certainly is Love. He created men that they might live forever in happy fellowship with Him, but men, by their own obstinacy, and by abuse of their free will have turned their faces away from Him, and have made hell for themselves. God neither casts any one into hell, nor will He ever do so, but man himself, by being entangled in sin, creates hell for himself. God never created any hell."[194] At that moment, the very gentle voice of one of the high angels said from above, "God gives permission that this man may be brought into heaven."[195] The man excitedly moved forward attended by two angels, but when he arrived at the door of heaven, he gazed at the holy and light-enveloped place, and the glorious and blessed inhabitants that reside there began to feel disconcerted. The angels told him, "See how beautiful a world is this! Go a little farther, and look at the dear Lord sitting on His throne."[196] While he looked standing from the door, the light of the Son of righteousness exposed the impurity of his sin-filled life. He stepped backward in an agony of shame and self-abhorrence, and fled so rashly that he swiftly passed through the intermediate state of the world of spirits and threw himself headlong into the bottomless pit. Then Jesus in His sweet and gentle voice said, "Look, My dear children, none is forbidden to come here, and no one forbade this man, nor has any one asked him to leave. It was his own impure life that forced him to flee from this holy place, for, 'unless a man be born anew, he cannot behold the Kingdom of God' (John 3:3)."[197]

We choose our destinies that are suitable for our natures. On Sundays, while some people are in church singing praises to God, others are drinking, carousing, and brawling at bars.[198] Likewise, after this life is over, some people yearn to be with God and with other God-loving people in heaven, while others want to be in hell with their own types of people: selfish, lustful, self-important, or greedy.

The World of Spirits

According to some NDErs and Christian mystics, after death all people except a few enter the world of spirits, an intermediate state between heaven and hell. From there, they usually wait and discern where they will spend their eternities. Those who like the life of love, light, and truth choose heaven, while those who like self-love, darkness, greed, and falsehood choose hell. Some advanced or doomed spirits go directly to heaven or hell without going through the world of spirits. Some people, who have disguised their natures by wearing many masks, slowly take off those masks one by one to reveal themselves, and finally choose according to their true natures. While they appear very caring and loving externally, internally they are doing everything out of their own self-interest. Because it may take time for them to reveal who they really are, they stay in the world of spirits for quite a while.[199]

In the Old Testament, *Sheol* meant the place where those that had died were believed to be congregated. It is described as our eternal house (Eccl.

12: 5).[200] *Sheol* is similar to the world of spirits in terms of the gathering place of the dead. They are different, however, in their functions. In the understanding of the Old Testament, all the dead stayed permanently in *Sheol*, while the world of spirits is only a temporary station.

The New Testament, in contrast, references a place called Hades, an interim stop for the dead on their journey to the afterlife. Hades receives spirits after death and delivers them to *Gehenna* at the resurrection (Rev. 20:13). The New Testament is not uniform, however, in its understanding of Hades. In some cases, Hades means the place where all the spirits of the dead stay until the resurrection (Ac. 2:27, 31), while in others it signifies the place only of the spirits of the ungodly (Lk. 16:23) or of non-Christians (Rev. 20:13 f.).[201] In brief, *Hades* in the New Testament is more similar to the world of spirits than *Gehenna* or the Old Testament's *Sheol* in terms of its purpose as an interim station, but *Hades* and the world of spirits are different in their functions.

God Throws No One into Hell

Since God desires eternal fellowship with everyone, God would never throw anyone into hell or deny them entrance into heaven. An evildoer, however, would not want to go there because of the breath of heavenly love and the inflow of heavenly light that would cause pain and hellish torment in their heart.[202] The evil within us is hell within us; it makes no difference whether we call it "evil" or "hell." It is we who lead ourselves into hell, not the Lord since we are responsible for our own evil. Our loves and desires stay with us after death.[203] People who have loved and intended what is evil in this world love and intend the same evil in the next life; but in the next life, they will no longer let themselves be led away from it. In fact, after death, evil craves to be with more evil. After death, therefore, it is not God, but they who cast themselves into hell.[204]

How would this work? When a gentleman enters the next life, he is first welcomed by angels who do everything for him, tell him about the Lord, heaven, and angelic life, and give him lessons in matters of truth and

goodness. However, if he is the kind of person who has denied truth or goodness during his earthly life or despised them at heart, then after some of this
conversation, he yearns to get away. When the angels see this, they leave
him. After spending some time with various other people, he eventually
joins with people who are engaged in similar evils. They not only enter hell
voluntarily out of a burning desire for evil, they dive into hell headfirst. This
is the reason why they look to be thrown into hell by divine power.[205]

This, understanding is, of course, very much at odds with the popular
view of hell that pictures the lock to hell on the outside of the door, with
God punishing evildoers unendingly. C. S. Lewis contradicts that popular
idea: "The doors of Hell are locked on the inside."[206]

Lewis' View of Hell

Apologist C. S. Lewis wrote *The Great Divorce* to reject the idea that God
sends sinners to hell, and to refute the concept of universalism (that everyone gets to heaven eventually). The book opens with a bus ride carrying a
group of people (ghosts) from a dismal gray town (hell) to a sunny, grassy
country (heaven), where they are offered a chance to stay. In the bright sun-
shine, while the new arrivals look transparent, the solid people in this sunny
land are bright, solid, and beautiful. The grass under the feet of the new
comers does not bend, causing walking to be hard and painful. They feel
uncomfortable with the beautiful land of heaven. The solid people contact
individual ghosts to encourage them to stay and travel toward the mountains
with them. They advise the ghosts to remain with them because they will
get adjusted to this new environment and grow solid themselves as they cope
with their minor problems. Some of the ghosts, however, are afraid and return to the bus and the others cluster together for protection. One by one
they choose to return to the gray town.[207]

The book centers on this theme: God does not condemn any soul to hell
as punishment. The souls choose their own destinies: "All that are in Hell,
choose it. Without that self-choice, there could be no Hell. No soul that
seriously and constantly desires joy will ever miss it."[208] Hell, for Lewis, is

chosen by the individual. The punishment endured in this place is not the active torture by God inflicted upon poor miserable sinners. On the contrary, the individual is on some level unable to deny their actions, the pain they have caused, the goodness and beauty of God, or the truth of their sin. This individual is also unable to reconcile their sin with the truth and spends eternity in conflict. Such recognition is in itself torment by rejecting God's grace. Furthermore, hell is a place where the individual is free to deny God, and where one is left with all that is not God. Self and self-delusion consume such an individual.

No one wants to go to hell; but, ironically, many feel comfortable living there. This is why some people choose to go to places where heavy metal music blasts from the speakers, and others go to listen to quiet classical music. It is comparable to this: No liar wants to be lied to by others, but there are many who love to lie to others. Such a contradictory place where liars gather together is hell.

It would have been greatly beneficial for Darwin or Russell to have had a chance to dialogue with Sundar Singh or with C. S. Lewis. Unlike Darwin's understanding, the reality of hell is not a damnable doctrine. It is instead the inconceivably gracious provision of the loving God for Darwin's family members and relatives. Contrary to Russell's understanding of the cruel hell of God, hell burns not with God's cruelty, but with people's intense hatred, vehement anger, obsessive greed, and filthy lust. Only the unreserved love of God buttresses the foundation of hell.

CHAPTER 4

Is There Any Experiential Evidence of Hell?

MOST PEOPLE WHO have experienced near-death experiences (NDErs) have reported feelings of peace, joy, and bliss. A number of NDErs with positive near-death experiences (NDEs), in fact, say that there is no hell or judgment after this life. Other NDErs, however, have shared their less-common negative NDEs that were dominated by emotionally painful feelings of fear, terror, horror, loneliness, isolation, anger, and/or guilt.[209] Although some NDErs repudiate the existence of hell, Howard Storm and many other NDEs actually experienced hell. Even though hellish NDEs are less common, such experiences are hard to deny. Howard Storm is one who had such a negative NDE.

Howard Storm

Storm was a Professor of Art at Northern Kentucky University. He said that he was not a very pleasant person and that he, as an avowed atheist, was hostile to theists and toward all religions. He had no faith in anything that couldn't be seen, touched, or felt. To him, the tangible and material world was all that existed, and all religions were illusions that manipulated people. Science was the only truth. He claimed that he lived a joyless life based on such a worldview, and often vented his anger and rage on others.

In 1985, a perforation of the stomach drove Howard Storm to a near-death experience (NDE) at the age of 38 in a Paris hospital. After barely being able to express his deep love to his spouse and say goodbye to her, he waited for the end of his life. He truly believed there was no life beyond death. But "the end" did not happen. Instead, he "drifted into darkness, a sleep into annihilation."[210] While in such a state, he felt weird, opened his eyes, and found himself standing between the hospital beds.

He thought it was a dream. He squeezed his fists and was surprised by the keen feeling in his hands. He "could feel the bones in his hands, the muscles expand and contract, skin pressed against skin."[211] He was more alive than ever before in his life.

He saw his roommate Monsieur Fleurin, whose eyes were half closed, his beloved Beverly sitting in the chair next to his bed, and a covered object in his bed. When he stooped down to see what it was, he was appalled to find out that it was a man with a face similar to his own. This object could not be him because he was standing over it and looking at it. It looked like a meaningless, hollow, lifeless husk. He was schizophrenic, yet more conscious than ever before. He frantically tried to get Beverly's attention, but she did not respond to his efforts. Even when he became very upset and screamed profanities at her, she responded with nothing. Then he yelled at his roommate Fleurin to get his attention, but again received no response at all.

Suddenly he heard certain persons calling him, "Howard, Howard," in clear English.[212] Their voices, male and female, young and old, were pleasant. These shadowy persons enticed him to follow them so that they could help him. They were pale, clad in gray. Since they did not reveal their identities, he did not want to follow them; but because his spouse and roommate ignored him, he reluctantly followed them by stepping out into the hallway. When he asked them where they were going, they evasively responded that he would find out soon. They surrounded him and led him through a misty road. He walked with these elusive beings for a significant distance. At first they were playful and jolly, and then a few of them slowly started to play rough and be aggressive. They made fun of him, and others hushed the aggressive ones, saying: "Shhh, he can hear you, he can hear you."[213]

As the fog became thicker and darker; they became rougher and meaner. Storm had hoped that his agony would end by death, but the situation grew worse as a mob of cruel beings drove him to move toward some unknown destination. He wished that it were a dream, but everything he had experienced in the world was a dream compared to the reality he was now undergoing.[214] As he finally refused to go any further, they changed and forced him with hostility to go with them. Many of them pushed and jostled him, and he responded by beginning to fight back. Then a crazy carousel of chaotic jeering, yelling, and punching arose. As the main attraction of their amusement, he was hurt by their tearing and biting. His throbbing became their pleasure. Although unable to see anything in such total darkness, he was aware that dozens or hundreds of them surrounded him. The more he attempted to fight back, the greater he pleased the crowd. Furthermore, they began to slowly rip off pieces of his flesh. He was horrified at the realization that he was being gradually taken apart and eaten alive for their pleasure. These vicious creatures were none other than former human beings. When they massed around him, he underwent intense physical contact with them in the dark. They had human bodies except for their long, sharp fingernails and their even longer teeth.[215] This mob of evil beings, driven by unrestrained brutality and fury, tortured him. After a long fight, he lay there exhausted, too broken to resist. By that time his body was badly dismembered, and the evil ones began to lose interest in a nonresponsive person, even though a few still picked at, mocked at, and gnawed at him.[216]

ALONE

While his tormentors flocked around him, a voice surfaced from his chest. It seemed like his voice, but it wasn't. "Pray to God," said the voice.[217] He thought, "Why? What a stupid idea. That doesn't work . . . I don't believe in God. This is utterly hopeless, and I am beyond my possible help whether I believe in God or not. I don't pray, period."[218] Although the voice from inside his chest said that he should pray to God, his mind replied to the voice by saying that he had not prayed and did not know how to pray. Three times the inner voice urged him to pray. So he tried to pray using phrases that had religious implications such as "The Lord is my shepherd . . . The Star-Spangled Banner, the Pledge of Allegiance, God bless America."[219] To his astonishment, something miraculous happened when he prayed with such broken words. The vicious creatures started yelling, and ordered him to stop calling on a non-existent and worthless God: "There is no God! Who do you think you're talking to? Nobody can hear you! Now we are really going to hurt you."[220] While hurling at him the most obscene, blasphemous language on earth, they nevertheless retreated from him as if he were formidable and awesome. As he kept uttering things about God, they became more furious and left him, "cursing and screaming against God."[221] While lying down hopelessly in a dark hell, he heard his own voice singing a childhood song, "Jesus loves me, da da, da . . ."[222] Then into the darkness he hollered, "Jesus, save me" with all his strength for first time in his entire life.[223]

Far away in the darkness, he saw a light approaching him, getting brighter and brighter. This light was a living being. The intense bright light penetrated his body, healing his agony, the torn pieces of his body, and all his wounds with miraculous ecstasy. This bright loving being embraced him and knew him intimately "better than I knew myself."[224] This being unconditionally accepted and loved him. "He was King of Kings, Lord of Lords, Christ Jesus the Savior."[225] His prayer was answered right away; Jesus came to rescue him and held him near, stroking his back. Then, like a football player lifting his fallen teammate off the field, Jesus put his arms around Howard, and Howard sobbed like a baby in His arms; "He carried me out of there and we headed to where God lives."[226] Believing that Jesus made a terrible mistake, Howard thought, "I'm garbage and I don't belong in heaven." "We don't make mistakes," Jesus replied gently.[227] "He could read everything in my mind and put His voice into my head," Howard recollected.[228]

In that place, he was asked whether he would like to see his life. When he agreed, he reviewed his life from beginning to end, together with Jesus, and the angels.[229] The whole review was not a session of judgment, but a learning session: "It was a terrible experience because my life deteriorated after adolescence. I saw I became a selfish, unloving person. I was successful, a full tenured art professor at 27, the department head, but I was a jerk."[230] In this review of his life, he witnessed his heavy drinking and adultery. "I cheated on my wife proudly. It was horrible."[231] While they watched together, Howard could perceive the pain and disappointment on the face of Jesus. "When I did these things it was like sticking a knife into his heart."[232] Before seeing the replay, he never knew that his sinful way of life hurt Jesus. "I was in the arms of the most wonderful, holy, loving, kind person and we're looking at this stuff. Embarrassing doesn't even begin to describe it."[233] He could cope with the life review, however, because of the love of Jesus and the angels. Even when they disapproved of his actions, they conveyed their unceasing love for him. After reviewing it, they asked, "Do you have any questions?"[234] He answered, "I have a million questions," and he proceeded to ask them. They kindly, and without wearying, answered Howard's questions.[235]

HIS RETURN

Howard reports that he did not see God and that he was not in heaven. Instead, he believes that the place he visited was an intermediary world: "I was not in Heaven. It was way out in the suburbs, and these are the things that they showed me. We talked for a long time, about many things, and then I looked at myself. When I saw me, I was glowing, I was radiant. I was becoming beautiful—not nearly as beautiful as them—but I had a certain sparkle that I never had before."[236]

Unwilling to face the earth again, he told the angels that he wished to be with them forever: "I'm ready, I'm ready to be like you and be here forever. This is great. I love it. I love you. You're wonderful."[237] Knowing that they loved him, he asked if he could eliminate his body and become like them with the powers they had shown him. They replied: "No, you have to go back."[238] They explained to him that he was very underdeveloped and that he would need to develop important characteristics in the world to become like them and to be involved with their work. Pleading with them to stay, he argued that he might end up in the pit again if he had to return to the world. To that, they said: "Do you think that we expect you to be perfect, after all the love we feel for you, even after you were on earth blaspheming God, and treating everyone around you like dirt? And this, despite the fact that we were sending people to try and help you, to teach you the truth? Do you really think we would be apart from you now?"[239] He replied: "But what about my own sense of failure? You've shown me how I can be better, and I'm sure I can't live up to that. I'm not that good. No way. I'm not going back."[240]

They responded to him, "There are people who care about you; your wife, your children, your mother and father. You should go back for them. Your children need your help." He said,

> You can help them. If you make me go back there are things that just won't work. If I go back there and make mistakes I won't be able to stand it because you've shown me I could be more loving and more compassionate and I'll forget. I'll be mean to someone or I'll do something awful to someone. I just know it's going to happen because I'm a human being. I'm going to blow it and I won't be able to stand it. I'll feel so bad I'll want to kill myself and I can't do that because life is precious. I might just go catatonic. So you can't send me back.[241]

Assuring him that mistakes are an acceptable portion of being human, they said, "Go and make all the mistakes you want. Mistakes are how you learn."[242] If he made a mistake, he should fully admit it as a mistake, then put it behind him and just try not to make the same mistake again. They said that the important thing is to try his best, keep his standards of goodness and truth, and avoid compromising those norms to win people's approval. "But," he mentioned, "Mistakes make me feel bad."[243] They told him, "We love you the way you are, mistakes and all. And you can feel our forgiveness. You can feel our love any time you want to."[244] He asked, "I don't understand. How do I do that?" "Just turn inward," they answered. "Just ask for our love and we'll give it to you if you ask from the heart."[245]

They instructed him to recognize his genuine mistakes and to ask for forgiveness, but he would need to accept forgiveness while learning from his mistakes. "However," he asked, "how will I know what is the right choice? How will I know what you want me to do?" They answered: "We want you to do what you want to do. That means making choices—and there isn't necessarily any right choice. There are spectrums of possibilities, and you should make the best choice you can from those possibilities. If you do that, we will be there helping you."[246] Although giving him no direct mission or purpose, they desired him to live his life to love people, not things. He told them that he was not good enough to live out what he had just experienced and learned from them on a worldly level. They assured him he would be given suitable help whenever he might need it. All he needed to do was to ask.[247]

"The luminous beings, my teachers, were very convincing. I was also acutely aware that not far away was the Great Being, what I knew to be the Creator. They never said, 'He wants it this way,' but that was implied behind everything they said. I didn't want to argue too much because the Great Entity was so wonderful and so awesome. The love that was emanated was overwhelming."[248] He told them that it would break his heart to come back to the world and that he would die if he had to leave them and their love. "Coming back would be so cruel, I said, that I couldn't stand it. I mentioned that the world was filled with hate and competition, and I didn't want to return to that maelstrom. I couldn't bear to leave them."[249] While the angels were explaining how to communicate with them, they told him to quiet himself inside and to ask for their love; then that love would come and that he would know they were there. They said, "You won't be away from us. We're with you. We've always been with you. We always will be right with you all the time."[250] After hearing these kind explanations, he exhausted his arguments and thought he could return to the world. And, just like that, he was back. As soon as he returned to his body, the pain was there and worse than before.

Storm received his second chance at life and returned to earth, although he strongly expressed his desire to stay in heaven. After his NDE, he drastically changed his lifestyle, and has since lived a life of care and love for God and others. His life was so immensely changed after his near-death experience that he resigned his professorship and devoted his life to preaching the gospel of Jesus Christ. This cost his marriage. His divorce was as painful as his experience of hell. He entered United Theological Seminary, completed its Masters of Divinity program in 1992, and has served several different churches as pastor since then.

Some people say that his NDE was a hallucination. To him, his NDE was more real than the reality of his earthly life. One thing is very clear: this

NDE must be true because of the way it drastically changed his life. I have known him personally since 2014. He is an amazing person, filled with the love of God, compassion, humility, wisdom, and integrity. His life is proof that he has been born from Above. This transformed life is the credible substantiation of his description of hell.

George Rodonaia

Rodonaia was a neuropathologist and a political dissident in the Soviet Union. In 1975, he received an invitation from the United States. In 1976, he obtained his exit visa. On the day he was leaving for New York, a car ran over him on the sidewalk while his family was waiting for him in the airport.[251] The KGB planned to kill him before his departure. He was taken to the hospital and the doctors did everything they could to save him, but he was pronounced dead. His body was left in the morgue. Since his case was highly political, an autopsy had to be done. His corpse was stored in a freezer cabinet for three days.[252]

The first thing he remembered about his NDE was that he found himself in a realm of total darkness: "I had no physical pain. I was still somehow aware of my existence as George, and all about me there was darkness, utter and complete darkness - the greatest darkness ever, darker than any dark, blacker than any black."[253] He was horrified because he never expected such a thing to happen in his life. This total darkness was an incredible experience. The scary thing was that the darkness existed, not beyond him, but within him. He felt that the darkness was pressing. He was terrified because he did not understand why and how this darkness existed.[254] During those three days, he saw "everything that was happening around, seeing myself, my body, seeing my birth, my parents, my wife, my child, and my friends. I saw their thoughts. I saw what they were thinking, how their thoughts move from one dimension to another."[255]

Then he saw a light. He went through a little hole into that light. The light was so powerful that he could not compare it to anything. No words could describe it: "The light was so burning, going through flesh. I didn't have a body. That was the most interesting part. And I was scared of the light, I wanted to go into the shade to save myself from this light. What is that light? I don't know. It can be called the light of God, it can be called the light of Life."[256] At first he found the brilliance of the light painful, and couldn't look directly at it: "But little by little I began to relax. I began to feel warm, comforted, and everything suddenly seemed fine."[257]

He had not been raised in a religious environment and was not familiar with all that was happening. He was confused and shocked that he still existed, although he did not know where he was: "I wasn't prepared for this at all. I was shocked to find that I still existed, but I didn't know where I was. The one thought that kept welling up in his mind and troubled him most was, 'How can I be when I'm not?'"[258] He tried to be positive even in such darkness and thought that light would be great in darkness: "Then, suddenly, I was in light; bright white, shiny and strong; a very bright light. I was like the flash of a camera, but not flickering—that bright. Constant brightness."[259]

The next thing he saw were molecules, atoms, protons, and neutrons flying everywhere. It was totally chaotic, yet joyful, for this chaos had a symmetry of its own. The symmetry was beautiful, unified, and whole. He saw the universal form of life and nature laid out before his eyes: "It was at this point that any concern I had for my body just slipped away because it was clear to me that I didn't need it anymore, that it was actually a limitation."[260] Beyond his concern for his absent physical body, he experienced the unified existence of the next life: "Everything in this experience merged together, so it is difficult for me to put an exact sequence to events. Time as I had known it came to a halt; past, present, and future were somehow fused together for me in the timeless unity of life."[261]

Next, he reviewed and participated in the holographic image of his real life drama from beginning to end. This life-review had no sense of past, present, and future: "It wasn't as though it started with birth and ran along to my life at the University of Moscow. It all appeared at once. There I was. This was my life. I didn't experience any sense of guilt or remorse for things I'd done."[262] He felt no sense of failures, faults, or achievements: "All I felt was my life for what it is. And I was content with that. I accepted my life for what it is."[263] Since he had no body, he could be anywhere and any period of time instantaneously. When he wanted something, he received it. And he had the desire to learn about the Bible and philosophy. He could be anywhere instantly, really there. He tried to communicate with the people he saw. Some noticed his presence but did nothing about it. He felt it necessary to learn about the Bible and philosophy. As he thought about it, it came to him:

> So I participated, I went back and lived in the minds of Jesus and his disciples. I heard their conversations, experienced eating, passing wine, smells, and tastes— yet I had no body. I was pure consciousness. If I didn't understand what was happening, an explanation would come. But no teacher spoke. I explored the Roman Empire, Babylon, the times of Noah and Abraham. Any era you can name, I went there.[264]

While he relished such incredible experiences, the doctor from Moscow began the autopsy and started to cut into his stomach. He felt that some great power grabbed his neck and pushed him down. The impact was so great that he opened his eyes and felt a great sense of pain. His body was shivering out of the cold. They immediately stopped the autopsy and moved him to the hospital. There he spent the next nine months largely in a respirator.[265]

Gradually he recovered his health. He would never be the same again, however, because all he wanted to pursue for the rest of his life was the study of wisdom. This new yearning led him to attend the University of Georgia where he earned his second PhD in the psychology of religion. Afterward, he became a priest in the Eastern Orthodox Church. In 1989, his family came to America, and he served as an associate pastor at the First United Methodist Church in Nederland, Texas.[266] He later served as a pastor at St. Paul United Methodist Church in Baytown, Texas.[267] He passed to the next life in 2004.

For him, his NDE pointed to one theme: the practice of the love of the Creator.

> Anyone who has had such an experience of God, who has felt such a profound sense of connection with reality, knows that there is

only one truly significant work to do in life, and that is love; to love nature, to love people, to love animals, to love creation itself, just because it is. To serve God's creation with a warm and loving hand of generosity and compassion—that is the only meaningful existence.[268]

He humbly acknowledged the fragmentary answers of NDEs and expected better answers in the next life: "Many people turn to those who have had NDEs because they sense we have the answers. But I know this is not true, at least not entirely. None of us will fully fathom the great truths of life until we finally unite with eternity at death. But occasionally we get glimpses of the answer here on Earth, and that alone is enough for me."[269] He was humble enough to be content with glimpses of the heavenly answer on earth.

Like Howard Storm, Rodonaia was an atheist, but he was not a militant one. Although he was a circumstantial atheist, he was not a vicious person. He experienced the spiritual world very differently from Storm. There were no physically tormenting, torturing, vicious spirits; only the deep presence of darkness in his experience of the spiritual realm. In fact, NDErs experience hell differently in accordance with their own states of the mind and their lives, leading to the conclusion that there must be many hells. His escape from the Soviet Union is an astonishing story, and his returning to life from his three-day death is an implausible reality. His coming out of the greatest inner darkness of hell is an exceptional and significant event that transformed him from an atheist to a strong believer.

Matthew Botsford

Here is another clearly negative NDE of a businessman. Matthew, his brother, and another colleague from work were attending a business convention in Atlanta, Georgia. in the spring of 1992. After dinner, they were waiting for a cab outside a restaurant when a gunman standing at the nearby corner suddenly opened fire, spraying bullets from an Uzi submachine gun at the innocent bystanders after he and his friends were denied entry to the restaurant.

One bullet struck Matthew in the right rear parietal area of his head and he almost died before he hit the ground. Matthew said, "I felt a hot, needle-like pierce, excruciatingly painful, for a brief instant at the top of my head; and then utter darkness enveloped me as if thick, black ink had been poured over my eyes."[270]

In the pitch darkness, Matthew experienced the evil of hell:

> Evil was present on all sides. It was an ever-present form of evil . . . Cold permeated to the very marrow of my bones—an icy, water-type cold in that it surrounded all of me, inside and out. It was in my lungs and stomach and head . . . Time was of no consequence here, confined in this evil cell of darkness. A cell in hell—yes, a cell in hell was where I was being kept.[271]

He was on the verge of death three times after his heart stopped, once on the sidewalk, once in the ambulance, and once in the emergency room of Piedmont Hospital. To reduce his brain swelling, doctors induced a coma that lasted twenty-seven days.

Before the incident, Matthew had little concern about God. "I knew there was a God and that Jesus is His son," he recollects. "But never had I made a commitment to say Jesus is the Way or made any effort to get to know Him. It was all about me. I had my own plans. At 28-years-old, I felt young, vibrant, and strong."[272]

When his life was hanging in the balance, Matthew entered a different dimension of life. "Immediately, I shifted from the temporal realm I lived in, to the eternal realm of hell," he remembers.[273]

Matthew further portrays a horrifying experience of hell "with his body suspended in midair, arms outstretched, shackled with ancient black chains clasped around his wrists and ankles suspended over a deep glowing red abyss."[274] He witnessed "four-legged creatures roaming about in apparent agony, as they attempted to stay clear of flowing lava. Smoke billowing up from the magma seemed to carry the souls of the lost. He heard awful screams emanating from the depths of hell. None of the screams were intelligible—just cries of pain, loss, and anguish."[275]

Hearing the countless screams, he was in his own torment; he was not alone, yet isolated and inaccessible.[276] The lava flow got closer to Matthew, and blobs of magma splashed on his shins and feet, which charred his flesh to the bone. "I smelled my own flesh searing and burning away. I saw and felt my flesh re-form only to be burned off again and again."[277]

Demons with dark oval eyes watched him, condemning and insulting him.

> I could see some of the faces of these demons, and bodies . . . short and stout covered with scales and horns of varying numbers, sizes and lengths upon their heads, denoting their levels of authority in Satan's realm. Demons with sharp teeth peeled the skin off his backside, which resulted in tremendous pain. I heard the sound of my skin being ripped off in ribbon-like fashion. I smelled their stench like rotten carcasses or rotten flesh. Over and over and over this repeated itself. There was to be no end to the torment. I understood this was to be an eternal existence for me.[278]

His experience of hell is compatible with Storm's. To him, hell is a really awful place where demons torment evildoers. It is hard to dismiss his experience or to treat his experience as a hallucination. His descriptions of demons are gruesome, but their appearances are very horrific only to outsiders because their internal minds externally appear, according to Emanuel Swedenborg. They look like normal human spirits to each other.[279]

John Bunyan

John Bunyan (1628–1688) was an English preacher imprisoned for his faith. He authored over forty books. His best-known work is *Pilgrim's Progress,* one of the most popular and recognized books in world literature. When he was a young man, he almost committed suicide, which was prompted by atheistic lures of an evil spirit. Upon the attempted suicide, an angel of God showed him a vision of spiritual realms.

PLANNING SUICIDE

When John Bunyan repeatedly heard that there is no God, devil, heaven, or hell, he was confused enough to consult the wrong friend, who laughed at his fears and pretended to pity his weakness.[280] He was further confused and decided to kill himself to find out the truth. One morning, he entered a nearby woods and was going to use a knife to end his life. Before the attempt, he heard a quiet voice whisper to him, "Do not fall into everlasting misery to gratify the enemy of your soul. The fatal stroke you are about to give yourself will seal your own damnation. For if there is a God, as surely as there is, how can you hope for mercy from Him if you willfully destroy yourself who were made in His image?"[281] Such a power-filled voice made him throw away the knife; and as he knelt down on the ground to worship God with great thanksgiving, he prayed that God would take away the darkness in his spirit so that he would never question God's being and greatness.[282] Suddenly a glorious light surrounded him. A bright angel appeared before him and told him that God would show him celestial realms. He was transferred into heaven where he experienced magnificent things beyond description. He met the prophet Elijah who imparted heavenly wisdom to him.[283] And before he returned home, the angel showed him the regions of the prince of darkness.[284]

As they descended to the lowest regions of the air, he saw a crowd of horrible figures and miserable dark beings that fled from the shining presence of his bright guardian.[285] Located in the caverns of the infernal depth, he saw hell's territories in a sulfurous lake of liquid fire. Lucifer sat on a flaming throne with eyes filled with hellish fury.[286]

He saw a number of spirits suffering from different tortures. One place was crowded with a vast number of tormenting demons. They were persistently lashing a large company of wretched spirits with knotted whips of fiery steel. The loud cries of the tormented prompted Bunyan to plead with one of the tormentors, "Oh, stop your whipping, and do not use such cruelty on those who are your fellow creatures, and whom you probably helped lead to all this misery."[287] "No," replied the tormentor very easily. "Though we are bad enough, no devil was as bad as them, nor were we guilty of such crimes as they were. We all know there is a God, although we hate Him; but these souls would never admit (until they came here) that there was such a Being."[288] "Then these," he said, "were atheists. They are wretched men, and tried to ruin me had not eternal grace prevented it."[289]

When Bunyan spoke, but one of the tortured cried out despondently, "Surely I know that voice. It must be John." Bunyan was astonished to hear his name mentioned and he responded, "Yes, I am John; but who are you?"[290] To this he answered, "I once knew you well upon the earth, and had almost persuaded you to be of my opinion. I am the author of that celebrated book entitled *Leviathan*." "What! The great Hobbes? Are you come here?"[291] asked Bunyan. "Alas, I am that unhappy man indeed. But I am so far from being great that I am one of the most wretched persons in all these dirty territories. For now I know there is a God. But oh! I wish there were not, for I am sure He will have no mercy on me. Nor is there any reason that He should. I do confess I was His foe on earth, and now He is mine in hell. It was that proud confidence I had in my own wisdom that has so betrayed me," Hobbes lamented.[292] "Your case is miserable, and yet you admit that you suffer justly. For how industrious were you to persuade others and try to bring them to the same damnation. No one can know this better than I, as I was almost taken in your snare to perish forever," said Bunyan.[293] "It is that," sighed he, "that stings me to the heart, to think how many will perish by my influence. I was afraid when I first heard your voice that you had also been cast into hell. Not that I wish any person happy, for it is my torment to think that anyone is happy while I am so miserable. But I did not want you to be cast into hell, because every soul that is brought here through my deceptions, increases my pains in hell."[294]

"But tell me, for I want to know the truth. Did you indeed believe there was no God when you lived upon earth?" asked Bunyan.[295] Hobbes confessed, saying:

> At first I believed there was a God but as I turned to sins which would lead me to His judgment, I hoped there was no God. For it is impossible to think there is a just God, and not also remember that He will punish those who disobey Him. But as I continued in

my sins, and found that justice did not swiftly come, I then began to hope there was no God. From those hopes I began to frame ideas in my own mind that could justify what I hoped. My ideas framed a new system of the world's origin, which excluded from it the existence of God. At last I found myself so fond of these new theories that I decided to believe them and convince others that they were true. But before this, I did find several checks in my own conscience. I felt that I could be wrong, but I ignored these warnings. Now I find that those checking thoughts that might have helped me then, are here the things that most of all torment me. I must confess that the love of sin hardened my heart against my Maker, and made me hate Him first, and then deny His being. Sin, that I so proudly embraced, has been the cursed cause of all this woe; it is the serpent that has stung my soul to death. For now I find, in spite of my vain philosophy, there is a God. I have also found that God will not be mocked, although it was my daily practice in the world to mock at heaven and all that is sacred, for this was the means that I found very successful to spread abroad my cursed ideas. For anyone that I could get to ridicule the truths of God, I looked upon as becoming one of my disciples. But now these thoughts are more tormenting to me than the sufferings I endure from these whips of burning steel.[296]

Bunyan responded. "Sad indeed. See what Almighty Power can inflict on those that violate His righteous law."[297] As Bunyan was going to make some more remarks, the unrelenting tormentor said to Bunyan. "Now you see what sort of men they were in the world. Do you not think they deserve their punishment now?"[298] To this Bunyan responded, "Doubtless it is the just reward of sin which they suffer, and which you will suffer also. For you, as well as they, have sinned against the ever-blessed God, and for your sin you shall suffer the just vengeance of eternal fire. Nor is it any excuse to say you never doubted the being of a God; for though you knew there was God, yet you rebelled against Him. Therefore you shall be justly punished with everlasting destruction from the presence of the Lord."[299] The fiend rejoined, "It is true we know we shall be punished, as you say. But if you say that mankind should have pity showed them, because they fell through the temptations of the devil, it is the same case with me and all the rest of the inferior spirits. For we were tempted by the Bright Sun of the Morning to rebel with him. And therefore, though this multiplies the crime of Lucifer, it should lessen that of the inferior spirits."[300]

Bunyan's guide countered with an irate countenance. "O you apostate, wicked, lying spirit! Can you say those things and see me here? You know it was your proud heart that made you rebel with Lucifer against the blessed God who had created you with glory! But since you proudly exalted yourself above your blessed Creator, and joined with Lucifer, you are justly cast down to hell. Your former beauty has changed to your present horrible form as the just punishment of your rebellious pride."[301] To this the apostate spirit retorted, "Why do you invade our territories, and come here to torment us before our time?"[302] After saying this, he slid out of the place as if he wanted to hear no response.

Based on his experience, Bunyan describes hell as the place where evildoers torture other evildoers, believing that they are more evil than they and deserve such tortures. This is the true nature of the torture of hell. The tormentors torture others because of their specks, not realizing their own logs (Luke 6:42).

Thomas Hobbes's confession is amazingly sobering. He regrets how gradually wrong rational convictions seeped into him and trapped him in his own lies. In Part IV of his *Leviathan,* he shared his belief that demons, evil, and good are nothing more than the imagery of the brain.[303] Ironically, he now suffers from the tortures of demons whose existence he once denied. His remorse speaks volumes about our current debates on the existence of hell and demons.

CHAPTER 5

Children's Near-Death and Mystical Experiences

CHILD NDERS SHARE something unique. They make the world much sunnier and more compassionate.

Diane M. Komp, MD discloses that children inspired her to turn to God. In her book, *A Window to Heaven*, Komp, an atheistic pediatric cancer specialist at Yale Hospital in New Haven, Connecticut, tells story after story of what dying youngsters say.[304] She met the child who saw Jesus driving a school bus and another who described the music of a chorus of angels. It is an interesting fact that there is little difference between reports from a child's deathbed and reports from a child NDEr. Books such as *A Window to Heaven* are becoming more accepted, as people feel free to discuss the topic of life after death more openly.[305] Since many of physicians take a friendlier look at things "paranormal," more physicians including Komp fear no longer being ridiculed by their peers.[306]

A Confused Child Near-Death Experiencer

A young man from New Zealand, with tears flooding his eyes, told Atwater about a time, when he was barely seven, that he died of a high fever from pneumonia.

> He had disobeyed his parents about playing outside, overdoing it, when he had not sufficiently recovered from a previous illness. Confined to bed, alone, frightened, and guilt-ridden, he left his painfully hot body and went in search of help.

He described "walking" through the house and seeing his father enter through the front door. He ran to his father with arms outstretched, believing that help had been found. His father looked him in the face, then ran right past him, ignoring his pleas. The boy was invisible to his father, but he didn't know it at that time. He was heart-broken by what his father did and decided that, because of this, he wasn't good enough to be loved anymore. He never saw how panic-stricken his father was once the boy's lifeless body was discovered, nor did he see the heroic efforts made to save him. When he revived in the hospital, all he remembered was pleading for help and being refused. He withdrew from his family after that and remained estranged from his father for many years. No amount of counseling made any difference until we spoke, and he could finally understand what had happened to him and why.[307]

Obviously, children are often confused by their NDEs because they have insufficient information about them.

A Child Gang Member

James, a black boy at the age of nine or ten from East St. Louis, was a member of a gang that was involved in the drug trade. However, James changed radically after his NDE which resulted from drowning: "And you know, when I floated out of my body and saw myself, suddenly I realized we are all the same. There ain't no black and there ain't no white. I saw that bright light and I knew it was all the colors there were, everything was in that light— everything good for me, that is."[308] His friends were already pushing drugs and he avoided them. He was very serious about school, and had quit talking trash: "I always thought that I had a dream. Then when I heard about these near-death experiences I knew that I'd had one. I feel better about myself. I know that I am different. I don't think about putting people down for fun like I used to."[309] He said that he was amazed by the fact that he could change his attitude of life: "I see life the way it really is. It is not meant to be played with. I don't want to end up here with all this gang violence and poverty. I believe in God very much. I believe God took me out of my body and kept me in a very safe place when I almost drowned."[310]

Dr. Melvin Morse was deeply moved when he heard, "Life is not to be played with. I want to better myself."[311] This disclosed how bigoted practices based on color have no place in the realm of true celestial life.

Infant SIDS (Sudden Infant Death Syndrome)

Dorothy M. Bernstein of North Olmsted, Ohio, had four NDEs, two as a child and two as an adult. Her childhood accounts focused on her stopping her breathing because of her choice to die. Today, we would say that she was a victim of SIDS. But her understanding of what happened to her is quite different from how SIDS has been understood:

> She claims, "I knew the truth about how my mother tried to abort me, and even again at five weeks before I was born, me, the seed of an alcoholic, a rapist, an adulterer, an abuser. Who could blame her?" While still a virgin, her mother had been raped. Dorothy, as a fetus in the womb, said she was aware and knew all that had happened. "I never cried as a young child. I remember being wet and hungry and thinking, 'Don't cry or she'll kill you.' My mother thought I was such a good baby, but I remembered the pain." Dorothy noted that her crib was kept in her parents' bedroom after her mother married. One day, at the age of ten months, she witnessed some sexual behavior she was not meant to see and was punished by her father. She can vividly recall the painful confusion that preceded her decision to "go home," and then knowing exactly how to kill herself: by expelling all the air from her lungs and constricting her chest muscles to make her heart stop. Her last remembered thought was, "Oh, God, how could he hurt me like that?" and God's mysterious reply, "Perhaps he was trying to protect you." As she explains it, that "voice" so startled

her that she gasped, which restarted the breathing process. Her account is filled with descriptions of a brilliant light, focusing on the mirror's reflection of an angel picture, having a spirited dialogue with a tiny person perched at the head of her crib, and promising God: "I will never forget from whence I came, nor will I ever deny you." Nonetheless, at the age of three and a half, badly traumatized by the neglect and abuse she received from her mother after the birth of her mother's "love child" (her half-sister), she recalled once again making the decision to "go home." She used the same method, with the same results. Only this time, Dorothy said, feelings of warmth and love coming from the crown of her head convinced her that God wanted her to live and to help her sister. Breath returned, but, sadly, the situation with her family worsened.[312]

When researcher P. M. H. Atwater spoke with Dorothy about her two bouts of breath stoppage as a child, she mentioned reading a newspaper article about sudden infant death syndrome. "The doctors suspect the infants die because they just forget how to breathe. Not true! I chose not to breathe!"[313] This view may be in conflict with present medical understandings and practices, but can still be potentially informative for medical practitioners.

Encountering the Unborn: Colton Burpo

Todd Burpo was a small-town pastor in Nebraska and his secular job was garage door installation. On their way to a family vacation, their four-year old Colton suffered from appendicitis, which later ruptured and he received emergency surgery. During that time he had an NDE and entered heaven. After a few setbacks, he miraculously recovered.

As months and years passed, Colton revealed what he experienced. At first, they could not believe his descriptions of the heavenly thrones, the triune God, and angels that were beyond the comprehension of a young boy. Colton continued his story about meeting his older sister whom his mother Sonja had miscarried. His parents had not told him about the miscarriage so he should not have known about it. He also met Todd's grandfather who had passed away long before Colton was born. Colton's descriptions of heaven amazed Todd because they aligned with biblical passages. Later Colton identified a painting of Jesus' face by Akiane as the correct representation of Him.[314] Akiane "began to describe to her mother her visits to heaven" at age four and started painting at age six.[315] In the epilogue, Todd says, "Just over seven years have passed since an ordinary family trip turned into a heavenly trip that changed all our lives."[316] When the editor of the book asked Colton what he wanted people to know from his story, he answered right away, "I want them to know that heaven is for real."[317]

Based on the book *Heaven Is for Real,* a drama film "Heaven is for Real" was made in 2014 and has captivated the world.

A Child Artist Trained by God: Akiane Kramarik

Akiane was a child art genius, who started drawing at the age of four. Born in Illinois in 1994, Akiane grew up in a poor family with three other siblings. She primarily is a self-taught painter.[318]

Her family was unique, having no friends, no relatives, and no television or radio. Their life was simple, they valued long walks in nature, open conversations, home-schooling, and hands-on exploration of knowledge in a nurturing environment. They were loving, idealistic, poor, and atheistic.[319]

Her mother, Forelli, is a Lithuanian immigrant educator raised as an atheist. Akiane's father, Mark, is a chef from Chicago. He is non-religious with a Catholic background. Her family never talked about religion, never prayed together, and never attended any church. Yet in the insular atheistic environment, her parents created – free from media influences or even outside babysitters – Akiane suddenly began to talk about God.[320]

Akiane told *Christianity Today* that the first time God began speaking to her was when she was three years old: "He said, 'You have to do this, and I'll help you.' He said, 'Now you can help people.' I said, 'Yes, I will.'"[321] Because of that conversation with God, Akiane has donated a considerable portion of the money received from art sales to charity. When asked why she believed she received the gift, Akiane answered that she has been blessed by God for one reason only, which is to help others.[322]

One very early morning when she was eight years old, her mother found Akiane looking through the window at the sky. Asked what she was doing, she answered:

I was with God again, and I was told to pray continually. He showed me where He lived, and it was so light. He was whiter than the whitest of whites. I was climbing transparent stairs; underneath I saw gushing waterfalls. As I approached my Father in paradise, His body was pure light. What impressed me most were His gigantic hands — they were full of maps and events. Then He told me to memorize thousands upon thousands of wisdom words on a scroll that didn't look like paper, but more like intense light. And in a few seconds I somehow got filled up. He showed me the endless universe, its past and its future, and He told me that from now on, I needed to get up very early and get ready for my mission. I hope one day I'll be able to paint what I've been shown.[323]

Akiane has also recounted the vibrancy and ethereal beauty that exists in Heaven. "All of the colors were out of this world. There are hundreds of millions of colors that we don't know yet. The flowers there were crystal clear …" Akiane told CNN in an interview a few years ago.[324]

Before she turned nine, Akiane painted her best-known masterpiece, the Prince of Peace, and between the ages of nine to twelve years, most of Akiane's drawings seem to have a spiritual theme and a visionary quality to them.[325]

When she was invited to *The Oprah Winfrey Show* at the age of nine, before her interview her mother pulled Akiane aside. "Remember," her mother whispered, "your new agent told us that you shouldn't focus on God so that you don't offend the viewers of different beliefs. Remember when I used to be very offended myself by just hearing the word God? Do you know who Oprah is?" "No, yes, no!"[326]

Before her mother knew it, Akiane was climbing onto the stage. At the conclusion of the interview, Oprah asked, "Where does your inspiration come from?" "From God."[327] Akiane couldn't prevent herself from mentioning the most important influence in her life: God. Oprah repeated, "From God," and hugged her.[328]

By then Akiane was ten years old, and she was invited to the Museum of Religious Art in Iowa. The three-day exhibition proved to be a notable event. There were masses of people standing in a line that wound from the outside doors down the road. The questions were posed to Akiane from all directions. "What church do you belong to? What denomination?" someone from the crowd asked loudly. "I belong to God," Akiane responded.[329] "I am a Buddhist. You called Jesus the 'Prince of Peace,' yet in His name so many people were massacred. How do you explain that?" She maturely answered with full wisdom: "Jesus is peace, just like calm water. But anyone can drop a stone into water and make it muddy."[330] "Why did you choose Christianity instead of another religion?"[331] She replied, "I didn't choose Christianity; I chose Jesus Christ. I am painting and writing what God shows me. I don't know much about the religions, but I know this: God looks at our love."[332] "Who taught you how to paint?" "I'm self-taught. In other words, God is my teacher."[333] "What message do you want people to get from your art and poetry?" "I want my art to draw people's attention to God, and I want my poetry to keep their attention on God."[334]

Akiane's discovery of God seems unique. "Since nobody told me who God was, I found God myself. He's been there for me through the years. I don't belong to any denomination or religion. I belong to God."[335] In explaining this further, Jesus is first in her mind. "He is the only way to God — the only way to heaven and joy," she says. "My personal views on Jesus have only matured and deepened since age 4. As I grow I see how vast and unlimited His love is."[336] "Jesus remains my highest authority, love, and God," she adds.[337] "I pray every day that people will one day follow Jesus, His teachings and feel His love."[338] She remarks further, "My art is only a representation of what I see — Jesus' glory is beyond any description!"[339]

It is extraordinary that no one led her to God, but God Godself led her to heaven and to God and Jesus. Akiane's experience would be in the category of 'mystical experience' rather than as an NDE.

Historical NDE Cases: Abraham Lincoln, Albert Einstein

LINCOLN

For a specific example of perhaps a quintessential child experiencer, let's consider Abraham Lincoln.[340]

When he was five years old, Lincoln was crossing on the narrow footbridge and fell in a rain-swollen creek and drowned. His older friend Austin Gollaher rescued him with a long pole. Once ashore "He was almost dead, and I was badly scared. I rolled and pounded him in good earnest. Then I got him by the arms and shook him, the water meanwhile pouring out of his mouth."[341] In spite of having no record of his telling an otherworld journey to anyone, Abe's family and friends made ample remarks about his sudden craving for knowledge, his persistence on learning to read, and his exhaustive effort to consume every book he could find.[342]

Five years later, one day, taking a bag of corn, he mounted the old gray mare and leisurely rode to Gorden's mill in Indiana. After arriving there, he hitched the old mare to the arm so that the mare might go around to grind the corn. Abe was mounted on the arm, urging his old mare with his whip to better speed, saying "Get up, you old hussy," when the resentful mare kicked him in the forehead, sending him sprawling to the ground.[343] "Miller Gordon hurried in, picked up the bleeding senseless boy, whom he took for dead, and at once sent for his father." Old Tomas Lincoln came as soon as possible and loaded the lifeless boy in a wagon and drove home. He was in bed all night unconscious, but the attendants noticed signs of his consciousness coming back toward the break of day.[344]

Later he refers to himself in the third person, "A mystery of the human mind. In his tenth year, he was kicked by a horse, and apparently killed for a time."[345]

Some features suggestive of a brain shift/spirit shift that Lincoln came to exhibit may be the following:

> The loss of the fear of death, a love of music and solitude, unusual sensitivity to sound and light and food, sensing in multiples, wildly prolific psychic abilities, a preference for mysticism over religion, absorption tendencies (merging), dissociation (detachment), susceptibility to depression and moodiness, increased allergies, regular future memory episodes, hauntingly accurate visions, the ability to abstract and concentrate intensely, clustered thinking, charisma, moral upliftment, a brilliant mind, perseverance in the face of problems and obstacles, and a driving passion about his life's destiny.[346]

Lincoln enhanced his physical and mental capacities to perceive things sharper, higher, and deeper after his NDE.

EINSTEIN

Let us explore the early life of Einstein. When he was five years old, he almost died of a serious illness. While still sick in bed, his father showed him a pocket compass. The mysterious property of the iron needle, always pointed in the same direction no matter how the campus case was turned, impressed upon him the fact that something in empty space must be influencing it.[347] Although speech fluency did not occur until around the age of ten (perhaps because of dyslexia), family members recall how deeply he would reflect before answering any question—a trait that made him appear subnormal. Interestingly, he learned to play the violin at six (later delighting with the mathematical structure of music), he taught himself calculus at fourteen and enrolled in a Zurich university at fifteen.

Like Lincoln, Einstein was afflicted with nervousness and stomach problems and almost died from these problems as an adult. Also like Lincoln, the unusual characteristics of his disposition and talent may trace back to the age of five and afterward.[348] NDE researcher J. Timothy Green, PhD, has a fascinating view concerning how Einstein might have been inspired to figure out a theory of relativity. When Einstein was a student in

Zurich, Switzerland at the age of seventeen, Albert von St. Gallen Heim was a distinguished professor of geology. Heim had once fallen while climbing the Alps and described a most peculiar NDE. After this incident, he collected accounts from others who had fallen or had similar accidents over a twenty-five year period. He presented his research findings to Swiss Alpine Club in 1892 and published them that same year. In so doing, Heim became the first person in modern history to publish a collection of what would later be referred to as near-death experiences.[349] Heim and his interviewees reported that "Time became greatly expanded," while they fell toward the ground.[350]

Green holds that Einstein was a student of Heim in the years immediately after the publication of this paper, and was aware of comments such as: "When people fall from a great height, they often report that time seemed to slow down or stop completely—as it expands."[351]

Years later, asked in a *New York Times* interview how he came to begin working on his theory of relativity, Einstein related the idea to a near-death incident he had witnessed. It was reported: "He [Einstein] had been triggered off . . . by seeing a man falling from a Berlin rooftop. The man had survived with little injury. Einstein had run from his house. The man said that he had not felt the effects of gravity—a pronouncement that led to a new view of the universe."[352] Green and Atwater have no doubt that these two men met and knew each other, and that Heim influenced the young Einstein.[353] It is realistic to suppose that the professor's NDE and his succeeding research paper on the subject had a profound effect on his probing student, laying the groundwork for Einstein's famous theory and maybe even validating what had previously occurred to him at the age of five.[354]

Child NDErs share lots of their lessons. Researcher Atwater conveys some of them in the following:

- No one ever dies. We just trade one body for another one. Sometimes that's a happy thing to do and sometimes it's not. Whatever we experience becomes God's experience, and God never forgets a thing.

- We are full of love because God is. So is everything else. It's a wonder how many people forget that, and they forget about having a soul. We each have one, that's our perfect part. Our soul makes certain we remember who we are, so we can always make our way back to the lifestream—our home—no matter how far away from it we travel.
- We only think we can be separated from God. Really, we can't. We each have a purpose in a Larger Plan, and we are important to that Plan.
- We each have a job to do. Large or small, it doesn't matter.
- We need to respect each other, too, even babies who aren't born yet.
- Mistakes can be corrected. We're never stuck.
- We think we can do everything by ourselves, but we can't. There are always helpers around us ready to pitch in.
- You can't laugh enough, or play and create things and sing and write poems and scrunch up your nose so your face tickles. Always be loyal and truthful. Lying hurts you or someone else, sooner or later.[355]

These summary points depict Atwater's insightful big picture of child NDEs well. Through her own NDEs, she could hear the depths of these youngsters' speaking, grasping unspoken messages between the lines. She depicts God as the center of child NDEs and points out the significance of the purposes of God's creation for everyone and the rest of God's creation.[356]

CHAPTER 6

What Would Happen to Suicides?

Suicide is when we direct violence at ourselves with the intent to end our lives. According to CDC (Center for Disease Control), suicide is a leading cause of death in the United States. In 2013, it was the second leading cause of death among young people aged 15-34 years.[357]

There exist documented reports of positive and negative near-death experiences resulting from attempted suicide. This may denote that rather than the act of suicide itself, one's personal life may determine one's positive or negative NDE. It may be possible for positive or negative spiritual conditions of a person to endure beyond death. Because of pre-existing negative circumstances, people usually attempt to commit suicide and such negative factors may influence their mindsets and spiritual conditions unless the brain generates such conditions.[358]

Six Types of Suicides

During his NDE, Dr. Ritchie, author of *Return From Tomorrow and My Life After Dying*, grasped what happens to some suicides. After visiting the astral realm (the world of spirits), Jesus and he were in another place (hell) where suicides arrive. He learned about four types of suicide through visiting the spiritual realm. I added two more to his four types.

The first type of suicide is those who kill themselves "out of hatred, jealousy, resentment, bitterness and total disdain for themselves and others."[359] This derives from a murderous intent. Because of their religious upbringing, they cannot murder others. So they kill themselves: "If I can't kill you, I shall kill myself to get even with you."[360] They have the same type of strong emotions as murderers.

The second type is those who kill themselves out of insanity and mental diseases. These people are incapable of being accountable for their actions.

The third type of suicide is those who kill themselves in the midst of a horribly long-suffering physical illness.

The fourth type is those who kill themselves because of chemical addictions. According to Ritchie, these people can become stuck in limbo trying in vain to satisfy their addiction until eventually something frees them. This condition is also called an earthbound condition, and Dr. Richie describes it thus:

> Jesus and Ritchie then went to a dingy bar and grill near a large naval base that was crowded with sailors drinking beer and belching whiskies. Spirits walled the sailors as they frantically attempted to lift the shot glasses to their lips in vain. Desperate nonsensical fights were constantly breaking out among them over their drinks. Other spirits tried to control the sailors' alcoholic behavior
>
> When a sailor passed out, a crack rapidly opened in the shielding aura round him and one of the spirits vanished as he hurled himself at that opening crack. Ritchie learned that the dependence on alcohol could go beyond the physical. It becomes mental and even spiritual. When the addicts lose their bodies, they could shortly possess other people's bodies. The thought that the addict could never stop hungering made him shudder.[361]

This type of earthbound spirits leave this earth after some time, move on to the world of spirits, and choose their own permanent places.

The fifth type of suicide is those who commit suicide out of their incredibly difficult circumstances and life tragedies.

Dr. Ritchie is convinced that we have a God of unfathomable love that is expressed in the life of Jesus. So this fifth type of suicide will be treated with understanding and love.

The sixth type is altruistic. Some people lay down their lives for others, their families, communities, and nations. Altruistic suicide can be praised or condemned, depending on perspectives. This type of suicide is complex in its ethical and religious evaluation (e.g. Samson and patriotic suicides). God understands the motivations of suicides.

All these suicides need our understanding, care, and love, not blaming, judgment, or condemnation.

George Ritchie's Witness to Suicide Cases

The Centers for Disease Control and Prevention (CDC) collects data about mortality in the U.S., including deaths by suicide. In 2013 (the most recent year for which full data are available), 41,149 suicides were reported, making suicide the 10th leading cause of death for Americans (Figure 1). In that year, someone in the country died by suicide every 12.8 minutes.[362]

After cancer and heart disease, suicide accounts for more years of life lost than any other cause of death.

During his NDE, George Ritchie witnessed some suicides undergoing agonizing experiences. It is an excerpt from his *Return From Tomorrow*:

In one house a younger man followed an older one from room to room. "I'm sorry, Pa!" he kept saying. "I didn't know what it would do to Mama! I didn't understand."

But though I could hear him clearly, it was obvious that the man he was speaking to could not. The old man was carrying a tray into a room where an elderly woman sat in bed.

"I'm sorry, Pa," the young man said again. "I'm sorry, Mama." Endlessly, over and over, to ears that could not hear.[363]

Several times we paused before similar scenes. A boy trailing a teen-aged girl through the corridors of a school. "I'm sorry, Nancy!"

A middle-aged woman begging a gray-haired man to forgive her.

"What are they so sorry for, Jesus?" I pleaded. "Why do they keep talking to people who can't hear them?" Then from the light beside me came the thought, "They are suicides, chained to every consequence of their act."[364]

Raymond Moody's Reflection on Life After Life

Raymond Moody discusses the topic of suicide in his book, *Reflection on Life After Life*. At the time he wrote the first book, *Life after Life*, he encountered few important cases of near-death emerging from attempted suicide. Since then, he accrued more additional cases. These attempted suicides have one common point: "They felt their suicidal attempts solved nothing. They found that they were involved in exactly the same problems from which they had been trying to extricate themselves by suicide. Whatever difficulty they had been trying to get away from was still there on the other side, unresolved."[365]

One woman who attempted suicide expressed her experience as that of being trapped. Her state of affairs before the suicide attempt was being repeated as if in a vicious cycle: "Well, the thing, was, it was still around, even when I was 'dead'. And it was like it was repeating itself, a return. I would go through it once and at the end I would think, 'Ho, I'm glad that's over', and then it would start all over again, and I would think, 'Oh, no, not this again'."[366]

Those who attempted suicide, after their experiences, would never contemplate suicide again; for their attempts were mistakes. One individual was asked whether he would ever try to kill himself again. He said:

> No. I would not do that again. I will die naturally next time, because one thing I realized at that time is that our life here is just such a small period of time and there is so much which needs to be done while you're here. And, when you die it's eternity.[367]

These people need to resolve problems and issues on earth. Otherwise, they will remain unresolved in heaven: "Truly I tell you, whatever you bind on earth will be bound in heaven, and whatever you loose on earth will be loosed in heaven (Mt 18:18)."

Angie Fenimore – NDE: Beyond the Darkness

When 27-year-old Angie Fenimore finally turned her back on her childhood of abuse, a lifetime of misery, she committed suicide on January 8, 1991.

Her life had started normally enough. Everything revolved around her family until her mother, who had suffered from emotional issues, went away to a camp to seek treatment. This move devastated their family with her mother ultimately moving out and her father beginning a period of reckless behavior that heavily influenced Angie's life.[368]

From the text, it is revealed that Angie suffered some sort of sexual abuse early in her childhood that created darkness within her soul.[369] Having an abusive stepmother try to fill the void left by her real mother widened that crevice until so much darkness had filled her inner being. Angie moved onto experimenting with drugs and alcohol and had to be rescued from herself in that regard. But the darkness crept deeper into her life.[370]

When she married, she thought that this would be the medicine that would make her well and move her away from her destructive behavior. She had been experiencing cycles of depression every summer and winter and these episodes became even more intense when she moved away from her home to join her husband who was serving in the Air Force.[371]

At one point she mirrored the behavior of her mother and ran away with her sons to get away from the life that had been suffocating her. Unable to comprehend the warning signs and advice that had been put in front of her, she lived apart from her husband for a period of time.

Unable to find anyone who could help her out of the malaise she was in, she ultimately overdosed on medication and had an NDE.[372] Her encounter is quite remarkable.

THE LIFE REVIEW & JUDGMENT

Angie's life review begins interestingly when she reviews all of the events of her childhood and the pleasantries that she associated with growing up in a healthy, happy home.[373]

As her darker years approached, the pictures became less detailed. It was at this point in the review that she felt someone alongside her reviewing each segment of her life. She felt no judgment from "the presence" and that person was male. The feeling she received from Him was: "This is the way it is. This is the life that you lived."[374]

THE DARKNESS

Angie describes a darkness that is unending and continued in all directions, seeming to have no end – "but it wasn't just darkness, it was an endless void, an absence of light."[375] It was during this part of her experience that Angie realized that "Oh, we must be the suicides."[376] The thought tumbled out without her speaking it and she realized this from the fact that she "recognized" most of those around her as teenagers.[377]

Angie then describes a secondary tunnel where she traveled at a very high speed. This trip propelled her deeper into the darkness and she was left with no idea of how far or how long she had traveled. It was at the end of this part of the journey that the word "Purgatory" whispered into her mind.[378]

She describes at this point entering what I would describe as a waiting room. There were pieces of furniture, tables & chairs, mirrors, etc. Her awareness of those around her in this place gave her the impression of all being completely self-absorbed, a characteristic that will weigh heavily in the revelation she had later in her encounter: "They were completely self-absorbed, every one of them too caught up in his or her own misery to engage in any mental or emotional exchange. They had the ability to connect with one another, but they were incapacitated by the darkness."[379]

It was in this place that she was able to pick up small exchanges of conversation people had as they reflected upon the woes of their lives. She even describes people wearing dirty white robes. Some were extremely filthy while others bore only a few stains.[380] This seems important as a one gets a sense of the magnitude of what they did in their lives.

It is at this point that she realizes the emptiness of her decision. She is completely cut off and as far away as she feels she could possibly be from the relief she had hoped for. One person she encountered gave her the impression that he had taken his own life. Her description, though, is a person whose clothing is so very old and dirty and he is completely void of thought. She asked herself if he could have been on the earth when Jesus was alive, maybe he could be Judas Iscariot.[381] This statement, like the issue of being self-absorbed, will have a bearing on the encounter.

An Encounter with God

It is at this point that Angie describes hearing a voice of incredible power, "crashing over me like a booming wave of sound; a voice that encompassed such ferocious anger that with one word it could destroy the universe, and that also encompassed such potent and unwavering love that, like the sun it could coax life from the earth."[382]

It is at this point in the encounter that God asks her directly – "Is this what you really want?"[383] Her description of God is very exact down to the detail. She is not sure, however, whether the light she saw emanating from God could or would not cross the barrier into darkness.[384]

Through the next phase of her conversation with God, He repeatedly asks her the same question but in different ways. Going from "Is this what you really want?" to "Do you realize this is the worst thing you could have done?"[385] As the pace of this exchange goes back and forth, she determines that Jesus is in her presence and He begins to make intercession on her behalf.

The moment she encountered Jesus she began to realize the depth of her issues paled in comparison to the depth Jesus had gone to save her life, to make atonement on her behalf. She had a sense that He had lived her life. Jesus' intercession with the Father came with a forensic feel: Jesus the defense attorney – presenting the facts of the case, and God the universal judge seeking justice for the universe for the deed she had committed. Jesus made the case in her defense: He had already paid for the sin she had committed.[386]

She described her entry into this place as a spiritual "time-out."[387] This is a very fitting remark in that God wanted her to understand in eternal terms the results of her decision. Her action caused the "Ripple Effect" in that she had a first-hand view of the impact on the world from her decision. Comparing this "Ripple Effect" action to a person not removing the first dandelion from their yard and the resulting impact of the widespread invasion they would make, she was able to pierce the future to a certain extent and capture the essence of the future she had molded with her suicide.[388]

On the opposite side of the damaging impact suicide would have on her family, she was able to gain insight into the nature of God and the missionary role God desires each of us to play. Her children would have been knocked off their stride in the roles they were to play in reaching out and completing the mission God had assigned to them. They would be damaged emotionally, mentally, and physically by the selfish act Angie had committed.[389] This caused her great despair.

This opposite side of the "Ripple Effect" gave her the opportunity to see what God's goodness does in the lives of people when it is given a chance. Each act of kindness and goodness begets another and this becomes a thread through which God has the greatest impact on our lives. That would be "Paying it Forward" but in reality this is God's way of sowing divine love into our everyday lives.[390]

Angie's case belongs to Type 5 of suicide, mentioned above, but God rhetorically asked her "Is this what you really want?" and "Do you realize this is the worst thing you could have done?" These were a kind of judgment upon her. Her leaving her children behind might have been the reason why she experienced the darkness of self-absorption and was sent back to life.

Peter R's NDE

To Peter, the three negative NDEs happened in mid '87 within a 3 month period. At that time he was using amphetamines.

#1: I had been living hard, & strained my heart to such a degree that it finally gave out. I felt difficulty breathing, & lay on the floor of my flat. I then felt an incredible pain, the like of which I had never experienced before. It was so severe, I reached for a knife to kill myself to get away from the pain. It felt like a steel band was tightened around my chest to such an extent, that I was crushed. I thought of crawling downstairs to a young girl that lived there to get help, but I KNEW I would not make it, & if somehow I did, I would die in front of her. I considered the effect my gruesome death would have on her, & [she was 21] thought it best to stay where I was & let nature take its course. [I had wet myself, & my nose & eyes were running] I then felt a curious detachment to what was happening, & I lost ALL sensation in my physical body. My hearing CEASED TO BE, & I could no longer move or focus my eyes, but I could still see.

Then I was outside my body. I don't know how I was just outside it. I was standing up, & there was a spirit waiting for me. I glanced behind me, & I saw a body lying on the floor. I was about to say to the spirit; hold on, there's someone on the floor... but the thought came out like a shout, & I realized that the body was me. I turned back to the Spirit realizing that I had died.

The Spirit said [by thought] "it was your fault that you died because you were not looking after yourself. That is considered a form of suicide, and there is a penalty that must be paid." A screen appeared far in front of me, depicting the negative aspects of my character in HUMAN FORMS. They became animated & started to attack me. I was kicked & punched. I felt the pain of each contact. Curiously, I felt no need to defend myself or fight off my attackers. They then moved backward as though they were on rewind & got back onto the screen as they were before they animated.

The Spirit then communicated; "YOU HAVE NO RIGHT TO HURT YOURSELF OR ANYONE ELSE, BECAUSE YOU AND EVERYONE ELSE ARE THE PERSONAL PROPERTY OF GOD" All this took place in a black void. There was nothing there. All negative aspects of my nature were magnified far more than what they are here in the physical realm. There was/is NO ESCAPING FROM MYSELF. I was then somehow put back in my body, & gradually began to pull myself together. It was not until many years later that I realized that I was given another chance to continue because I had put a young girl's welfare ahead of my own, even though I was dying.

#2: My heart & lungs gave out again & I went through very much the same physical reactions as the first experience. I knew I was going into that black void again, & I prayed; I won't ask for mercy or anything like that, all I have to say is that I am not FULLY RESPONSIBLE for the mental & emotional state that I am in. That was enough to allow the dying process to be reversed.

#3: Heart/lung failure again. I went into the black void. I was in a hell of my own making. I was emotionally & mentally (?) 'damned'. I had no choice but to face up to myself and knew I was doomed to stay where I was until I did, & made an effort to get my thinking & living straight. All the experiences had a timelessness about them, & if 2 seconds pass here in the physical, an 'eternity' is there. I hope I have made myself reasonably clear. I cannot prove what I experienced, as it always remains subjective for the experiencer. Even if I could prove with medical records all illnesses, it still won't prove the actual out of body experiences. I know this will be of help to some people out there. We all go somewhere after leaving the physical.[391]

On the first case, Peter does not know what medications killed him. God pointed out the fact that he needed to take care of his body better. God gave him a second opportunity to live life through for his kind heart and his potential.

The first case belongs to the first type of killing oneself for self-disdain and the fifth type of drug addictions. He said that he was taking amphetamines at the time of NDEs. We don't know what led him to commit suicide each time.

Peter is convinced that the Spirit was sent to help him, and those animated aspects of his character were simply he turning against himself to teach him a lesson. It was self-judgment.

On the second case, we don't know the state of Peter's mental and emotional state. Obviously, his physical, mental, and emotional state (the second type of suicide) produced the collapse of his heart and lungs. So he was exonerated from being fully accountable for his suicide.

On the third case, Peter committed suicide because of his illness. Yet, his main concern is to help other potential suicides. Peter suggests the following:

> I sincerely hope that I have been of some benefit to someone. (actually, I know I have because a lot of people are ashamed to admit that they were/are so dysfunctional that their NDE was negative). In actual fact, it is these people who have a responsibility to tell others what could befall others if they persist in destructive behavior. They are actually BEACONS showing the way to the truth.

The important lesson he learned from his NDEs is to love ourselves. That is an indication on how well we can love others.

Peter appreciates NDERF (Near Death Experience Research Foundation) for providing him an opportunity to share his experiences with others.

Carl Knighton

Carl was raised in the Christian church and was taught that heaven and hell were real. Even as a child, he was sensitive to the subjects of God. He recalls, "All through the power of God, I've seen angels, even at an early age. They let me know that God was with me."[392] After high school, Carl got married and joined the army. Both his marriage and his military career did not last long. His superiors told him that he had performed poorly on his job and that he needed to do better or he would not be promoted. He got so frustrated that he made the decision to go AWOL. He hitchhiked to Ohio to see an old friend. While there, he went on a drug binge for two weeks.

One night he went to a crack house in the worst part of Columbus. He recalls, "You could smell the stench of the crack cocaine and marijuana. People were high and lying all over the floors."[393] He smoked some crack, drank some alcohol, and took other drugs. But, he believes it was a Valium pill that killed him. He remembers:

> When I took that Valium pill, I collapsed onto the floor. Everything went pitch-black dark. I began to quiver. I got the shakes, and I started going down and down into a deep pit. I began to smell the stench of hell. It was the most rotten smell you could ever imagine. More than you could imagine. Hell is real. It's real. It's just like the Bible says; you're in torment. I could feel myself being tugged and pulled at like the demons were pulling at me and calling my name, 'We gotcha! We gotcha! We gotcha! You belong to us now!' I saw souls, lost souls that were in torment. They were in the lake of fire. They were crying and calling on God. They were hopeless. I called on the Lord. Jesus! Jesus! Jesus! As soon as I called His name, I saw the hand of God snatch me out of hell, and my spirit went back into my body.[394]

Carl thinks he was in hell for longer than half an hour. He says, "I was shaking and trembling. I was dead, but there was a God and a Jesus that loved me so much."[395]

Three days later he returned to Ft. Eustis, Virginia to face the penalties of his AWOL. He was demoted and confined to the barracks for thirty days. During his time of confinement, he completely surrendered his life to Jesus Christ. He says, "God loved me so much that he gave me a second life. I'm here to tell His story. Don't throw your life away."[396] Today Carl s married again and on a mission to share his story of the reality of heaven and hell.

Carl's suicide is of the fourth type, due to chemical addiction. Since his drug binge was voluntary, he was accountable for his own death. That could be the reason why he went straight to hell. Even though his suicide was accidental, he killed himself, no one else did it. In point of fact, drug addicts cannot fully control their own wills. Drugs can shift addicts' brain structures.[397] As Dr. George Ritchie witnessed, spirits of alcohol/drug addictions can occupy addicts. Many suicides that result from chemical addiction regret their actions after killing themselves, because of the temptation of spirits within. Carl was delivered from hell by God's sheer grace. His case is similar to that of Howard Storm.

In fact, most drug addicts' suicides are, strictly speaking, involuntary in terms of the enormous controlling power of drugs. Drug epidemics are sweeping the country. According to preliminary data compiled by The New York Times, 59,000 to 65,000 people died from drug overdoses in 2016, the largest annual jump ever recorded in the U.S. history. And all evidence suggests the problem has continued to worsen in 2017.[398] Since Carl's case is a suicidal death caused by drug overdose, his story may have an impact upon drug users.

Carl's case also may shed light on suicidal veterans. About 20 veterans a day commit suicide nationwide, according to new data from the Department of Veterans Affairs.[399] Since Carl was a struggling veteran, his story may inspire struggling veterans with drug/alcohol addictions, mental issues, or other problems. The God of love can help them pursue their destinies in spite of their tragic lives.

A Suicide Case of a Certain Man: Swedenborg

Here is a case of suicide Swedenborg mentioned in his writing. This man committed suicide from his despair:

> It appears that whatever happens at the hour of death, is carried into the other life, and the state is continued for some time. Thus we read in the "Spiritual Diary" of a person who had been reduced by melancholy to despair, until being instigated by diabolical spirits, he destroyed himself, by thrusting a knife into his body. "This spirit came to me," writes Swedenborg, "complaining that he was miserably treated by evil spirits. He was seen by me, holding a knife in his hand, as though he would plunge it into his breast. "With this knife he labored very hard, as wishing rather to cast it from him, but in vain."[400]

Although circumstances at the event of our death stay with us for a while, they do not permanently determine our destinies in Swedenborg's view.

Swedenborg upheld that God does not judge us after death, even suicidal deaths. We come to choose heaven and hell by our hearts. Our random actions will not decide our final dwelling places, but our hearts of love and ways of life will. Swedenborg had a compassionate understanding of the mental illness of suicides. The following explains his thoughtfulness:

> No one is reformed in a state of mental illness because such illness takes away rationality and thus the liberty of acting in accord with reason. The whole mind is sick and not sane; the sane mind is rational, but not a sick one. Such disorders are melancholy, a spurious or a false conscience, fantasies of different kinds, mental grief over misfortune, anxiety and anguish of the mind over a bodily defect.[401]

Swedenborg would have concurred with Dr. Ritchie on the fact that all suicides do not go to hell. In accordance with the motivations and circumstances of suicide, their inner selves will lead them to their proper places.

To Atwater, suicide near-death experiencers clarify the confusions and misunderstandings of suicide by sharing their own episodes. They typically return with a feeling that suicide solves no problem and that they need to remain in earth to deal with their problems. They are notably rehabilitated and refreshed by that feeling, using their near-death events as the sources of the courage, strength, and inspiration of their renewed lives.[402]

In brief, we cannot escape from our problems by committing suicides. Thus, our life on earth is a precious opportunity to solve and heal all physical, mental, and spiritual issues of earthly life. Otherwise, these problems will persist on another level in the next life.

What a Big Picture of Heaven and Hell Does Emanuel Swedenborg Draw?

CHRISTIAN MYSTICS[403] HAVE set the foundation of Christian spirituality for over two thousand years. While Christian theologians have generally pursued divine truth with a goal of formulating church doctrines mainly through the Scriptures and reason, Christian mystics have endeavored to meet God directly through the Scriptures and prayer without going through theology. Christian mystics have even reached the realms of heaven and hell through their communion with God. While the Scriptures describe the next life in a limited way, the mystics have expanded that picture of heaven and hell through their direct access to God in prayers.

Among the mystics, Emanuel Swedenborg and Sundar Singh stand out concerning heaven and hell. Their extensive mystical experiences have described the spiritual realms beyond NDErs and theologians. While Swedenborg and Singh disagree with NDErs on several issues concerning heaven and hell, they do mainly complement NDERs' understandings. By no means are their understandings whole. However, their pictures of the spiritual world are much clearer and bigger than others. We will explore Swedenborg's understanding of the spiritual world in this chapter and Singh's in the next. Swedenborg wrote in Swedish and Singh wrote in Hindi.

His Life

Emanuel Swedenborg was born in Stockholm, Sweden, on January 29, 1688. His mother, Sara Behm, died when he was eight years old but her quiet, benevolent spirit formed Emanuel's character. His father, Jesper Swedberg, was professor of theology at the University of Uppsala and later became Bishop of Skara. At the age of eleven, Emanuel attended the University of Uppsala, where his father was teaching.[404] On completing his studies in 1709, he journeyed abroad. His first stop was England where he studied natural sciences, both under scientists such as Isaac Newton and Edmund Halley and on his own. Next he went to Holland and studied economics, politics, cosmology, mathematics, anatomy, physiology, metallurgy, mineralogy, geology, mining engineering, and chemistry.[405] In 1716 when he returned to Sweden, he worked with Swedish inventor Christopher Polhem, and King Charles XII appointed him to the post of Extraordinary Assessor in the Royal College of Mines and to a position at the Board of Mines. At that time, the mines were a crucial part of Sweden's economy. Queen Ulrika Eleonora later elevated the Swedberg family to nobility, changing their name to Swedenborg in 1718.[406]

Swedenborg's first book was a philosophic work titled Principles of Chemistry (1720), and his first major publication was *Philosophical and Metallurgical Works* (*Opera Philosophica et Mineralia*). The first of a series of books on anatomy was the two-volume *Dynamics of the Soul's Domain* (*Oeconomia Regni Animalisss*) published in 1740 and 1741.

From 1743 to 1744, Swedenborg underwent his first transcendent experiences in Holland and England. They were intense dreams and visions which he logged in his diary. On April 6, 1744, Swedenborg went to bed at ten o'clock, and thirty minutes later he heard a noise under his head. He then thought that the Tempter (Satan) [407] was gone. Immediately afterward a tremor came over him, powerfully affecting him from the head over the whole body, accompanied by some sound.[408] This happened several times. He felt that something holy had come over him. He then fell asleep again, and about twelve, one, or two o'clock at night a strong tremor seized his whole body, with the sound of many winds. With such an indescribable sound, he was thrown from the bed on his face and became wide-awake, opening his spiritual eyes.[409] While Swedenborg prayed and lifted up his hands, a hand came and firmly pressed his hands. He then continued his prayer, laid on Jesus, and looked at Him face to face; "It was a countenance with a holy expression, and so that it cannot be described; it was also smiling, and I really believe that His countenance was such during His life upon earth."[410] This occurrence was his first meeting with Jesus.

In 1745, he received Jesus' call to bring a new revelation to the world in London, England. From that year until his death, he spent most of his time adding theological writings to his long previous scientific and philosophical works.[411] In 1747, he declined a promotion that had been granted to him by the King. He instead petitioned the king to release him from his service on the Board of Mines so that he could allow time for theological writing. Between 1747 and 1756, Swedenborg published his twelve-volume theological work, *Secrets of Heaven (Arcana Coelestia)*. Theological writings continually flowed from his pen. By 1758 he completed more new titles: *Heaven and Hell*, a description of the afterlife of their residents; *White Horse*, on the inner meaning of the Bible; *Last Judgment* and *New Jerusalem*, distinctive aspects of his theology.[412]

From 1759, a series of supernatural incidents took place and Swedenborg drew international attention. In 1759, while Swedenborg was attending a dinner party in the Swedish city of Göteborg about 300 miles away from home, he suddenly became pale and disturbed and described a fire in Stockholm that was menacing his house. He feared that some of his manuscripts would be destroyed. Two hours later, he told his friends that the fire had been put out three doors down from his house. Two days later, messengers from Stockholm arrived in Göteborg and confirmed what Swedenborg had said to them.[413]

Because of this incident, some others made Swedenborg widely known not only in Sweden but in continental Europe as well.

The following year, the widow of the recently deceased Dutch ambassador in Stockholm received a bill for a very expensive silver service her husband had purchased. She was sure he had paid the bill, but could not locate the receipt. She asked Swedenborg for help and so he met her husband in the spiritual world. The ambassador told him to tell her that he would reveal its location. Eight days later she had a dream in which her husband told her the location of the receipt and she found it.[414]

When Swedenborg was introduced to Sweden's Queen Louisa Ulrika in 1761, she asked him whether he could communicate with her recently deceased brother, Prince Augustus Wilhelm of Prussia. After agreeing to do so, Swedenborg returned to court a few days later and told her something privately. On hearing the statement, she exclaimed that only her brother would have known what Swedenborg had just told her.[415]

In December 1771, Swedenborg suffered a stroke that impeded his ability to speak and caused him to be unconscious for almost three weeks. During January and February, he gradually recovered and received visitors. In February, in response to a letter from noted minister John Wesley suggesting a meeting after his six-month journey, Swedenborg responded that it would be impossible, because he would permanently enter the world of spirits on March 29, 1772, at the age of eighty-four.[416]

The Afterlife

His grasp of heavens, hells, and the world of spirits is the most comprehensive and profound in the history of humanity. His heavens are where God, angels, and good spirits reside and they are open to anyone who wants to reside there. His hells are most fitting places for those who like to live the life of darkness and nights. Their residents opt to live there than live in heavens. The world of spirits is the intermediary place where people would take their own final destinies in keeping with their natures (see chapter 3).

WHAT HAPPENS WHEN WE ENTER INTO THE NEXT LIFE?
We awaken from the dead and enter the world of spirits first. We think, breathe, talk, and work. Our thought and affections consist of our personhood. When we die, the presence of angels is perceived as an aromatic odor around us to keep evil spirits from coming near us.[417]

People who have not believed in a life after death are very embarrassed by the fact that they are still alive, and reject the divine and the reality of their life after life. They join others of like mind and move away from people of faith. Most of them are attached to some hellish community.[418] Swedenborg had met some newcomers from the world and had recognized them by their faces and voices; but when he met them later, he could not recognize them.

People who were involved in good affections had lovely faces, while people who were absorbed in evil affections had threatening ones.[419]

How do We Live in Heaven?

People live an authentic life in a real spiritual body and a real world. They read, work, sleep and waken, recreate, and worship. They relish an active life of service to others.

We come after death into that hell or into that heaven in which we have been while in the world. Heaven or hell cannot be outside us; it is within us.[420] Hell has three universal loves: the love of ruling from selfish love, the love of greed from worldly love, and lewd love. Heaven has the three universal loves opposite to these: the love of serving others from the love of usefulness, the love of attaining goods from the love of using them well, and pure love.[421]

The World of Spirits and Its Three States

After death, we pass through three states in the world of spirits to expose who we are. The first state engages our more outward natures, the second engages our more inward natures, and the third engages a state of preparation.[422]

Our First State After Death

In the first state, we will be jubilantly welcomed to the world of spirits by our family members, relatives, friends, and others whom we have known in the world.[423] The first state after our death is similar to our state in the world, for we would keep our externals such as our faces, speech, and dispositions, having much the same moral and civil life.[424] The faces of hypocrites change more slowly than those of other people, because of their lifetime practice of arranging their inner minds into a counterfeit of good affections.[425] This first state of life can last for days, months, or a year depending on the person, but rarely beyond a year for anyone.[426]

Our Second State After Death

The second state after our death is the state of our interiors—our minds, our wills, and our thoughts. Because all are free from bodily restraints, those who were good and wise internally in the world act better and more wisely than before, while those who were evil act more foolishly and insanely.[427]

Our Third State After Death

The third state after death is a state of instruction. This state is for those who enter heaven. Good spirits are led into the third state where they prepare for heaven through instruction. Those who are bound for hell do not go through the third state because they cannot be instructed on account of their own selfish love.[428]

The senses of the spirits are far more acute than those living on earth. They have great sight, living in a really bright light. Spirits also have more sensitive hearing, smell, and touch when compared with their earthly perceptions. They have desires and affections. Spirits think more clearly and distinctively than they did on earth. They lie down, eat and, drink as in the former world. Death is not the destruction of life but its full continuation.[429]

George Ritchie's Intermediary Space: Astral, Purgatory, or Terrestrial?

In the late 1960s, Dr. Ritchie's NDE testimony fascinated Raymond Moody at the University of Virginia and led him to publish his book, *Life After Life.* Dr. Ritchie is unique in mentioning the intermediary place, even though he was not quite sure what kind of place that was. That is why he wonders whether it is "astral, purgatory, or terrestrial"?[430] Swedenborg calls it the "world of spirits." Ritchie saw another city superimposed on our physical city in his vision. He came to understand that this city belonged to astral beings. Most of the residents of one realm weren't aware of the existence of the other.[431]

As our earthly cities are divided by ethnicity and moral values, so are the cities in the astral realm: "Birds of a feather flock together."[432] People gather together because of the fear of others who disagree with them. Ritchie says that one of the places he observed deep in this realm appeared to be a receiving station. When he observed this, it was during the middle of the World War Two and he saw many young beings arrive there as results of their physical deaths. He also saw angels working with them trying to help them realize that God is truly a God of the living. He wondered whether this realm could be the paradise Jesus referred to in Luke 23.[433]

Besides Ritchie and Marietta Davis, I do not know any contemporary NDErs who describe the intermediary place extensively.

CAN OUR WHOLE BODY REMEMBER?

We leave nothing behind except our bodies. When we are faced with our deeds after death, the angels who are given responsibility for examining us look carefully, beginning with the fingers of one hand, then of the other, and then the whole body. When Swedenborg wondered why this was so, it was explained to him. The reason is that the details of our thought and intention move out from there into the whole body. The entire body is our "Book of life" mentioned in the Bible.[434] Each and everything we have done will be visible as if in broad daylight.[435] A great deal of Swedenborg's experience has affirmed that we consist of our love or intention after death.[436] After death we are engaged in every sense, memory, thought, and affection.

After this life, there is judgment for all: "And just as it is appointed for mortals to die once, and after that the judgment" (Heb 9:27). NDEr Andy, however, said that in heaven there was "no ledger of good and bad deeds. Only warmth, peace, joy, happiness, forgiveness, and love in the Light. I'm one with the unconditionally loving Light. I'm home forever."[437] Andy's idea has been supported by many fellow NDErs.

Dr. Long's God Study found that NDErs typically did not sense being judged by God. Some examples are the following:

- When I was enveloped in this clear white light, the love and acceptance of me was way beyond any love I have felt on earth. There was no judgment of me; there was only acceptance of me as a unique self.
- God does not judge anyone. He loves unconditionally.
- Powerful, unconditional love—the feeling of just knowing what it is. I felt like I was a sinner, and I was amazed that God would show me such love despite my mistakes in life that may have hurt others or myself.[438]

It is very rare that NDErs feel judged by another being even when they re-view every action of their life. God seldom expressed disapproval of the life of the near-death experiencer.[439]

Some NDErs, however, believe that there may be some kind of a device of judgment in the next life. Here is a good example:

> Although Sharon experienced God as not judging at all, she also learned that we judge ourselves and that what we put out to the universe returns to us in some way. This gives rise to the intriguing idea that, although God might not serve as our judge, nonetheless there might be a mechanism whereby judgment is built into the universe's fabric. Could goodness and morality be more like scientific laws than we suspected? It is a fascinating idea.[440]

Sharon is right in thinking that there might be a mechanism of judgment built in the universe. That mechanism is our own body memories. Thus, we judge ourselves from our own memories. Indeed, God does not directly judge evildoers, but their whole bodies remember what they have done. Not during NDEs, but in the next life their sins will be exposed in public. Also, the evil spirits torment other evil spirits in hell. Such an ironical place is hell, where evil spirits judge and torture other evil spirits. This is the view of judgment for both Swedenborg and Singh. This can be somewhat illumi-nated by evil deeds and their punishments in the world, where they are also closely tied. The one difference is that in the world, evil can be hidden, but evil cannot be covered up in the next life.[441]

Repentance

To Swedenborg, it is impossible to grant the life of heaven to a person who has led his or her life opposed to it while in the world. Some people believed that they would readily accept divine truths after death, after hearing them from angels, that they would become believers and live changed lives, so that they could be admitted into heaven. However, this has been tested with some people with this kind of belief, so that they could learn that no repentance after death exists. These people eventually returned to the lives that they loved. There is no way to change their evil ways of lives after death.[442] If they followed divine truths, yet occasionally fall into wrong doing, they are able to turn around and move toward heaven. But, if their basic natures are evil, they are unable to turn around.

Swedenborg's Heaven

Swedenborg never mentions the superiority of Christianity. However, his view of the Trinity discloses the indispensability of our acceptance of the Trinity in entering heaven. If we deny the Trinity, we will be outside of heaven because the Triune God is the contents of heaven and Jesus is the visible manifestation of the Triune God Most NDErs are silent about the doctrine of the Trinity.

WHO IS THE GOD OF HEAVEN?

In his explanation of heaven, Swedenborg starts his book with the most important issue: who the God of heaven is. Everything else depends on this issue. He states that no one is acknowledged as God except the Lord, just as God taught in the book of John that, "He is one with the Father; that anyone who sees Him sees the Father; and that everything holy comes from Him" (John 10:30, 38; 14:9-11; 16:13-15).[443] For Swedenborg, the "Lord" means Jesus.

WHY IS THE TRINITY THE MOST IMPORTANT ISSUE?

To Swedenborg, the reality of the Trinity is the most important issue in our discussion of heaven and hell. He often talked with angels about this issue, and they consistently said that they are incapable of dividing the Divine into three, for they know that the Divine is one and that this oneness is in the Lord. The angels also told Swedenborg that as believers arrive from earth with the idea of three divine beings, they are unable to enter heaven until they accept the reality of the Triune God since their thought vacillates from one to the other and since in heaven they cannot think "three and say 'one.'"[444]

In heaven, people essentially speak directly from their thoughts, so that they have a kind of thought-speech (telepathy) or vocal thought. In such heavenly communication of all thoughts, if people think "three" and say "one," they are immediately known for what they are and are repelled right away.[445]

Thought about one God opens heaven to people since there is but one God. On the contrary, thought about multiple gods closes heaven since the idea of multiple gods ends the idea of one God. Thought about the true God opens heaven since heaven and everything hinging on it is from the true God. Instead, thought about a false God closes heaven, since only the true God is acknowledged in heaven.[446]

Swedenborg underscores the real importance of our thought about God: "Thought about *God the Creator, the Redeemer, and the Enlightener* opens heaven, for this is the trinity of the one and true God. Again, thought about God infinite, eternal, uncreated, omnipotent, omnipresent, and omniscient opens heaven, for these are attributes of the essence of the one and true God."[447] Swedenborg also explains the Trinity with the components of a person: "*The Divine of the Father*, which constitutes *the soul*, and *the Divine of the Son*, which constitutes *the body* and t*he Divine of the Holy Spirit or the proceeding Divine, which constitutes the operatio*n, are the three essentials of the one God. . . . In every man there is soul, body, and operation; so also in the Lord."[448] A number of Christians would be reinstructed on the Trinity if they have some misunderstanding on the Trinity and are willing to be corrected by the Holy Spirit.[449]

His idea of the Trinity affirms the oneness of the Trinity: "In the Lord is the Trinity-*the Divine Itself, the Divine Human, and the proceeding Divine Holy*-and these are a one."[450] He thinks that numerous Christians have the images of the three Gods because of the term "the three persons." God is not three persons, but One.[451]

If believers have disregarded the Lord Jesus, recognized only divine the Creator, and have hardened their minds to the Trinity, they are outside heaven. Likewise, those who have denied the Lord's divine nature and have recognized only his human nature (such as the Socinians: early Unitarians) are also outside heaven by default.[452]

There are also those who claim to believe in the invisible Divine, called the Reality of the Universe, as the source of all beings and reject any faith in the Lord. When examined, it turns out that they do not believe in any God at all, since the invisible Divine is practically equivalent to nature. This is incompatible with faith and love because it is not adequate substance for thought. These people are ended up being with those called naturalists.[453]

In our time, naturalists are similar to New Age people who believe in God as the source of all beings and the impersonal energy. A number of NDErs think of God as the impersonal energy or universal principle. Their idea of God is incongruent with the essential belief of the Christianity that Swedenborg upholds. Even though they thought that they had experienced heaven, some of them could have been in an intermediary place (the world of spirits) between heaven and hell.

In his book, *God and the Afterlife,* Dr. Long reports a remarkable increase of NDErs' belief in God after their NDEs: "Before their experience 64 percent of NDErs believed 'God exists.'"[454] After their NDEs, the percentage of the believers of God's existence leaps to the big 81.9 percent.[455]

These 81.9 percent of NDErs experienced the existence of God, but they rarely talk about the Trinity. They probably did not stay in the spiritual realm long enough to find out the truth of the Trinity. Thus, mystics may help such NDErs understand the reality the Trinity further.

CAN PEOPLE ENTER HEAVEN THROUGH DIRECT DIVINE MERCY?

Some people believe that acceptance into heaven is a matter of divine mercy given to those who have faith.[456] This divine mercy is available to the whole human family; it is never withdrawn from anyone.[457] The Lord never does anything against the divine design. That design is heaven within a person.[458] Any person who accepts heaven into himself or herself enters heaven.[459] The Lord never rejects anyone from heaven, but an evildoer would not stay there because of the breath of heavenly love and the inflow of heavenly light that cause hellish torment in them.[460]

Furthermore, Swedenborg warns of the danger of teaching justification by faith *alone* and underscores the pivotal importance of the life of faith and love. Many Christians come to the Lord and expect to get into heaven by faith alone without changing their wicked nature. They don't know that faith without love is just knowledge and that no one can enter heaven by knowledge alone. Gnostics in the early centuries believed that they would be saved by knowledge alone. That's the reason why Jesus said to the "Lord-Lord"ers, "Not everyone who says to me, 'Lord, Lord,' will enter the kingdom of heaven, but only the one who does the will of my Father in heaven. . . . Then I will declare to them, 'I never knew you; go away from me, you evildoers'" (Matt. 7:21-13). Swedenborg points out the significance of the nature of our love in heavenly living, which is not by faith alone.

Martin Luther's *justification by faith alone* can mislead people. Angels are distressed that the people of faith alone are unaware of the fact of the impossibility of faith alone because faith without its source, love, is a piece of knowledge.[461] Angels said that no one is accepted into heaven by faith alone, but by one's own life of love and faith.[462] Paul says, "The only thing that counts is faith working through love" (Gal 5:6). It is our transformed heart in the life of *faith and love* that leads us to heavenly salvation.

Does the Lord's Divine Nature Make Heaven?

The nature of God springing from the Lord is the *good* deep-rooted in love and the *truth* deep-rooted in faith.[463] Everyone in the heavens knows, believes, and even perceives that nothing good is designed and fulfilled by the self and that nothing true is deliberated and believed by the self.

Everything comes from the Lord. Anything good and true from the self is not good or true because there is no life within it. Angels of the inmost heaven perceive clearly and feel the divine inflow. The more they accept it, the more they seem to be in heaven; for they are more fully absorbed in love and faith, in the light of intelligence, wisdom, and the measure of their subsequent heavenly joy.[464] All life is from the Lord and everything in the universe flows back to the good and the true. Our life of love returns to the good and our life of faith or intelligence goes back to the true. Thus, as everything good and true comes from the Lord, so does all life.[465] Since angels know and believe this, they dismiss any thanks offered them for the good they have done. In fact, they feel offended and go away if anyone credits them for anything good. Heaven cannot accept those spirits who during their earthly lives had persuaded themselves that their *good deeds* and *true beliefs* stemmed from themselves or claimed credit for them. These are people who regard merit as good deeds and claim righteousness for themselves.[466]

Many NDErs experience the unconditional love of God. Therefore, coming back to this world, they really believe in the power of this unconditional love and want to implement such love in their lives. It is true that our good deeds and our true beliefs come from the God of unconditional love so that there is no place for self-righteousness in heaven.

WHAT IS PROPER DESTINY OF HUMAN BEINGS?

We are born not for the sake of ourselves but for the sake of others. We are created to serve our fellow-citizens, society, country, the church, and therefore the Lord.[467]

We can be perfected in knowledge, intelligence, and wisdom to eternity.[468] When we are gifted with truths, we are perfected in intelligence and wisdom. When we are perfected in intelligence and wisdom, we are blessed with happiness to eternity.[469] Each of us is destined for eternal happiness in heaven. Yet we must first live through this valley of the shadow of sorrow, suffering, and death.[470]

The state of our inner natures makes heaven, and heaven is within each one of us, not outside us. This is what the Lord teaches in saying, "Once Jesus was asked by the Pharisees when the kingdom of God was coming, and he answered, 'The kingdom of God is not coming with things that can be observed; nor will they say, "Look, here it is!" or "There it is!" For, in fact, the kingdom of God is among you'" (Luke 17:20-21).

All perfection increases as we move inward and decreases as we move outward because more inward things are closer to the Lord and are intrinsically purer, while more outward things are more remote from the Lord and are intrinsically cruder. Angelic perfection is composed of intelligence, wisdom, love, and everything good, with happiness as their result. It does not involve happiness alone, for happiness in the absence of the rest is not inward and is superficial.[471]

THREE HEAVENS AND TWO DISTINCTIVE LOVES IN HEAVEN

The three heavens are quite clearly distinguished from each other. There is an inmost or third heaven, an intermediate or second one, and an outmost or first heaven.[472] We have an inmost nature (spirit), an intermediate nature (mind) and an outmost nature (body). This is because when human beings were created, the whole divine design was copied into them and they are, therefore, a heaven in miniature.[473]

Love for the Lord abides in the third or inmost heaven, while love for our neighbor abides in the second or intermediate heaven. Both come from the Lord, and each makes a heaven. Loving the Lord does not mean loving Him in His role, but signifies loving the good that flows from Him. Loving the good means intending and doing what is good, out of love. Jesus himself teaches the truth of this in the Gospel of John: "They who have my commandments and keep them are those who love me; and those who love me will be loved by my Father, and I will love them and reveal myself to them . . . Those who love me will keep my word, and my Father will love them, and we will come to them and make our home with them" (14:21, 23). [474]

DOES EVERYTHING ON EARTH DERIVE FROM HEAVEN: THE PRINCIPLE OF CORRESPONDENCE

Whatever happens in the natural world emerges from the spiritual world.[475] Heaven is yoked with earth in everything.[476] Earth depends on heaven in all things. This is the principle of correspondence. We are unaware of this relation of correspondence because we have moved away from heaven to love for the world.[477] Everything in the natural world corresponds to the spiritual world, not just in general but in detail.[478] This is the reason Moses built the tabernacle according to the pattern God showed to him in the mountain (Exod. 25:40). NDErs agree with Swedenborg that in the spiritual realm all things, such as trees, grass, and flowers are there and they are truly alive and are more real than things on earth.[479]

All correspondence with heaven is correspondence with the Lord because heaven is from Him and He is heaven.[480] As everything agreeing with the divine plan corresponds to heaven, everything disagreeing with the divine plan corresponds to hell. Everything that corresponds to heaven reveals what is good and true, while that which corresponds to hell exposes what is evil and false.[481] Furthermore, the sun of the earth came into being from the sun of heaven: "The Lord created everything by means of the spiritual world's sun, but not by means of the physical world's sun, since this latter sun is far beneath the former one."[482] While the sun of heaven has life, the sun of the earth is essentially lifeless. Our spirit provides life to the lifeless body.[483] "This sun is the first emanation of divine love and wisdom, and as explained above, everything comes from divine love and wisdom."[484] This means that our cosmologists will not fully understand the origin of our sun without knowing its heavenly origin.

Is There Time in Heaven?

Scripture says, "With the Lord a day is like a thousand years, and a thousand years are like a day" (2 Peter 3:8). Here Peter refers to *kairos* (God's time). *Kairos* is used eighty-six times in the New Testament[485] while *chronos* (clock time) is used fifty-four times in the New Testament.[486]

Paul Tillich describes *kairos* as the right time or qualitative time and *chronos* as the measurable or quantifiable time.[487] But, the tree of life on the new earth will be "yielding its fruit every month" (Revelation 22:2). What does Revelation mean by every month? Does this indicate that there are twelve months in a year in heaven? Revelation 8:1 says, "There was silence in heaven for about half an hour." Does this indicate that there are twenty-four hours a day in heaven? I don't believe that heaven has twenty-four earthly hours. In these sentences, the author uses the category of earthly time to express unquantifiable heavenly time. Heavenly time is eternity.

It is clear that in the next life we'll no longer live in *chronos* but in *kairos*. In heaven instead of years and days there are changes of state; where years and days exist, there are times. Where changes of state exist, there are only states.[488] As angels have no notion of time, but they do have an idea of eternity different from persons on the earth. There is no earthly *chronos* time in heaven. There are, however, events happening in the heavens. Quantifiable time is not there, but the change of state in sequences of events is present. Instead of hours, days, and years, heaven has changes of state.[489] Eternity does not mean an infinite time, but the infinite state. With no concept of time, angels have a different concept of eternity than we do. They perceive eternity as an infinite state whereas we perceive it as infinite time.[490] Although things continuously take place in sequence and develop in heaven the way they do in the world, angels do not have a notion or concept of time and space. While years and days exist with time, changes of state occur in different events. The reason we have time in our world is that the earth revolves around the sun. It is different for heaven's sun. It does not make years and days by sequential motions and rotations but makes apparent changes of state.[491]

In his earlier days when Swedenborg was using a concept of time, not changing states, he could not grasp what eternity meant. He could not understand what God had been doing before creation from eternity. His anxiety level would go up because of this until he came to perceive the notion of eternity from the perspective of the angels, which shed light for him that we must not think about eternity in terms of time but in terms of state.[492] NDErs testify that there is no time in heaven like there is on earth. However, they do not deny the sequence of events.

Is There Space in Heaven?

"In my Father's house there are many dwelling places. If it were not so, would I have told you that I go to prepare a place for you?" (John 14:2). Jesus says that there are places in heaven. He confirms this by saying, "Then he will send out the angels, and gather his elect from the four winds, from the ends of the earth to the ends of heaven" (Mark 13:27). The ends of heaven indicate some measurement of location. The ends can signify particular locations.

Numerous communities are founded according to the nature of the love and faith in which they are involved. People involved in a similar good build a single community. The distances between communities are established on the state of their love or good that is prevailing in them. Persons who differ greatly fall apart from each other; persons who differ slightly come closer together; the likeness among them brings unity. Persons within given communities are distinguished from one another in a like way, with the wisest and most loving of them living in the center and the simpler, less remarkable ones toward the fringes. As individuals on earth recognize family members, relatives, and friends, all angels involved in similar practices of good recognize one another. They all generally have a similar appearance.[493]

In the spiritual world no space exists but appearances of space do; and these are in line with the states of love. For this reason, no one but us can dwell in our own houses, which are provided and assigned to us in accordance with the quality of our love.[494]

Space in heaven refers to the state of the interiors. Spaces or places do not exist, but states do. In heaven those in similar states are close to each other while those in dissimilar states are at a distance. The spaces in heaven depend on the internal states of consciousness. This is the reason why the heaven is far from hell, due to their contrary states. They are separated from each other. Space is not there, but the intimacy of people's hearts or empathy measures space.[495]

All movements by the angels are done not in space but in the internal state of consciousness in spirit. No measurable distance exists between them; so they have no material spaces. Changing from place to place signifies changing from state to state in this context.

God in all time is without time, and God in all space is without space. God apart from time is in all time. God is not in space. God apart from space fills all the spaces of the universe.[496]

HOW IS HEAVEN RUN?

Administration in the heavens is the administration of mutual love.[497] The form of governance in the Lord's celestial kingdom is called justice because all the people there are engaged in love to the Lord from the Lord. Anything emerging from this love is called just.[498] Governance in the Lord's spiritual kingdom is called judgment because they are engaged in spiritual "good," which is that of love toward the neighbor. What is true is an issue of judgment, and what is good is an issue of justice.[499]

All people in hell want to control others and to be on top. They hate the people who disagree with them, and use vicious means to reciprocate them because this is what selfishness is like. As a result, vicious people rule and others obey out of fear.

In heaven all the forms of governance emphasize the public good as their objective, and within this good, the good of each person.[500] Egoism rules in hell, but common goals and good rules in heaven.

WHAT DO CHILDREN DO IN HEAVEN?

All little children who form a third part of heaven are led first into a recognition and trust that the Lord is their Parent.[501] Some people believe that only children born in the church enter heaven. They say this because they believe that without baptism and church catechism, they cannot be saved. The Lord, however, accepts every child regardless of parental background and brings her or him into heaven, teaching the divine design and filling her or him with affection.[502] Understanding and wisdom form an angel, and children do not have these yet. They grow up with angels and once they are equipped with understanding and wisdom, they become angels.[503]

NDErs concur with Swedenborg on the understanding of the destiny of infants and children. They are greatly welcomed into heaven whether they are baptized in the church or not. For Augustine, unbaptized children go to *limbo* because of their original sin. Thanks be to God for the acceptance of all children into God's heaven in Swedenborg's understanding! Even Pope Benedict XVI said in 2007 that *the limbo* of infants is not the teaching of the Roman Catholic Church.[504] Infants and children are the joy of the world and heaven and are accepted into heaven without infant baptism.

WHAT ARE HEAVENLY DELIGHT AND HAPPINESS?

All delights stream out of love; whatever we love, we feel as delightful. Love is the only source of any delight. It follows from this that the quality of love determines the quality of delight. Pleasures of the flesh flow out of love of self and out of love of the world, and these are also the source of our yearnings and pleasures. All the delights of the spirit stream out of love for the

Lord and neighbor, which are also the source of affections for our deeper forms of happiness. These loves and their delights stream from the Lord and heaven by an inner path from above and move our deeper natures. The other loves and their pleasures flow in from the flesh and the world along with an outer path from below and move our outward natures.[505]

We may gather the magnitude of heaven's delight simply from the fact that everyone there joyfully shares his or her delight and blessedness with someone else. Since everyone in the heavens is like this, we can see how huge heaven's delight is.[506] In the heavens, doing good for others is pleasurable; doing good for oneself is not pleasing unless it is done so that the good may benefit someone else. This is how we love our neighbors more than ourselves.[507]

Heavenly joy is an affection composed of countless delights and joys that unite to present a single united affection. This contains a harmony of countless affections that do not come through from individual consciousness to general consciousness. Joy and delight, according to Swedenborg, seem to well up from the heart and disperse very gently through all the fibers with such a deep feeling of pleasure that the fibers are virtually nothing other than pure joy and delight.[508]

Swedenborg conversed with some spirits who thought that heaven and heavenly joy involve being great, but they were told that in heaven the greatest is the least. The term least is used to describe persons who have no power and wisdom except from the Lord. Such a person has the greatest happiness; she or he is greatest because greatness is from the Lord .[509]

People in heaven are steadily advancing toward the springtime of life. The longer they enjoy living, the more pleasant and happy is their springtime. This goes on forever, increasing in accordance with the growth and level of their love, thoughtfulness, and faith.[510] In short, to grow old in heaven means to grow young.[511]

For mystic Meister Eckhart, God is "most new" or "forever young" and God invites us into our newness.[512] The soul is created young by God in accordance with the image of God. By moving away from God we grow deteriorate.[513]

Why does the Lord Need to be Worshipped?

The essence of spiritual love is to do good to others. The essence of God's love is like the love of parents for their children. Parents love their children out of love for their children, not out of self-love. This is clearly seen in the love of a mother toward an infant. Because the Lord is to be worshipped, adored, and glorified, it seems that He loves worship, adoration, and glory from us for His own sake. In reality, He loves them for our sake, because by means of them we come into such a state that the Divine can flow into us and be felt. For by doing these activities, we remove the focus on our own self that prevents the acceptance of God. For the focus on self is self-love, which hardens and shuts off the heart. This is removed by the acknowledgment that in our own right we are nothing but evil and nothing but good comes from the Lord. This results in a softening of the heart and humiliation, from which flow forth adoration and worship.[514] God is not a megalomaniac who demands and commands us to worship Godself, but we are self-absorbed. We tend to worship ourselves. The God of unconditional love is helping us grow out of that by encouraging us to worship the ultimate Reality than our own idols. By worshipping God, we grow loving God and others in blessedness.

Swedenborg's Hell

Who Manages Hell?

Swedenborg learned that God oversees both heaven and hell. Under God's authority, every relationship between heaven and hell requires a balance. Unless God contains the attacks of hell and their madness, the balance will be lost; and if the balance were wrecked, everything else would go.[515]

There are three heavens overall; so are there also three hells overall. The deepest hell counterbalances the inmost or third heaven; a middle hell is opposite to the middle or second heaven; and the outmost hell counterweights the outmost or first heaven.[516] Overall, the hells are overseen by a general impact of divine good and divine truth from the heavens. Specifically, the hells are managed by measures of angels who are given the ability to look into the hells and check the insanities and riots there.

In a broad sense, though, all the people in the hells are ruled by their fears, some by fears sown and rooted in them by the world. However, since these fears are not adequate and gradually weaken, they are controlled through fears of punishment, which are the primary means of deterring them from doing evil. There are many kinds of punishment there, milder or more severe depending on the evil they have practiced. For the most part, the more malevolent spirits are given power over the others. They have gained control by their cunning and their schemes, being able to keep the rest in servile obedience by punishments and the resulting fears. These dominant spirits do not dare go beyond limits set for them. [517]

No Hell?

Some NDErs believe that there is no hell. There is only one home, heaven. Here is a case posted on the IANDS (International Association For Near Death Studies) website:

> I was hit by a car while riding my motorcycle. I died on the operating table.
>
> I went through the dark into the light--a soft bluish light. An entity (Jesus to me) was of the light, and the light was a doorway . . . I was relieved to know it is real! Jesus said, "I know it hurts and I know it is bad. You have not done what you said you would do and must go back." I refused. Jesus said, "You will come here, just not now . . . not yet. I am sorry." Then I was on the operating table and heard someone say, "We got him" and then "Oh my God he is awake."
>
> I am now an ordained minister and preach. I was shown there is no hell. We all go home. [518]

It is clear that he was shown there is no hell and that he experienced no hell. His experience is so real that he became an ordained minister. When he said that there is no hell, he perhaps means that he experienced the loving God who did not send him to hell. It is undeniable that he had a limited experience of heaven and hell in comparison with other NDErs and Swedenborg. In line with the Bible, Swedenborg and many other NDErs testify that hell is real and that many of them underwent hell's torments.

WHY DO EVIL SPIRITS LOOK MONSTROUS?

Seen in any of heaven's light, all the spirits in the hell appear in the form of their own degree of evil. Generally, they are forms of contempt for others, menaces against people who do not admire them; they are forms of various grades of hatred, of various forms of vengefulness. When others praise or adore and worship them, their faces compose themselves and they look almost happy and content.[519]

Swedenborg was not allowed to see hell in its overall form but was told that, like heaven, hell is in the form of a single person. However, he often saw particular forms of hells or hellish communities at their entrances; a monster appears at the gate of hell and usually gives the picture of the form of the people within. The barbarity of its residents can be imagined by things too appalling and sickening to mention.

Even though hellish spirits look like monsters in heaven's light, they look like normal people to each other. It is due to the Lord's grace that they do not look disgusting to each other.[520]

CHARACTERS OF SELF-LOVE

If hellish spirits see no prospect of esteem and glory in useful and good efforts, they would become sluggish. People ask, "Whoever did anything worthwhile, anything useful, anything worth mentioning, except for applause and prestige from other people, or in other people's minds? And what other source does this have than the fire of a love for glory and prestige—that is, then a love of self?"[521] This is why people in the world do not realize that, in its own right, love of self is the love that rules in hell and that constitutes hell within us.[522] Absorbed in self-love, we do not genuinely love our church, country, community, or any constructive activity, but we love only ourselves. Our pleasure simply lies in self-love. Self-love also leads us to love our own, specifically our children, grandchildren, and, more broadly, those people who support us. Loving our families and supporters is actually loving ourselves, for we regard the other's being in ourselves, and center on ourselves in others. These "others" include all who praise, respect, and admire us.[523]

Being led by ourselves is being led by our own self, and that we claim ourselves as our own is nothing but evil. It is actually our evil inheritance that involves loving ourselves more than God and the world more than heaven.[524] We regard people outside our group and who oppose out evildoing as worthless; we are also treated the same by our enemies.[525]

HELLFIRE AND GNASHING OF TEETH

Some people understand hellfire to be material fire while others think of it as torment in general, the pangs of conscience, or just a phrase to scare people. Some understand the gnashing of teeth to signify an actual grinding while other think of it as the kind of shudder we feel when we hear teeth chatter that way.[526]

Every word in the Word has a spiritual meaning in it. Fire essentially means love in the Word. *Heavenly fire denotes love for the Lord and love for neighbors while hellish fire means self-love and love of the world.*[527] Hellish fire has the same source as heavenly fire, namely, heaven's sun or the Lord. Because hellfire is self-love and love of the world, it includes all the cravings that belong to those loves. These cravings are an extension of love, for we crave what we love. It is also our delight to get what we love or crave. This is the sole source of our hearty delight.

So hellfire includes the cravings that well up from these two loves.[528] These evils are disdain for others, animosity and hostility towards people who do not support us, envy, hatred, and vengefulness; and viciousness and cruelty as a result. In the perspective of the Divine, they are denial, a consequent contempt, ridicule, and blasphemy of the holy values of the church. After death, when we become spirits, these turn into rage and hatred against holy values.

All the hells are communities like this, so people there enjoy contempt toward others in their hearts and vent their wrath on others. These demonstrations of viciousness and torment are what is implied by hellfire, on the grounds that they are the aftereffects of their obsessions.[529]

The Worst Hellish Spirits: Genii or Demons

The worst people of all are the ones who have been engaged in evil pursuits because of their self-love and whose inward behavior, spite, and skill have been deceitful throughout their lives. This is because their deceit utterly permeates their thoughts and infects them with venom, destroying all their spiritual life. Many of these people are in the deepest hell with those called "demons" or "genii."[530]

People engrossed in evils for their love of the world are in the hells toward the front, though, and are called "spirits."[531] When a mob of "demons" arrives in the next life after death, these are instantly tossed into their hell. When they are examined as to their guile and craft, they look like serpents.[532]

Genii's Skills and Unspeakable Arts

Their arts are unidentified in the world. One type has to do with the abuse of correspondences.[533] This type of demon or genii tries to destroy heaven by attacking the principle of correspondence that yields the balance of heaven and hell;[534] a second type has to do with the misuse of the lowest elements of the divine plan; a third type with the communication and instillation of thoughts and affections by distractions, inward focusing, and the use of decoy spirits as well as by emissaries; a fourth type involves manipulation by hallucinations; a fifth type with projection beyond themselves so that they appear to be where their bodies are not; a sixth type with various impersonations, persuasions, and deceptions.[535]

Why Each of Us has Two Evil Spirits and Two Good Angels

Every person has good spirits and evil spirits. We have our alliance with heaven through the good spirits and our alliance with hell through the evil ones.[536] To moderate and control the two evil spirits, the Lord assigns two angelic spirits at the head of each person.[537]

There are two kinds of spirits in hell, and two kinds of angels in heaven. We also have the two faculties--the will and understanding. The first kind of evil spirits are simply called spirits; and they are involved in the things of understanding. The other kind is called genii or demons; and these are involved in the things of the will. They are also most distinct from each other. The first kind of evil spirits pour in falsities. They distort the truth and are delighted when they can twist truth into falsity and falsity into truth. But the genii pour in evils and act upon our affections and lusts. They detect in a moment what we desire. If this be good, they turn it most deftly into evil, and relish when they can make good appear as evil and evil as good. The genii share nothing common with the spirits. The genii care nothing for what we think, but only for what we want; the spirits care nothing for what we want, but for what we think. The genii are in the depths of the hells, and they are almost invisible to the spirits, but the spirits are in the hells at the sides and in front.[538]

On the other hand, each of us has two angels. One kind of angels cares for our will and our love, influencing our good. The other cares for our understanding, influencing our truths. They are also most distinct from each other. Those who act upon the things of our will are called celestial angels; and those who act upon our understanding are called spiritual angels. To the celestial angels the genii are opposed; to the spiritual angels, the spirits.[539]

THE LORD'S PROVIDENTIAL GUARDIANSHIP OF US FROM EVIL SPIRITS IN SLEEP

Evil spirits strongly desire and burn to infest and assault us while sleeping, but God watches over us; for God's love never sleeps. The spirits who thus infest are miserably punished by angels. The spirits mainly plague us during the night and attempt to pour themselves into our inner thoughts and affections. These spirits are sirens, who are interior magicians. But by the most grievous punishments, angels continually keep them away from us and deter them from infesting us. The sirens have even talked to us in the night just as if from someone we know, as it were his or her speech so that it could not be distinguished from him or her, while they are pouring forth filthy things, and persuading us to fallacies.[540] The sirens are punished by angels more often than can be told.

Swedenborg's Heavenly Insights

ARE INNER VOICES AND THOUGHTS FROM HEAVEN OR HELL?
We think that our natural mind autonomously thinks independent of anyone. In fact, we do not think by ourselves. Our thoughts flow from either heaven or hell. When people who long for something to flow in from heaven, they receive their answers "through a vivid impression or a subtle voice in their thinking, but rarely through anything obvious."[541] If some thoughts or voices tell us what to do or what to believe clearly, that is not from the Lord or angels in heaven, but from some fanatical spirits in hell.[542]

God or an angel communicates with us indirectly or subtly so that we may use our free will to think, believe, or act, but evil sprits dictate to us what to think and what to do, depriving us of the use of our free will. People in heaven desire goodness and truth while people in hell are obsessed with evil and the consequential illusions of fallacy.[543]

ALL WE THINK AND DO IS FROM GOD OR FROM THE DEVIL
We believe that we think, resolve, speak, and act from ourselves. In Angelic Wisdom about Divine Love and Wisdom, however, it was disclosed that there is only one Life and that we are recipients of Life. Our *will* receives God's love, and our *understanding* receives God's wisdom. Our love and wisdom flow from the One Life; "Every generous act of giving, with every perfect gift, is from above, coming down from the Father of lights, with whom there is no variation or shadow due to change" (James 1:17). We need to know "that all good and truth, all wisdom and thus all faith and charity are from the Lord, also that all evil."[544]

DOES LOVE MAKE US WISE?
All things in the universe were created by divine love and divine wisdom.[545] Divine love and divine wisdom are one. The love of God is the source of our

wisdom because the God of love gives a birth to wisdom. If we love God, we grow wiser. So the person who loves God and others becomes intelligent and wise. Swedenborg shares his understanding of wisdom and love in his book, Secrets of Heaven:

> Wisdom is the term for everything that charity fathers, because whatever charity fathers comes by way of charity from the Lord, who is the source of all wisdom, since he is wisdom itself. This is the origin of true understanding, which is the origin of true learning, which is the origin of true knowledge. All three are the offspring of charity, or in other words, children of the Lord by way of charity.[546]

Wisdom originates in love from God. That is, God's love generates true understanding, true learning, true knowledge. God is Love itself and Wisdom itself.[547] The more nearly we walk with the Lord the wiser we become. The more nearly we walked with the Lord the happier we become. The more nearly we walk with the Lord the more distinctly we seem to ourselves as if we were our own, and the more clearly we recognize that He is the Lord's.[548]

PRAYER

We wonder to what prayers God would answer. Our prayers are not answered when we pray for ourselves against the well-being of the human family. Some spirits reasoned with Swedenborg about why the Lord does not answer their prayers. Swedenborg was allowed to answer to them: "They could not be heard, because they had as their end such things as are contrary to the welfare of the human race; and because they pray for themselves against all others; and that when they pray in this manner heaven is closed, for they who are in heaven attend solely to the ends of those who are praying."[549] If all of our selfish prayers are answered, that can risk the welfare of others.

When our prayers are aligned with God's Will, they will be answered. Thus, our prayers like our true worship should arise from the Lord: "But the worship which is from man is not worship, consequently the confessions, adorations, and prayers which are from man, are not confessions, adorations, and prayers which are heard and received by the Lord; but they must be from the Lord himself with man."[550] Our true prayer should derive from God, not from ourselves. When we ask not from ourselves but from the Lord we will receive whatever we ask. The ultimate meaning of prayer is not to fulfill our own wills but is to discern and follow God's Will.

Swedenborg describes heaven, hell, and the world of spirits in detail. He has presented the most comprehensive picture of the spiritual realm among mystics and NDErs. He is profound and truthful in his imparting of the ineffable heavenly truths. He genuinely shared what he learned from the Bible, angels, his own experience, and observations.

He has influenced numerous people, including German philosopher Immanuel Kant (1724–1804), British poet and artist William Blake (1757–1827), poet and philosopher Samuel Taylor Coleridge (1772–1834), Irish poet William Butler Yeats (1865–1939), the New England transcendentalist Ralph Waldo Emerson (1803–82), the Zen author D. T. Suzuki (1870–1966), writers like Honoré de Balzac (1799–1850), Fyodor Dostoevsky (1821–81), Charles Baudelaire (1821–67), poet Elizabeth Barrett Browning (1806–81), and religious leader Mary Baker Eddy (1821–1910). Notable Swedenborgians include Helen Keller (1880–1968), the American poet Robert Frost (1874–1963), John Chapman (Johnny Appleseed) (1774–1845), theologian Henry James Sr. (1811–82), his son psychologist William James (1842–1910) and novelist Henry James Jr. (1843–1916).

Several NDE scholars, including Dr. Raymond Moody and Dr. Eben Alexander, have used Swedenborg's materials for their own works and they appreciate him. Swedenborg is one of those wise people who have led many to God, shining like the stars and the brightness of the sky forever and ever (Dan. 12:3).

What a Big Picture of the Life after Life Does Sundar Singh Portray?

His Life

SUNDAR WAS A very Christ-like person in the twentieth century. In the midst of the diversity of Indian religions and cultures, he was born into a Sikh family in 1889. During the early part of his life, Sundar's mother fostered and nurtured his unique spiritual quest. She used to take him to a, an ascetic holy man, who lived afar in the rainforest.[551]

But with the death of his beloved mother when he was fourteen years old, the young Sundar grew gradually despondent and aggressive. He had others throw stones at Christian preachers.[552] He tore up the Christian Scripture and burned it. Although he was faithful to his own religion, he found no satisfaction or peace in it. So he decided to leave everything behind and commit suicide. Three days after he burnt the Scripture, he rose up around 3 am, took his ceremonial bath, and prayed, "O God, if there is a God, wilt thou show me the right way or I will kill myself."[553] He planned to place his head on the railroad track when the 5:00 am Lothian Express passed by, if he received no satisfaction in life. With a firm determination, he prayed. At 4:30 am, he saw a bright light in the room. He thought that a fire had broken out, but there was no fire.

He imagined that God had sent this light to answer his request. So he continually prayed and looked into the light, and saw the form of the Lord Jesus Christ in a manifestation of glory and love. Had it been a Hindu god, he could have prostrated before it. But it was the Lord Jesus Christ whom he had insulted a few days before. Sundar saw, "in a shining cloud of light . .

. the glorious loving face of Jesus Christ."[554] Jesus asked him in Hindustani, "How long will you persecute me? I have come to save you."[555] He realized that Jesus is living. Thus he fell at His feet and felt wonderful, unmatchable peace and joy. When he got up, the peace and joy remained with him, although the vision faded away.[556]

When he had made up his mind to follow Christ, his family tried to bring him back to his old faith. His father's tears almost broke his heart. One day his wealthy and honored uncle took him to a deep cellar below his mansion. He unlocked a secret, large safe, showed his priceless jewels, quantities of money, and rolls of bank notes. Then taking off his turban and laying it on Sundar's feet as his humblest supplication, his uncle begged him not to shame the family name by becoming a Christian and said to him, "All these shall be yours if you will remain with us."[557]

Moved by his uncle's condescension in humiliating himself to the youngest son of the household, he keenly felt the temptation. Filled with tears, he expressed his love for the uncle, yet remained firm about this decision. After that event, family persecution followed and he was disowned by his father and poisoned with food; yet he survived the deadly poison and so the physician who diagnosed him read the New Testament and became a Christian missionary.[558]

From that time, Sundar Singh became a Christ-like itinerant preacher.

From this encounter, his incredible faith journey started with unbearable persecutions. His family rejected him and his father poisoned him, but he miraculously survived it. Before his death, his father came to Sundar to be baptized, coming home with his repenting heart.

Wearing the saffron robes of the sadhu, he began to spread the simple gospel of repentance, rebirth, love, and peace through Jesus Christ. He carried no money or other possessions, but only a New Testament.

Stories from those years are astonishing and sometimes incredible. Indeed, there were those who insisted that they were mythological rather than real happenings.

In the summer of 1912, he travelled through the Kailas of the Himalayas alone, on foot and often weary, but rejuvenated by the beautiful scenery.

One day when struck by a blinding snow storm and almost exhausted to death, he staggered drearily on over snowy and stony crags not knowing his direction. All of sudden he lost his balance and fell. Recovering from the fall he awoke to one of his greatest experiences. He was rescued by the legendary Maharishi of Kailash in a deep cave. Clothed with long hair he appeared to be an animal, he had spent over three hundred-fifty years in meditation and prayer. He told Sundar "Let us kneel and pray."[559] Then followed a most earnest prayer ending in the name of Jesus. He unrolled a bulky copy of the Gospels in Greek, read Matthew 5, and mentioned the role that had come down to him from Spanish Jesuit missionary Francis Xavier (1506-52). Sundar heard from him wondrous wisdom and revelations of God and visited the saint three times.[560]

At a town called Rasar he was arrested, accused, and found guilty of entering the country illegally and preaching the gospel of Christ. They threw him into a dry well full of bones and rotting flesh and left to die. On the third night, just when he was crying to God in prayer he heard a rough sound of someone opening the locked lid of his dreary prison.

Then a voice spoke to him from the top of the well, telling him to take hold of the rope that was being let down. So he did and arrived at the top of the well. The lid was covered over again and locked. On looking round, he found nobody. Later he went back to town, preached the gospel, and was arrested again amidst a great commotion. The head Lama was flabbergasted with the fact that the key was still on his girdle and released him out of fear of God's curse on him and his people.[561]

On a severely cold snowy day, Sundar was taking a journey across some mountains in Tibet.

He had a Tibetan travel companion. On the road, they were nearly frozen to death, and wondered about the possibility of reaching their destiny alive. They came to a deep crag to find a person lying there apparently frozen. Sundar suggested they should take him to a safe place, but his companion opposed it, saying that all they could do was to get themselves into safety, and he walked on his way. In spite of the difficulty, Sundar carried the man on his back, and struggled to move forward with his heavy load. Soon Sundar's body became warm and his body heat began to thaw the frozen man. Before he had gone very far, he found his Tibetan companion who had turned into a frozen stone across the path. The event reminded him of Jesus' saying: "For those who want to save their life will lose it, and those who lose their life for my sake will find it" (Matt. 16:25).[562]

On another day, Sundar went to the forest to pray, sat on a rock, and started to consider for what blessings he should pray. While he was doing this, another person appeared and stood next to him. Guessing by his behavior, dress, and manner of speech, he appeared to be an honorable and devoted servant of God; but his eyes gleamed with craft and guile, and he breathed an odor of hell in his speech. He said:

> Holy and Honoured Sir, pardon me for interrupting your prayers and breaking in on your privacy; but it is one's duty to seek to promote the advantage of others, and therefore I have come to lay an important matter before you. Your pure and unselfish life has made a deep impression not only on me, but upon a great number of devout persons. But although in the Name of God you have sacrificed yourself body and soul for others, you have never been truly appreciated. My meaning is that being a Christian only a few thousand Christians have come under your influence, and some even of these distrust you. How much better would it be if you became a Hindu or a Muslim, and thus become a great leader indeed? They are in search of such a spiritual head. If you accept this suggestion of mine, then three hundred and ten millions of Hindus and Muslims will become your followers, and render you reverent homage.[563]

On hearing this, his lips outpoured these words:

> Thou Satan! Get thee hence. I knew at once that thou wert a wolf in sheep's clothing! Thy one wish is that I should give up the cross and the narrow path that leads to life, and choose the broad road of death.

My Master Himself is my lot and my portion, who Himself gave His life for me, and it behooves me to offer as a sacrifice my life and all I have to Him who is all in all to me. Get you gone therefore, for with you I have nothing to do.[564]

When hearing this, Satan went away grumbling and growling in his rage. Sikhism is a combination of Hinduism and Islam. To a former Sikh, Satan's offer could be very reasonable, for Sundar wore a yellow saffron robe of Hindu Sadhus (holy men) for the purpose of his evangelism.

Throughout his prayer life, Sundar Singh experienced a lot of celestial revelations. He shared how his experience of celestial visions started:

At Kotgarh, fourteen years ago, while I was praying, my eyes were opened to the heavenly vision. So vividly did I see it all that I thought I must have died, and that my soul had passed into the glory of heaven; but throughout the intervening years these visions have continued to enrich my life. I cannot call them up at will, but, usually when I am praying or meditating, sometimes as often as eight or ten times in a month, my spiritual eyes are opened to see within the heavens, and, for an hour or two, I walk in the glory of the heavenly sphere with Christ Jesus, and hold converse with angels and spirits.[565]

He sometimes had more than two trances in a week. As a homeless evangelist, he did not have enough time or settings to write down his supernatural experiences and visions.[566] Furthermore, it is difficult to articulate deep indescribable or ineffable experiences.

With only his Bible he traveled to India, Tibet, Malaysia, Japan, and China, and the rest of the world. He visited the West twice, traveling to Britain, the United States, Australia in 1920, and Europe again in 1922. Facing the world of value confusions and materialism, he lived a very Christlike life of simplicity, love, and freedom. "I am not worthy to follow in the steps of my Lord," he said, "but like Him, I want no home, no possessions. Like Him I will belong to the road, sharing the suffering of my people, eating with those who will give me shelter, and telling all people of the love of God."[567] In April 1929, Sadhu Sundar Singh left for Tibet for a missionary journey. No one heard from him after that. He vanished, leaving behind a legend.[568] Singh's influence went far and wide, impacting on important spiritual leaders, such as Mahatma Gandhi and C.S. Lewis.[569]

The Next Life

THE TRINITY

At one time, perplexed about the doctrine of the Trinity, Sundar had thought of three independent persons sitting on three thrones, but a vision made everything clear to him: "I entered in an Ecstasy into the third heaven. . . . And there I saw Christ in a glorious spiritual body sitting on a throne. Whenever I go there it is the same. Christ is always in the center, a figure ineffable and indescribable."[570]

When he saw Christ for the first time, he felt there were some old and forgotten relationship between Jesus and him: "His face shining like the sun, but in no way dazzling, and so sweet that without any difficulty I can gaze at it—always smiling a loving glorious smile. . . . He had said, but not in words, 'I am He, through whom you were created.'"[571]

The first time Sundar entered Heaven, he looked round and he asked the saints and angels where God was:

And they told me, "God is not to be seen here any more than on earth, for God is Infinite. But there is Christ, He is God, He is the Image of the Invisible God, and it is only in Him that we can see God, in Heaven as on earth." And streaming out from Christ I saw, as it were, waves shining and peace-giving, and going through and among the Saints and Angels, and everywhere bringing refreshment, just as in hot weather water refreshes trees. And this I understood to be the Holy Spirit.[572]

Here God is the invisible, Jesus is the image of God, and the Holy Spirit is the waves shining, giving peace, and bringing refreshment. Another way to explain the Trinity is the analogy of the sun to him:

> Muhammadan and Hindu mystics have mistakenly sought an absorption into the Great Spirit like the sinking of the river in the ocean . . . But they are apt to be confused by their Pantheism. Christ s oneness with the Father and His oneness with ourselves is different. Light is Sun, and Sun is Light. Heat is Sun, and Sun is Heat. But you cannot say Heat is Light. Christ is the Light of the World. The Holy Spirit is the Heat of the World. Christ is not the Holy Spirit.[573]

To Singh, the sun can illustrate the Trinity. The flame of the sun is the Father, The light is Jesus, and the Holy Spirit is the heat. These three distinctive beings are inseparable, but one.

LIFE

Only one source of life exists. That is an infinite and almighty life. The power of this infinite and almighty source created uncountable other lives. All creatures live in the life and will remain in the life forever.[574]

DEATH

These lives can transform from one form into another, which is called "death," but they can never be annihilated. A thing may disappear from our sight, but it never ceases to be; it resurfaces, but in another form and state.[575]

THREE MAIN TYPES OF DEATH EXPERIENCES

There are three main types of the states of death. Its first type is a neutral state of the experience of death. Its second type is a celestial state of the experience of death. The third type is a hellish state of the experience of death.

Sundar saw that from all over the world thousands upon thousands of people attended by angels were constantly arriving in the world of spirits, a midway state between heaven and hell. Most people after death come here first. The wicked were led by only evil sprits to this place. In accordance with their likings, they choose either their destinies of heaven or hell in this state.

The second type of death is the death of sincere believers. Just before death, people usually see with their spiritual eyes. Only angels and good spirits led the good from their death-beds. Evil spirits were prevented to come near them, but watched them at a distance. The believers are welcomed by angels, good spirits, their family members, relatives, and friends. They are embraced by warmth, light, love, and a hearty welcome of the beloved to the world of spirits. Many of them experience the approach of Lord Jesus in dazzling light welcoming them to the city of God.

The third type of death is that of the wicked. They see evil spirits waiting at their deathbeds, scaring them to death. They are frozen in fear and in terror. Many of them try to avoid these evil spirits who menace them. At death, the evil spirits drag them to their place called "hell" and brutalize them. The evil spirits can harass those spirits that are similar to their mindsets:

> I saw also that there were no good spirits with the souls of the really wicked, but about them were evil spirits, who had come with them from their death-beds, while angels, too, stood by and prevented the evil spirits from giving free play to the spite of their malicious natures in harassing them. The evil spirits almost immediately led these souls away towards the darkness, for when in the flesh, they had consistently allowed evil spirits to influence them for evil, and had willingly permitted themselves to be enticed to all kinds of wickedness.[576]

Although they do not necessarily choose to go to hell, their lives make choices for them. In this sense, the wicked experience hell while living in the world by associating with evil spirits and doing evil.

The World of Spirits

Most people are not aware of whether they die or not because of the smooth transition of life after life. Death is like a deep sleep when we are really tired. At the time of death the spirit leaves the body.

The Spirits of the Good

When spirits arrive in the world of spirits, the good immediately split from the evil. In the world all are mingled together, but it is not so in the spiritual world. Sundar observed many times that on arriving in the world of spirits, the good spirits initially bathe in the mysterious air-like waters of a crystal clear ocean, and by doing this they find a deep and exhilarating refreshment. Within these inexplicable waters they move around as if in open air, but neither are they drowned under them, nor do the waters wet them. Instead, they are wonderfully washed, rejuvenated, and fully purified; they enter into the world of glory and light, where they will forever stay in the presence of their Lord, and in the fellowship of countless saints and angels.[577]

The Spirits of the Evil

In contrast to good spirits, the spirits of the evil are tormented by the all-revealing light of glory and strive to hide themselves in places where their adulterated and sin-stained natures will not be displayed. In their effort to hide themselves from the revealing light, the evil spirits go down and throw themselves headlong into the lowest and darkest part of the world of spirits, from where a gloomy and evil-smelling smoke arises and the bitter wails of remorse and anguish are heard constantly. From heaven, however, the spirits cannot see the smoke or hear the moans of anguish, unless any of them should see the horrible plight of those souls in darkness because of some special reason.[578]

Unexpectedly transferred into the world of spirits, many spirits are confused and in a state of great anguish at their fate, for they were not thinking of or preparing for the next life at all. So, they usually remain in the lower and darker levels of the intermediate state of the world of spirits for a considerable period. The spirits of these lower spheres often haunt and harass people in the world. The people that they can injure are, however, those who are like-minded to themselves, who open their hearts to treat them with their own free will. These evil spirits would do immense harm in the world if not had not God dispatched innumerable angels everywhere to protect God's people and God's creation.[579]

DEATH OF A CHILD

Sundar describes the following experience of a child's death and his reunion with his mother he witnessed in his vision.

> The little child Theodore died of pneumonia, and a band of angels came to accompany his soul to the next life. The angels led Theodore's spirit to the beautiful and light-filled part of heaven—the children's heaven where they cared for him and nurtured him with in heavenly wisdom until he gradually became like the angels.
>
> Later his mother also died. Grown up like an angel, Theodore came with other angels to welcome his mother. As soon as he identified himself to her, "Mother, do you not know me? I am your son Theodore," her heart was overwhelmed with joy. As they hugged each other, their joy-filled tears dropped like flowers.
>
> After this meeting, walking along together, Theodore gave her a tour around there and stayed with her during her appointed time in the intermediate state. When the period of instruction for that world was fulfilled, Theodore took her to higher realm of his residing place where there were peerless and extraordinarily gorgeous mountains, springs and the gardens of all kinds of fragrant flowers and delicious fruits. What the heart desires was available there. Then Theodore told his mother, "In the world, which is the dim reflection of this real world, our dear ones are grieving over us, but, tell me, is this death, or the real life for which every heart yearns?" She replied, "Son, this is the true life. If I had known in the world the whole truth about heaven, I would never have grieved over your death. What a pity it is those in the world are so blind! In spite of the

fact that Jesus has explained quite clearly about this state of glory, and that the Gospels again and again tell of this eternal Kingdom of the Father, yet, not only ignorant people, but many enlightened believers as well, still remain altogether unaware of its glory. May God grant that all may enter into the abiding joy of this place!"[580]

This story may comfort many mothers who lost their babies. Indeed, babies can grow in statue and knowledge in heaven.

Hells

THE JUDGMENT OF SINNERS

Contrary to the general idea that committing sins in secret will be unknown forever, all sins will be eventually disclosed and sinners will face consequences of their sins in the end.

Sundar asked once, "Will the dead stand in a line all together and be judged?"[581] The answer came: "No, after leaving the body the soul knows everything that has happened to it. The memory of it all is clear and fresh, and thereby they are judged. The heavenly light shows the wicked to themselves."[582] They begin to see at once that they are unable to live in that fellowship of saints and angels. They feel so unfit there and find everything so disagreeable that they ask to be allowed to go away from heaven.[583]

The real judgment is internal. It is going on everyday, not affected by an act of God intervening between ourselves and God. Our bodies like a carbon-copy paper remember what we are doing every day:

I was also told that in this world our spiritual bodies are inside our material bodies, and that when we sin it is like when we press with a point on paper behind which is a sheet of carbon; on the outside of the paper there is a very slight mark, but inside there is a clear black mark. Thus our sins mark and scar our spiritual bodies, and the result of this will be seen when, after death, the spiritual body escapes

123

from the material; and the revelation of the injury it has sustained will in itself be a large part of the judgment.[584]

We are judging ourselves according to our own record written on our bodies.

SECRET SINS

Sundar saw the following incident in a vision. A person was engaged in a sinful act in his own room, assuming that his secret sin is concealed from others. What he did not see was that a number of angels, saints, and some spirits of his dear ones were present in the room. They all grieved over his shameful conduct. One of the saints regretted, "How I wish that the spiritual eyes of this man had been open at the time, then he would never have dared to commit this sin." Another sighed, "We came to help him, but now we will have to be witnesses against him at the time of his judgment. He cannot see us, but we can all see him indulging in this sin. Would that this man would repent, and be saved from the punishment to come."[585]

WASTED OPPORTUNITIES

Once in the world of spirits, Sundar saw a spirit who was shrieking like a madman with cries of regret. An angel explained:

> In the world this man had many chances of repenting and turning towards God, but whenever his conscience began to trouble him he used to drown its pricking in drink. He wasted all his property, ruined his family, and in the end committed suicide, and now in the world of spirits he rushes frantically about like a mad dog and writhes in remorse at the thought of his lost opportunities. We are all willing to help him, but his own perverted nature prevents him from repenting, for sin has hardened his heart, though the memory of his sin is always fresh to him. In the world, he drank to make himself forget the voice of his conscience, but here there is no possible chance of covering up anything. Now his soul is so naked that he himself, and all the inhabitants of the spiritual world, can see his

sinful life. For him, in his sin-hardened state, no other course is possible but that he must hide himself in the darkness with other evil spirits, and so to some extent escape the torture of the light.[586]

THE SPIRIT OF THE LIAR

When a habitual liar died and arrived in the world of spirits, he attempted to lie as usual, but was truly embarrassed and mortified by the fact that all knew his thoughts even before he spoke. It is impossible for anyone to be a hypocrite or a liar there, for no thought of our heart can remain hidden. As our spirit leaves the world, our spiritual body bears the imprint of all the sin in it and turns out to be a witness against it.

This man in the world repeatedly distorted right and wrong, but in the world of spirits he learned that the possibility of twisting truth and untruth is impossible. The one who lies deceives and harms no one but himself. By lying habitually he skewed his inner perception of truth that had been implanted in him.

Intricately entangled in his own deception, this man shunned the celestial light and rushed down into the darkness, where his foul love of lying could be hidden from everyone, except from those like-minded. Truth alone convicted him as a liar.[587]

THE SPIRIT OF THE ADULTERER

Sundar Singh saw an adulterer, who had come to the world of spirits a short time before. His ue was sagging out like a person completely exhausted by thirst, his nostrils were swollen, and he smote his arms as if some sort of fire burned within him. Looking at his abhorrent appearance was very nauseating and repulsive.

After leaving all the garnishes of lust and indulgence behind in the world, he ran madly around, and wailed, "Curse on this life! There is no death here to put an end to all this pain. And here the spirit cannot die; otherwise, I should again kill myself, as I did with a pistol in the world in order to escape from my troubles there. But this pain is far greater than the pain of the world. What shall I do?"[588] Muttering this, he rushed toward and disappeared into the darkness where many other compatible spirits were.

One of the Saints mentioned, "Not only is an evil act sin, but an evil thought, and an evil look is also sin. This sin is not confined only to trafficking with strange women, but excess and animalism in relation to one's wife is also sin. A man and his wife are truly joined together not for sensualism but for mutual help and support, that they with their children may spend their lives in the service of mankind and for the glory of God. But he who departs from this aim in life is guilty of the adulterer's sin."[589]

THE SPIRIT OF A MURDERER

Some years before, a person murdered a Christian preacher. Later he was bitten by a poisonous snake and died. As he entered the world of spirits, good and bad spirits gathered around him. When the whole characteristic of his spirit exhibited that he was a person of darkness, the evil spirits soon claimed custody of him and shoved him along with them toward the darkness. One of the saints stated, "He killed a man of God by the poison of his anger, and now he is killed by the poison of a snake. The old Serpent, the devil, by means of this man, killed an innocent man. Now, by means of another snake, which is like him, he has killed this man, for 'he was from the beginning a murderer'" (John 8:44).[590]

THE SPIRIT OF THE PERSON MURDERED

As he was being led away, one good spirit from among others came to help him, saying to him, "I have forgiven you with all my heart. Now can I do anything to help you?"[591] The murderer immediately recognized him as the preacher whom he had murdered. Struck by shame and fear he fell down before him, and soon the evil spirits started to uproar noisily, but the angels who stood farther admonished and hushed them. Then the murderer said to the murdered,

> How I wish that, in the world, I could have seen your unselfish and loving life as I see it now! I regret that through my blindness, and

because your body screened your real spiritual life, I could not then see the inner beauty of your life. Also, by killing you I deprived many of the blessings and benefit that you would have given them. Now I am forever a sinner in God's sight, and fully deserve my punishment. I don't know what I can do except hide myself in some dark cave, because I cannot bear this light. In it, not only does my own heart make me miserable, but all can see every detail of my sinful life.[592]

To this the murdered responded, "You should truly repent, and turn to God, for if you do there is hope that the Lamb of God will wash you in His own blood, and give you new life that you may live with us in heaven, and be saved frown the torment of Gehenna."[593]

The murderer lamented, "There is no need for me to confess my sins for they are open to all. In the world, I could hide them, but not here. I want to live with Saints like you in heaven, but when I cannot bear the dimness of the self-revealing light in the world of spirits, then what will be my state in the searching brightness and glory of that light-filled place? My greatest hindrance is that, through my sins, my conscience is so dull and hardened that my nature will not incline towards God and repentance. I seem to have no power to repent left in me. Now there is nothing for it, but that I shall be driven out from here forever. Alas for my unhappy state!"[594]

As he stated this, overwhelmed by fear he fell down and his fellow evil spirits hauled him off to the darkness. On this one of the angels made comments, "See! There is no need for anyone to pronounce a sentence of doom. Of itself, the life of any sinner proves him guilty. There is no need to tell him, or to put forward witnesses against him. To a certain extent, punishment begins in the heart of every sinner while in the world, but here they feel the full effect of it. And God's arrangement here is such that goats and sheep, that is, sinners and righteous, separate of their own accord."

"God created man to live in light in which his spiritual health and joy are made permanent forever. Therefore, no man can be happy in the darkness of Sheol, nor, because of his sin- perverted life, can he be happy in the light. So, wherever a sinner may go, he will find himself in a hell. How opposite to this is the state of the righteous, who freed from sin, is in heaven everywhere!"[595]

THE SOUL OF A ROBBER

A rough robber died and entered into the world of spirits. From the beginning he paid no attention to his state and to other spirits around him. Instead, he instantly got down to his business of helping himself to the valuables of the place as he used to do it in the world. He was, however, startled and dumbfounded by the fact that these valuables appeared to be talking and reproving him for his disgraceful behavior. So severely warped was his nature that he never learned the real usefulness of things nor attained the knowledge of the proper way of their usage.

In the world, his tendencies had been so uncontrollable that in a rage he had injured or murdered any one who offended him for trifling causes. Now in the world of spirits, he started to undertake the same way of harming others. When good spirits came to help and teach him, he suddenly attacked them in a rage as though he would have ripped them to pieces like a violent dog. Regarding such a spirit, one of the angels commented, "If spirits of this kind were not kept down in the darkness or the bottomless pit, then they would cause immense harm wherever they might go. This man's conscience is so dead, that even after he has reached the world of spirits, he fails to recognize that, by murdering and robbing in the world, he has wasted his own spiritual discernment and life. He killed and destroyed others, but in reality, he has destroyed himself. God alone knows if this man, and those who are like him, will remain in torment for ages or forever."[596]

After this incident, the angels assigned to the duty "took him and shut him down in the darkness from which he is not permitted to come out."[597] The state of evildoers in such a hellish place is so appalling and the torment there is so inexpressibly severe that those who see the conditions shiver at the sight.

Where he is, there is nothing but throbbing that does not stop for a moment. Dark fire constantly blazes and afflicts these spirits, but they are not consumed nor does the fire exhaust itself. According to the magnitude and character of their sins, these spirits stay in their own grades and planes of hellish communities. In spite of the fact that God created these spirits all in God's own image (Gen. 1:26, 27; Col. 1:15), they have contorted that image by indulging themselves in sins and evil and have molded it to be horrible and wicked. In fact, the images of their spiritual bodies are exceedingly despicable and dreadful. If their images are not restored on earth by genuine repentance, they must remain in such frightful forms forever.[598]

In this account, Sundar shares his understanding of the involuntary aspects of hell-bound spirits. If spirits are out of control, angels may reluctantly regulate them. This is not done to imprison them for the sake of punishment, but to keep them where they cannot harm others and to let them burn their rage as fuel.

Heaven

The Worth of People: Usefulness

Our greatness is not contingent on our knowledge and position. We are as great as we can be useful to others, and the usefulness of our lives to others involves our service to others. Consequently, in so far as we can serve others in love, just so far are we great. Thus, Jesus said, "It will not be so among you; but whoever wishes to be great among you must be your servant" (Matt 20:26). They serve one another in love and in joy and remain forever in the Presence of God, fulfilling the purpose of their lives.[599]

Heavenly Life

In heaven, people can never be hypocrites, for all can see the minds and lives of others as they are. The all-revealing light that emits from Christ in glory gratifies the righteous with the utmost joy to be in the kingdom of light. There their goodness is evident to all and it proliferates more and more, for nothing can thwart their growth, and everything sustains them and assists them.[600]

In heaven, jealousy dissipates. People are glad to see the spiritual increase and glory of others and put their efforts, at all times, to serve one another without any ulterior motives. All the countless gifts and blessings of heaven are for the common use of all. People think of keeping nothing for themselves out of selfishness. God, who is love, is seen in the person of Jesus sitting on the throne in the highest heaven. His throne appears as the center of all things.[601]

All kinds of sweet and delicious flowers and fruits, and many kinds of spiritual food are ready to be consumed. While eating these foods, the residents experience an exquisite flavor and pleasure. After consuming them, the residents experience a delicate scent, which perfumes the air around and exudes from their bodies.

In brief, there is an invariable experience of wonderful joy and blessedness for everyone because in every life, God's will is made perfect at every stage of heaven and under all circumstances.[602]

THE STATE OF THE RIGHTEOUS AND THEIR GLORIOUS END
The lives of all true believers inaugurate heaven or God's kingdom in the world. For God as the source of all peace and joy dwells in their hearts, they are always filled with peace and joy, regardless of persecutions and troubles. Death is not the end of life for them, but a glorious door through which they walk into their eternal home. When the day comes for them to leave this world behind, they will be born into the life eternal in unfathomable joy. The following episodes will amply speak to such blessings of death.[603]

THE DEATH OF A RIGHTEOUS MAN
An angel showed Sundar how a true Christian who had wholeheartedly served God for thirty years died. Just before his death God opened his spiritual eyes so that he might observe the spiritual world. He saw heaven open, a party of angels and saints come out to welcome him, and the Savior at the door with outstretched hands waiting to embrace him. As such a scene revealed itself to him, he exclaimed his joy and his family and friends at his bedside were alarmed. "What a joyful hour it is for me," he shouted, "I have long been waiting that I might see my Lord, and go to Him. Oh friends! Look at His face all lighted by love, and see that company of angels that has

come for me. What a glorious place it is! Friends, I am setting out for my real home, do not grieve over my departure, but rejoice!"[604] A friend whispered, "His mind is wandering." He heard it and responded, "No, it is not. I am quite conscious. I wish you could see this wonderful sight. I am sorry it is hidden from your eyes. Good-bye, we will meet again in the next world. Lord I commend my soul into your hands."[605] After bidding his farewell to his folks and committing his spirit to God, he closed his eyes, falling asleep.

Comforting His Dear Ones

Once his spirit had departed from his body, the angels took him and were about to leave for heaven, but he requested them to wait a few minutes. Seeing his lifeless body, he told the angels, "I did not know that the spirit after leaving the body could see his own body and his friends. I wish my friends could see me, as well as I can see them, then these would never count me as dead, nor mourn for me as they do."[606]

Next he observed his spiritual body and realized that it was exquisitely light, delicate, and utterly different from his coarse physical body. Then he started to stop his wife and children from weeping and kissing his icy, stony body. With great love he stretched out his delicate spiritual hands to press them away from it, but they could not see him, hear him, or feel him at all. As if they were air, his hands passed through their bodies. Afterward, an angel solaced him, "Come, let us take you to your everlasting home. Do not be sorry for them. The Lord Himself, and we also, will comfort them. This separation is but for a few days."[607]

Then he and the angels left for heaven. On the way to heaven they met a band of angels, joyously greeting "Welcome."[608] They had gone forward only a little way when another band of angels met them with cries of "Welcome." Further on, seeing dear ones and many good friends, his joy was heightened. As soon as he reached the gate of heaven, the angels and saints lined up in silence on either side. On entering the doorway he was met by Christ. Immediately, he prostrated before His feet to worship Him, but the Lord raised him up, hugged him, and said, "Well done, good and faithful servant, enter into the joy of thy Lord."[609]

Hearing such breathtaking words, his joy grew unutterably. Tears of joy started to overflow from his eyes; with great love the Lord wiped away those tears. The Lord said to the angels, "Take him to that most glorious mansion that, from the beginning, has been prepared for him."[610] He hesitated to do this because he was concerned about the fact that following the angels might cause him to turn his back on the Lord and that such an act might dishonor Him. Eventually, when he turned his face toward the mansion, he was amazed to learn that whichever direction he looked he could see the Lord. For Lord Jesus is present and seen everywhere.[611]

It was delightful for him to see every side of his surroundings fill him with joy. So those whose positions are lowest in rank see without jealousy and envy those whose positions are higher and those whose position is more raised reckon themselves blessed to be able to serve their sisters and brothers in lower positions because of the nature of the reign of God and of love.[612]

Every part of heaven is beautified with splendid gardens that constantly blossom every variety of sweet and succulent fruit and bloom with all kinds of sweet scented flowers that do not fade. In them all kinds of creatures render praise to God without end. Colorful and gorgeous birds sing their sweet songs of praise. Sweet singing of angels and saints captures hearers with a wonderful rapture of joy. Wherever one may turn there is nothing but panoramas of boundless ecstasy.

This is the paradise that the Lord has prepared for those who love God and are called according to God's will, where there is no fear of death, sorrow, sin, and agony, but bountiful peace and joy.[613]

TIME AND ETERNITY

Sundar understands the relation between time and eternity in three ways. First, time in its relation to Reality is eternity.[614] Earthly time is a passing shadow of the real time. For God, everything is present, neither past nor future. The past and the future stand bare before the God who is infinite in knowledge. The present without subsistent existence is only a passing away of the future into the past. Every moment appears from the future and rapidly flies into the past. The past and the future also do not exist for us, for they are beyond our reach. Thus time has no reality for us: "When we awake from sleep, we are hardly able to tell how much Time has passed during our sleep. Even in our waking moments, Time is so unreal."[615] In trouble and suffering, an hour seems to be a year; in delight, a year an hour. While time has no reality, only "Reality is real under all circumstances, and we have no sense for Time as we have been created for Reality, which is Eternal."[616]

Second, changes of objects in space creates time: "When the change is taking place, it is Present; when the change has taken place, it is Past; when the change is still to take place, it is Future." Year, month, day and hour, minute, second change, but Reality and eternity do not change.[617]

Third, although time may change and be gone in forgetfulness, whatever we have done in time will never be obliterated, but pass into eternity. He quotes, "And the world and its desire are passing away, but those who do the will of God live forever" (1 John 2:17).[618]

DISTANCE

Sundar asked, "How far from one another are the various heavenly spheres of existence? If one cannot go to stay in other spheres is he permitted to visit them?"[619] A saint answered:

> The place of residence is appointed for each soul in that plane to which his spiritual development has fitted him, but for short periods he can go to visit other spheres. When those of the higher spheres come down to the lower, a kind of spiritual covering is given to them, that the glory of their appearance may not be disconcerting to the inhabitants of the lower and darker spheres. So when one from a lower sphere goes to a higher, he also gets a kind of spiritual covering that he may be able to bear the light and glory of that place.[620]

In heaven we feel no distance, for as soon as we want to go to a certain place we will be there at once. If we wish to see someone, either we will be there in a moment of thinking or the person appears in our presence.[621]

THE MANSIONS OF HEAVEN

Later, Sundar saw a person of God from a great distance and surveyed his prearranged mansion. On arriving at the door of his home, he saw written on it in bright letters the word "Welcome," and heard "Welcome, Welcome," from the letters themselves in audible sound repeated again and again.[622] When walking into his home, much to his surprise, he discovered Jesus Christ there before him. Seeing Jesus, out of his sheer joy he shouted, "I left The Lord's presence and came here at His command, but I find that The Lord Himself is here to dwell with me."[623] The mansion was well-adorned with things that his mind could have imagined, and everyone was ready to attend his need. His neighbors similar to his sainthood were ready to live in happy fellowship. Such a glorious future awaits every true disciple of Lord Jesus.[624]

A PROUD MINISTER AND A HUMBLE WORKMAN

A minister with a very high self-esteem and sanctimonious piety passed away at an advanced old age. He indisputably was a good man. As appointed for him, the angels took him to the intermediate state of heaven and left him there with recently arrived good spirits in charge of those angels who are appointed to instruct them, while the original angels returned to usher in another good spirit. In that intermediate heaven can be found grades upon grades right up to the higher heavens, and the quality of one's life on earth determines which grade any spirit is admitted to for instruction.

When on their way to a higher plane, the original angels brought the other spirit up beyond the grade where the minister was, the minister in a vociferous voice called out, "What right have you to leave me half-way up to that glorious country, while You take this other man away up near to it? Neither in holiness, nor in anything else, am I in any way less than this man, or than you yourselves."[625] The angels responded to his reproach, "There is no question here of great or small, or of more or less, but a man is put into whatever grade he has merited by his life and faith. You are not quite ready yet for that upper grade, so you will have to remain here for a while, and learn some of the things that our fellow-workers are appointed to teach.

Then, when The Lord commands us, we will, with great pleasure, take you with us to that higher sphere."[626] The minister rejoined, "I have been teaching people all my life about the way to reach heaven. What more have I to learn? I know all about it."[627]

Then the instructing angels replied, "They must go up now, we can't detain them, but we will answer your question. My friend, do not be offended if we speak plainly, for it is for your good. You think you are alone here, but the Lord is also here though you cannot see Him. The pride that you displayed when you said, 'I know all about it' prevents you from seeing Him, and from going up higher. Humility is the cure for this pride. Practice it and your desire will be granted."[628] Afterward, one of the angels spoke to him, "The man who has just been promoted above you, was no learned or famous man. You did not look at him very carefully. He was a member of your own congregation. People hardly knew him at all, for he was an ordinary laborer, and had little leisure from his work. But in his workshop, many knew him as an industrious and honest worker. All who came in contact with him recognized his Messiah-like character. In the war, he was called up for service in France. There, one day, as he was helping a wounded comrade, he was struck by a bullet and killed. Though his death was sudden, he was ready for it, so he did not have to remain in the intermediate state as long as you will have to do. His promotion depends, not on favoritism, but on his spiritual worthiness. His life of prayer and humility, while he was in the world, prepared him to a great extent for the spiritual world. Now he is rejoicing at having reached his appointed place, and is thanking and praising the Lord, who, in His mercy, has saved him, and given him eternal life."[629]

NAMES IN HEAVEN

Sundar asked the angels, "Can you tell me by what names you are known?"[630] An angel answered, "Each of us has been given a new name, which none knows except the Lord and the one who has received it. All of us here have served the Lord in different lands and in different ages, and there is no need that any know what our names are. Nor is there any necessity that we should tell our former earthly names. It might be interesting to know them, but what would be the use of it? And then we do not want people to know our names, lest they should imagine us great and give honor to us, instead of to the Lord, who has so loved us that He has lifted us up out of our fallen state, and has brought us into our eternal home, where we will forever sing praises in His loving fellowship - and this is the object for which He has created us."[631]

SEEING GOD

Sundar asked the saints, "Do the angels and saints who live in the highest spheres of heaven, always look on the face of God? And, if they see Him, in what form and state does He appear?"[632] One of the Saints answered:

> As the sea is full of water, so is the whole universe filled with God, and every inhabitant of heaven feels His presence about him on every side. When one dives under water, above and below and round about there is nothing but water, so in heaven is the presence of God felt. And just as in the water of the sea, there are uncounted living creatures, so in the Infinite Being of God His creatures exist.
>
> Because He is Infinite, His children, who are finite, can see Him only in the form of Christ. As Our Lord Himself has said, "He that has seen Me has seen the Father" (John 14:9). In this world of spirits, the spiritual progress of any one governs the degree to which he is able to know and feel God; and Christ also reveals His glorious form to each one according to his spiritual enlightenment and capacity. If Christ were to appear in the same glorious light to-the dwellers of the darkened lower spheres of the spiritual world, as he appears to those in the higher planes, then they would not be able to bear it. So He tempers the glory of His manifestation to the state of progress, and to the capacity, of each individual soul.[633]

Then another saint further replied:

> God's presence can indeed be felt and enjoyed but it cannot be expressed in words. As the sweetness of the sweet is enjoyed by tasting,

and not by the most graphic descriptive phrasing, so every one in heaven experiences the joy of the Presence of God, and every one in the spiritual world knows that his experience of God is real, and has no need that any should attempt to help him with a verbal description of it.[634]

To Sundar, Jesus is the visible image of God for the invisible God. It was one of the needs that God had to become a human being. We will see only Jesus in heaven even though we will experience God's Presence ubiquitously.

THE MANIFESTATION OF DIVINE LOVE

A saint said, "All the inhabitants of heaven know that God is Love, but it had been hidden from all eternity that His love is so wonderful that He would become man to save sinners, and for their cleansing would die on the Cross. He suffered thus that He might save men, and all creation, which is in subjection to vanity. Thus God, in becoming as a man, has shown His heart to His children, but had any other means been used His infinite love would have remained forever hidden."[635] The whole creation expects to be restored and glorified with the manifestation of the children of God in its full obedience to God until God will be all in all (Rom. 8:18-23).

OUR PERFECTION

Sundar asked one of the spirits about the meaning of the passage in John: "Jesus answered them, Is it not written in your law, I said, Ye are gods?" (John 10:34, KJV)

The spirit answered that we have innumerable desires and that these disclose that we are going to make infinite progress in heaven. Another time he asked the meaning of becoming perfect as God is. The spirits answered that God desires us to be equal to Godself, because love always wants a subject for affection equal to itself. If we become so, we would not rebel, for we should then have an infinite knowledge of the Love of God and that would bring with it infinite thankfulness: "Our Heavenly Father wants us to be made equal to Him, There is no jealousy in Heaven."[636]

When we reach God's degree of perfection in love, we will understand the humility of God to be one of us and to die on the cross for us in love: "Let the same mind be in you that was in Christ Jesus, who, though he was in the form of God, did not regard equality with God as something to be exploited, but emptied himself, taking the form of a slave, being born in human likeness. And being found in human form, he humbled himself and became obedient to the point of death—even death on a cross" (Phil. 2:5-8).

If we become perfect like God, we will not rebel against God, but will genuinely humble ourselves to be God's servants and servants of all in love and humility.

Sundar's visions and experiences are quite extensive, genuinely biblical, deeply transformative, and lucid. He is one of the most significant Christian mystics who draw big pictures of the spiritual life. His life itself is a very extraordinary and moving story. His illustrative teaching is penetrating, too. His teaching on prayer exemplifies such an illustrative instruction of simplicity and profundity. For him, the heart of prayer does not lie in asking for things, but in opening our hearts to God. Prayer is our longing for God Godself, the giver of life:

> A little child will run to his mother exclaiming: "Mother! Mother!" The child does not necessarily want anything in particular. He only wants to be near his mother, to sit on her lap, or to follow her about the house. The child longs for the sheer pleasure of being near her, talking to her, hearing her voice. This is what makes him happy. It is just the same with those who are truly God's children. They do not trouble themselves with asking for spiritual blessings. They only want to sit at the Master's feet, to be in living touch with him; then they are supremely content.[637]

Prayer is breathing, wanting, and living in God, the giver of everything. In it, we cannot stop loving and yearning for God.

Sundar came to be known as the apostle with bleeding feet in the missionary regions of North India because his feet became torn from the rough trails. When asked whether the stones had cut his feet, he answered that his feet cut the stones.[638] He carried with him a blanket and an Urdu New Testament for his traveling. In spite of beatings, arrests, being robbed, imprisonment, and stoning for proclaiming the love of God in Jesus, he faithfully followed Jesus all the way of his life's journey.[639]

Reflection

So far, we have explored the visions of Swedenborg and Singh to understand Christian views on the afterlife. Their views are broader than NDErs'. Here are a couple of NDE summaries and some salient points from Swedenborg and Singh. It is my opinion that their visions of the next life can help NDErs in their limited understanding.

From the research instruments and interviews of his study (total participants: 111 persons), Dr. Kenneth Ring has found seven essential elements of the following consistent world view of NDErs:

1. A tendency to characterize oneself as spiritual rather than religious. 2. A feeling of being inwardly close to God. 3. A de-emphasis of the formal aspects of religious life and worship. 4. A conviction that there is life after death, regardless of religious belief. 5. An openness to the doctrine of reincarnation (and a general sympathy toward Eastern religions). 6. A belief in the essential underlying unity of all religions. 7. A desire for a universal religion embracing all humanity.[640]

The main point to grasp is a shift toward spiritual universalism. Ring reports that this tendency is strongest for all groups of NDErs.[641]

Furthermore, it is noticeable that near-death experiencers in the God Study of *God and the Afterlife* come from every walk of life. From the wide-ranging backgrounds of 420 NDErs (physicians, scientists, nurses, teachers, business executives, homemakers, children, pastors, and others), Dr. Jeffrey Long collected their experiences of God and the divine.

Here are just a few NDErs' thoughts on their renewed sense of life and meaning after their near-death experience:

- All we need on earth is our belief and faith in God and to love, forgive, and accept one another. God loves all creatures.
- We can learn and grow, ultimately learning the power we have within us to create our lives if we honor our calling, our divine purpose.
- I came to understand that life is an opportunity for us to express and experience love.[642]

It is a sign of hope that these NDErs direct their orientation of life to their divine purpose and calling and grow in love, forgiveness, and acceptance. Their brief NDEs have drastically changed their hearts and lives.

In contrast to these NDErs' views, let us see how mystics Swedenborg and Singh have made their several viewpoints noteworthy.

First, they emphasize the importance of the reality of the Trinity because the Trinity consists of heaven. That is, the contents of heaven are the Trinity. By denying it, we are automatically outside heaven. Those who accept the reality of the Trinity simultaneously engage in heaven.

Regarding the Trinity, there are not three gods seating on three thrones. Only one God, the incarnate God, is on the throne. We will never see the face of the creator God in this life or in the next life forever because God is not a physical being, but spirit and love. So many people want to see God and to meet God personally. That's one of the major reasons God became a human being. Jesus Christ is the image of God. Both Swedenborg and Singh are adamant about this truth of the invisible God and of Jesus as the visible God.

God is love. This love is not an abstract love, but a concrete and incarnate love in person through Jesus. The spirit of this love overflows the visible and invisible worlds. Thus, by accepting this reality of the Trinity, people dwell in the Trinity by default, for where God is, there is heaven, or where the Trinity is, heaven transpires. The core of the Trinity is the love of God. This means, anyone who rejects this love of God is outside heaven.

Many NDErs aspire for a universal religion embracing all humanity. That is a noble desire for the unity of the human family. Let us briefly look into this issue. In Buddhism, there is no God; so Buddhism is atheistic. Buddha is not God, but is the first enlightened one. All of us should be enlightened ones like him. In Hinduism, there are many gods—at least five hundred major gods although there is one Brahman, the supreme existence or absolute reality.[643] Brahman is impersonal. In Islam, there is only one God Allah and His messenger is Mohamed. We need to submit to Allah. So there is no visible God in Islam. Confucianism is a more ethical religion than a spiritual one. Confucius is a wise sage, not a god. In Judaism, there is only one God, YHWH (Yahweh). We must worship, love, and serve the only true God of YHWH. In Christianity, the God of love (YHWH) became incarnate in Jesus Christ to redeem humanity. Jesus is the way of love, the truth of love, and the life of love to God. Among the major religions, there is no ultimate God who appeared in the form of a person except Jesus. Besides Christianity, all other religions do not claim the personal incarnation of the God of love.[644]

Some NDErs and NDE researchers believe that NDErs of different religious orientations would see their own religious figures. Buddhists would see Buddha, Hindus would see their own gods, Muslims would meet the prophet Mohammed, and Christians would see Jesus. Children of different religious backgrounds use terms typical to their family of origin in describing the "extra special being."[645] This is natural.

We need to understand, accept, and respect everyone's experience and belief. To pursue a universal religion that embraces all humanity or to seek the ultimate truth of God, however, we need to have interreligious dialogue not only on an intellectual and natural level, as religious scholars have done so far, but also at the spiritual and supernatural level of NDEs. This new approach to interreligious dialogue may treat the theme of the love of God or the ultimate Reality that NDErs have experienced. In this approach, God who is not unconditional love is theoretical and unreal. Swedenborg's and Singh's understanding of the Trinity of love should be included in this new approach to interreligious dialogue.

Second, Swedenborg and Singh clarify the world of spirits, the intermediary place between heaven and hell. This is different from purgatory. For Roman Catholics, purgatory is "A place or condition of temporal punishment for those who, departing this life in God's grace, are, not entirely free from venial faults, or have not fully paid the satisfaction due to their transgressions."[646] The world of spirits is not a place of punishment for purification, but a waiting room or a green room for heaven or hell.

A number of NDErs visited this place and thought that they had visited heaven. Swedenborg and Singh explain the nature of this intermediary place in detail, clarifying the confusion between the world of spirits and heaven and correcting the idea of purgatory. No one else has described the world of spirits as they have done.

Third, they sufficiently explain the necessity of the existence of hell for the sake of evildoers who want to go away from God. Hell has been allowed and sustained by God's grace and love. Hell is not the place where God punishes evildoers, but the place where evil spirits choose to be and where evil spirits torment other evil spirits.

Many NDErs acknowledged the existence of heaven, but have denied the existence of hell because they experienced no hell. If hell does not exist, there is no place where evil spirits can go to be themselves.

Fourth, why are there some different experiences of heaven and hell among NDErs? For Swedenborg and Singh, there are, at least, two reasons: the vastness of heaven and hell and our different understandings of the same reality.

Thus those NDErs who visited heaven and hell saw different parts of heaven and hell. To Swedenborg, people mistakenly think that heaven is a single place where everyone is gathered together; in actuality, heaven is vast, consisting of countless communities. There are also as many hells as there are angelic communities in the heavens, because a hellish community corresponds to each heavenly one.[647]

Even for those that visit the same places, the descriptions of their experiences can be diverse according to their levels of understanding. For instance, a first grader and a geologist go together to the Grand Canyon and write their experiences of it. Their reports would be quite different according to their levels of understanding, experiences, and observations. To Singh, truths have come by way of visions, yet people with different temperaments and different intellectual presuppositions will understand the truths through their own perceptions.[648]

Howard Storm explains this issue with his own earthly experience:

> If one sent 15 million tourists on a tour of a foreign country there would be 15 million different reports of the experience. The range of experience would be from the most negative to extremely positive. What are the many factors that predispose an individual to be sensitive or repelled by cultural differences. Having led more than two dozen mission trips to the same village in Belize, I am amazed at the response of the individuals to the people and circumstances. The range of reactions to a foreign culture have been extreme. How much more misunderstanding of a mystical NDE is possible? It is surprising there is so much agreement on essentials."[649]

It would be natural for people to report differently about heaven and hell. Those different NDE reports can be authentic and precious gifts from God.

Fifth, Swedenborg and Singh reject the idea of reincarnation. Many NDErs have not observed reincarnation. The term *reincarnation* has been used in a variety of ways. At least, Eastern religions have used it quite differently from Western philosophies and cults. So we are limited here to discuss this issue. Christianity, however, has opposed the idea of reincarnation for a long time because it disparages the authority of the Bible, the meaning of Christian salvation, the idea of judgment, and the resurrection of the body.[650]

Sixth, heaven is the place where we can grow up to God's holiness, mercy, and perfection. God is not threatened by our pursuit to be perfect but yearns for us to grow up to God's level of perfection.

Seventh, they disclose that our beliefs and transformed hearts work together for our entrance to heaven. We enter heaven not by our faith alone, but also our changed nature supported by fruits of our changed hearts, the lives of love, and authentic beliefs. The doctrine of justification by faith *alone* has misled many. Swedenborg and Singh teach justification by faith and love.

Eighth, Swedenborg unravels the meaning of eternity in light of the changes of state. Time and space collapse into eternity. To Singh, everything is present for God. So, eternity means now before God. Eternity takes place in our relation to God.

True, eternity is not independent of God. It is a relational event in our interaction with God. Our loving relationship with God and others turns a moment to an eternity of bliss, while our separated relation from God and others turns a moment to an eternity of displeasure. Even though we live thousands of years for our own sake, those thousand years can turn into the emptiness of a fleeting moment and eternal death. However, if we live a minute for God and others, that minute can turn into the blissful eternity of thousand years and eternal life.

Closing Remarks

WHAT ARE THE most inspirational and conspicuous points NDErs and Christian mystics make? A short list of them would include unconditional love, a God-centered transcendental life, the significance of the Trinity, hell emerging from God's love, our proper destiny, and no judgment by God.

Unconditional Love

The most important value that almost all mystics underscore and almost all NDErs have learned from the other side is unconditional love. NDErs really felt it from God or from the "Light," angels, and good spirits.

One NDEr experienced receiving unconditional love from ten thousand good spirits on the other side, which he reciprocated to them.[651] It felt like he was in an ocean of love. Wave after wave crashed over him, encircling him to the point of ecstasy. This went on for some time. Love expended itself incredibly. All of them were building one another up to such incredible peaks, hundreds of times grander than the human mind could expect.[652] Jesus kept on gathering more good spirits before him, with the numbers proliferating, until he was before hundreds of thousands of good spirits. These good spirits kept on growing to millions of words cannot describe how good this spirit felt, and how loved he felt.[653] Another person expressed it in the following way: "The only human emotion I could feel was pure, unrelenting, unconditional love. Take the unconditional love a mother has for a child and amplify it a thousand fold, then multiply exponentially. The result of your equation would be as a grain of sand is to all the beaches in the world. So, too, is the comparison between the love we experience on earth to what I felt during my experience. This love is so strong, that words like 'love' make the description seem obscene."[654]   Another NDEr described it as follows: "*The parts of the 'movie' where I had harmed others felt almost unbearable . . . At the same time it was all surrounded with unconditional love and forgiveness because it was all about lessons and never about retribution.*"[655] When we just love one person unconditionally, it causes a butterfly effect[656] that becomes unpredictable. When millions of people practice loving jointly, its overwhelming impact will be unutterable.

What is the purpose of the incarnation of Jesus? Jesus came to earth to redeem all of us from our sins so that we may love God with all our heart, our mind, and our strength and love our neighbors as ourselves. If we had done these two, Jesus would not have had to be crucified. In heaven, people practice these, too. It is a great opportunity to practice God's unconditional love on earth. In heaven, people live these out and don't need to practice them.

In Matthew 5:46-48, Jesus says, "For if you love those who love you, what reward do you have? Do not even the tax collectors do the same? And if you greet only your brothers and sisters, what more are you doing than others? Do not even the Gentiles do the same? Be perfect, therefore, as your heavenly Father is perfect."

To emulate Christ's example is to love God wholeheartedly and others unconditionally, which is our ultimate goal in life on earth.

A God-Centered Transcendent Life

Most NDErs experience an encounter with God or seeing the light. In his "God Study," Dr. Jeffrey Long finds a few thoughts NDErs would agree on: God loves all of us. All we need in this life is our trusting, loving, forgiving, and accepting one another in God. If we honor our divine purpose and divine calling, we can learn the God-given power within us to create our lives and grow in God. Life is our opportunity to experience and express God's love.[657]

In his book, *Near-Death Experiences as Evidence for the Existence of God and Heaven*, Miller shares his understanding of the major common messages of

NDEs. They are: God is love, personal, just, and light. What really matters is that our choices matter to God, that material things are temporary and not worth obsessing over, that a huge part of why we are here is to love people, that it is important to love God and to seek knowledge, and that prayers seem to be taken into account. Thus, we should not lust for power or be consumed with cultural norms, but we should forgive, tell the truth, and give to charities.[658]

The one thing that impresses Professor Bruce Greyson most about NDErs is their unfading spiritual attitudes, beliefs, and values after their experiences: "They have more compassion for others, a greater desire to help others, a greater appreciation for life, and a stronger sense of meaning or purpose in life."[659] Also, an overwhelming majority of NDErs has no longer any fear of death, have lost interest in material possessions, and no longer have any interest in personal prestige, status, or competition.[660]

The Significance of the Trinity

The two mystics, Swedenborg and Singh, rightly stress the significance of the reality of the Trinity in the sense that God is the essence of heaven. Where God is, there establishes heaven. By being ignorant of God, people cannot reside in God. Anyone who believes in the idea of three Gods will be outside of heaven. Many people say they believe in one God, but think as if there are three Gods. This should be corrected before they enter heaven. God is love. We cannot see love in an image. That's one of the reasons why God became a human being. That person is Jesus. Among all founders of major religions, no one claimed that he or she is the incarnate God of love. Jesus is the only God we will see in heaven forever. He is the image of the invisible God (Col. 1:15). The sun is a good metaphor for the reality of the Trinity: the base (the Creator), its rays (Jesus Christ), and its heat (the Holy Spirit).

Our Proper Destiny

There is only one source of life, which is an infinite and unlimited life. This life has created countless lives, different in kind, and in the stages of their progress. We human beings are created in God's own image so that we might enjoy divine happiness in God's holy presence.[661] This life created by God cannot be destroyed but may be transformed into another form.[662]

We are born not for our own sake, but for others' sake to serve our society, our church, our country, and thus the Lord.[663] Serving the Lord by obeying his commandments does not make a person a servant but makes them free. All who possess this freedom in the Lord will relish inexpressible happiness. By obeying the Lord we can be perfect in knowledge, intelligence, and wisdom to eternity. When we are gifted with truths, we can be perfected in intelligence and wisdom. Then we will be blessed with happiness for eternity.[664]

What Does the Bible Say about Heaven, Hell, and Universal Salvation?

FOR ATHEISTS, SKEPTICS, and agnostics, we have shown **in chapter 3** that there is life after life, using data that are verifiable. Among those who believe in the next life, however, many accept the existence of heaven while denying the existence of hell. Some of them think that hell is metaphorical rather than real. Others hold that hell is temporary and will close down. Concerning the existence of hell, we will discuss both hell and heaven in view of the Scriptures.

Since the term *heaven* is the English translation of *shamayim* (Hebrew), *ouranos*, and *palingenesis* (Greek) and since the term *hellll* is the English transla-tion of *sheololol* (Hebrew), *hades, gehenna,* and *tartarus* (Greek), we will look into these terms to understand their meanings better.

Furthermore, we will deal with the issue of whether hell is temporary or permanent in connection with "everlastingness" or "eternity" and universal salvation. Numerous Christians are universalists.[665] Thus, we will unravel the issues of universalism, taking note of God's love and sovereignty and our freedom.

Jesus, Heaven, and Hell

First of all, we will discuss what Jesus says about heaven and hell, exploring what he meant by them. It is important for us to know whether He uses the terms *heaven* and *hell* as real or metaphorical.

THE RICH MAN AND LAZARUS (LUKE 16:19-31)

The story of a rich man and Lazarus is the most detailed picture of the afterlife anywhere in the Scriptures. The following is a summary: There was a rich man who was well dressed and feasted lavishly every day. And at his gate lay a poor man (Lazarus), covered with sores, longing to fill his stomach with crumbs from the rich man's table. Lazarus died and the angels carried him to be with Abraham. The rich man also died and went to Hades, where he was being tormented in the fire, and looked up and saw Abraham and Lazarus. He pleaded with Father Abraham to send Lazarus to dip the tip of his finger in water and cool his tongue. But Abraham reminded him of his sumptuous life while Lazarus languished in poverty. He also mentioned an impassable great chasm, fixed between them. Then the rich man begged Abraham to send Lazarus to his father's house to warn his brothers not to come into his place of torment. Abraham replied that such a job belongs to Moses and the prophets.

This story raises the question whether we should interpret it as a realistic depiction of the afterlife or as an edifying parable.

I can see Jesus tell us through this narrative that heaven and hell are real places because his previous parables in Luke 15 (the parables of the lost sheep, the lost coin, and the lost son) are based on realistic settings, although they may not be actual occurrences. This story is also in a realistic setting. Furthermore, the parable is unique because two of its three characters are named and identified. This fact reinforces the realistic setting of this story.

This story must be a parable, too, for it warns us not to live for ourselves alone in this life. Jesus wants us to know that our actions or inactions in this life have consequences in the next life.

Beyond the controversy of the category of this story, there are some lessons we can learn from this account.

First, while heaven is the place where comfortless Lazarus may find comfort, hell is the place where the uncaring rich man is tormented by fire. Second, hell's torment by fire is not metaphorical for the rich man, but real.

Hell's flame was too hot for him to bear. Third, even Father Abraham could not help his own descendent from languishing in the fire of hell. No one could help the rich man who was isolated from others and suffered in flames alone.

For Swedenborg, flames in hell are not imposed upon us from outside but spew out from our own selfish love and love for the world as seen in envy, hatred, vengefulness, savagery, lust, greed, and cravings.[666]

Presently, a number of people illustrate this parable persuasively with their own NDEs. After coming back to life, they speak of God's unconditional love for all peoples and creation. God seeks only the best for all of us and desires us to use our resources and time for the purposes of love and growth in wisdom and knowledge.

NDEs have drastically changed people's lives. For example, Gordon Allen was a rich businessman and private investment banker founding his own firm that expanded to Europe.[667] During his first NDE (1993), he learned deeply spiritual lessons. These revelatory lessons radically changed him and his life. A wealthy and influential businessman turned into a humble counselor and minister that loves and serves his fellow human beings. Now, after his another significant NDE, he is pouring all of his energy and resources into the mission of Jesus Christ. He is the founder of Completion Ministries.[668]

In addition to this afterlife story, Jesus mentions hell several times in the Gospel of Matthew alone: 5:22, "the hell of fire"; 5:29, "to be thrown into hell"; 5:30, "your whole body to go into hell"; 10:28, "both soul and body in hell"; 18:19, "to be thrown into the hell of fire"; and 23:33, "being sentenced to hell." Jesus mentions "hell" more than twenty times. Next, let us see what the Scriptures say about heaven and hell in general.

Heaven and Its Features

The OT and NT describe heaven as God's abode, the community of the redeemed, the space of worship, God's Presence in our praises, and the place of perfecting God's love.

HEAVEN AS GOD'S DWELLING PLACES

The Hebrew Bible says that heaven is the abode of God: "Hear the plea of your servant . . . O hear in heaven your dwelling place; heed and forgive" (1 Kings 8:30). God resides in heaven and hears our prayers. Jesus says, "Our Father in heaven, hallowed be your name" (Matt. 6:9). Jesus confirms heaven as God's dwelling place, although God is omnipresent.

Jesus says further that heaven will be our abode, too, because there are many dwelling places in God's house and He will come back to take us there after making it ready: "In my Father's house there are many dwelling places. If it were not so, would I have told you that I go to prepare a place for you? . . . I will come again and will take you to myself, so that where I am, there you may be also" (John 14:2-3). Jesus will welcome people to the heavenly home.

That house of God is heaven, which is where we will be with Jesus for eternity. Heaven is where God makes his home among mortals: "See, the home of God is among mortals. He will dwell with them . . . He will wipe every tear from their eyes.

Death will be no more; mourning and crying and pain will be no more, for the first things have passed away" (Rev. 21:3-4). Heaven is our true home in which peace, warm-heartedness, comfort, joy, healing, and love overflow. Heaven is not a pie in the sky, but a tangible place where God's people will dwell and enjoy.

THE COMMUNITY OF THE REDEEMED

There will be no more blind eyes, no more deaf ears, no more speechless tongues, no more incapacitated legs, no more sighs, and no more grieving, but there will be everlasting joy and gladness in heaven. There will be no one unclean, but only the redeemed:

> "Then the eyes of the blind shall be opened,
>   and the ears of the deaf unstopped;
> then the lame shall leap like a deer,
>   and the tongue of the speechless sing for joy . . .

A highway shall be there,
    and it shall be called the Holy Way;
the unclean shall not travel on it,
    but it shall be for God's people . . .
they (ravenous animals) shall not be found there,
    but the redeemed shall walk there.
And the ransomed of the LORD shall return,
    and come to Zion with singing;
everlasting joy shall be upon their heads;
    they shall obtain joy and gladness,
and sorrow and sighing shall flee away" (Isa. 35:5-10).

HEAVEN AS THE SPACE OF WORSHIP (HEB. 4:14-16)

In the Hebrew Bible, Isaiah describes heaven as a real place where angels worship God, declaring the holiness of the Lord all day and night (Isaiah 6:3). When Isaiah got a glimpse of heaven, he fell to the ground and felt that he would be struck dead. In Isaiah 6:1-3, he reports an amazing view that he had of the throne of heaven:

> In the year that King Uzziah died, I saw the Lord sitting on a throne, high and lofty; and the hem of his robe filled the temple. Seraphs were in attendance above him; each had six wings: with two they covered their faces, and with two they covered their feet, and with two they flew. And one called to another and said: "Holy, holy, holy is the Lord of hosts; the whole earth is full of his glory."

It is the awesome place of holiness and of worship by angels incessantly. In the Book of Revelation John portrays, "And the four living creatures, each of them with six wings, are full of eyes all around and inside. Day and night without ceasing they sing, 'Holy, holy, holy, the Lord God the Almighty, who was and is and is to come'" (Rev. 4:8).

John's witness corresponds to Isaiah's. Isaiah saw seraphs with six wings praising the Lord of hosts continually. John saw the four living creatures with six wings worshipping the Lord God Almighty day and night without ceasing. The Bible clearly describes the throne room of God through the lips of Isaiah and John, confirming heaven as the place of continual praising and worship.

HEAVENS AS GOD'S PRESENCE IN THE PRAISES OF ISRAEL

The Bible clearly says that God cannot be bounded by any one geographical place and transcends time and space: "Even heaven and the highest heaven cannot contain you" (1 Kings 8:27). Although God's throne is in the heavens (Heb. 8:1, "the throne of the Majesty in the heavens"), God does not only reside in a particular location, but also in our praises: "Yet you are holy, enthroned in the praises of Israel" (Ps. 22:3). Heaven is the blessed space where God is Present: "For Christ did not enter a sanctuary made by human hands, a mere copy of the true one, but he entered into heaven itself, now to appear in the presence of God on our behalf" (Hebrews 9:24). Thus, we cannot say that God's heaven is here or there (Luke 17:21), but that God's presence makes heaven everywhere.

THE PLACE OF PERFECTING GOD'S LOVE

God's love makes the redeemed love and perfects them there: "No one has ever seen God; if we love one another, God lives in us, and his love is perfected in us" (1Jn. 4:12). Lovers of Jesus will observe his will: "If you love me, you will keep my commandments" (John14:15). They are delighted to obey Jesus' mandates because of their internal love for Jesus.

Terms for Heaven

THE HEAVENS, THE SKY (SHAMAYIM: HEBREW)

This term points to a visible heaven where the stars are (Judge 5:20, Gen. 15:5), before which fowl fly (Gen. 1:20), the abode of God (1 Kings 8:30, 32), and where Elijah was taken up (2 Kings 2:1).[669]

NEW CREATION (*PALINGENESIS: GREEK*)

This word derives from new (*palin*) and creation (*genesis*) and denotes "new genesis" either in the sense of "return to existence," "coming back from death to life," "renewal to a higher existence," or "regeneration" in the ordinary sense.[670]

The new heavens and the new earth do not involve creation out of nothing. In 2 Peter 3:12-13 they entail a purified universe out of the old one: ". . .waiting for and hastening the coming of the day of God, because of which the heavens will be set ablaze and dissolved, and the elements will melt with fire? But according to his promise we are waiting for new heavens and a new earth in which righteousness dwells."[671] Jesus said to them, "Truly I tell you, at the renewal of all things, when the Son of Man is seated on the throne of his glory, you who have followed me will also sit on twelve thrones, judging the twelve tribes of Israel" (Matt. 19:28). When Jesus is ready, he will renew God's creation (*palingenesis*) and his twelve apostles will judge the twelve tribes of Israel.

The term *new creation* is used twice in the NT referring to the re-birth of *physical creation* at Christ's return (Advent), which inaugurates His millennial kingdom (Matt. 19:28; cf. Rom. 8:18-25), and the re-birth all believers experience at conversion (Tit. 3:5).[672]

The term *new creation* signifies the renewal of the state of affairs. Scripture teaches that a new cosmic heaven and a new earth will be established and be the dwelling-place of the eschatological human beings around the center of God's permanent heaven.[673]

Although in the fourth Gospel and in the Pauline Epistles the emphasis on the heaven-centered character of the future life by renewing earth fades into the background, the book of Revelation acknowledges this part with its imagery of "the new Jerusalem" coming down from God from heaven upon earth.[674]

Revelation presents the prevalent imageries of the new heaven and the new earth in the OT (the Old Testament) and NT (the New Testament), particularly with the picture of the "new heavens and the new earth" of Isaiah and John. The renewal of all creation is comparable to creation out of nothing (*creatio ex nihilo*).

155

THE NEW JERUSALEM

Revelation 21:1-2 is about a new heaven and a new earth in contrast with the first heaven and the first earth: "Then I saw a new heaven and a new earth; for the first heaven and the first earth had passed away, and the sea was no more. And I saw the holy city, the new Jerusalem, coming down out of heaven from God, prepared as a bride adorned for her husband."

The central point of the new heaven and the new earth is the New Jerusalem. God will live with mortals and will comfort them. In the presence of God, mourning, crying, and pain will disappear with death itself. The passing of these was the vision of the prophet Isaiah: "For I am about to create new heavens and a new earth; the former things shall not be remembered or come to mind" (65:17).

The vision of Isaiah was fulfilled with the arrival of Jesus. He would lead us into the New Jerusalem which foundations are Jesus and his disciples:

> And had a wall great and high, and had twelve gates, and at the gates twelve angels, and names written thereon, which are the names of the twelve tribes of the children of Israel: On the east three gates; on the north three gates; on the south three gates; and on the west three gates. And the wall of the city had twelve foundations, and in them the names of the twelve apostles of the Lamb . . . . And I saw no temple therein: for the Lord God Almighty and the Lamb are the temple of it (Rev. 21:12-14, 22).

This New Jerusalem of heaven fulfills the aspiration of the Hebrew Bible and the New Testament by the incarnation of Jesus.

THE THREE HEAVENS

The idea of three levels of the heavens appears in rabbinic sources.[675] In the NT the third heaven was recognized by Paul (2 Cor. 12:2-4).

Before his own testimony of the third heaven, Paul includes the idea of the three heavens in his writing about the resurrection. He states that the resurrection of the dead corresponds to the different glory of earthy bodies and heavenly bodies.

> There are both heavenly bodies and earthly bodies, but the glory of the heavenly is one thing, and that of the earthly is another.[41] There is one glory of the sun, and another glory of the moon, and another glory of the stars; indeed, star differs from star in glory. So it is with the resurrection of the dead (1 Cor. 15:40-42).

The glory of the sun, the glory of the moon, and the glory of the stars offer the foundation for the three heavens. The first one is earth's atmosphere, the second is outer space, and the third is the home where God dwells.

First Heaven: Atmosphere
It is the sky that surrounds the earth and contains clouds and the air where birds fly: "And God said, "Let the waters bring forth swarms of living creatures, and let birds fly above the earth across the dome of the sky" (Gen. 1:20).

God has provided rain, food, and blessings from this heaven: "Yet he commanded the skies above, and opened the doors of heaven; he rained down on them manna to eat, and gave them the grain of heaven" (Psalms 78:23-24).

God opens the first heavens and sends rain on the land: "The LORD will open for you his rich storehouse, the heavens, to give the rain of your land in its season and to bless all your undertakings" (Deut. 28:12).

Second Heaven: Outer Space
The second heaven consists of the starry heavens of outer space (Deuteronomy 17:3; Jeremiah 8:2; Matthew 24:29) and starts from the end of the earth's atmosphere: "And God said, "Let there be lights in the dome of the sky to separate the day from the night; and let them be for signs and for seasons and for days and years" (Gen. 1:14).

The dome, firmament, or expanse is the second heaven: "So God made the dome and separated the waters that were under the dome from the waters that were above the dome. And it was so. God called the dome Sky" (Gen. 1:7-8).

God placed the sun, moon, stars, and constellations in the dome of heaven:

"God set them in the dome of the sky to give light upon the earth" (Gen. 1:17).

The Psalmist was inspired and awestruck by God's presence in the starry heavens:

"The heavens are telling the glory of God; and the firmament proclaims his handiwork" (Ps. 19:1).

Third Heaven: The Home for God

Beyond the space and stars, the third heaven is the home where God, God's angels, and God' just people dwells (1 Kings 8:30, Rev. 21:3-4). It is the "Father's house" in Jesus' words (John 14:2). The third heaven is called "the highest heaven" (1 Kings 8:27), "The heaven of heavens" (Deuteronomy 10:14),), and the location of the throne of God (Ps. 2:4; Rev. 4:6).

Furthermore, Paul notes his experience of the third heaven: "I know a person in Christ who fourteen years ago was caught up to the third heaven— whether in the body or out of the body I do not know; God knows. And I know that such a person . . . was caught up into paradise and heard things that are not to be told, that no mortal is permitted to repeat" (2 Cor. 12:2-4). In the third heaven, he heard something not to be disclosed. It is noticeable that Paul equates the third heaven with paradise. It is hardly possible to say anything more explicitly on the nature of the third heaven.[676] It must be the highest heaven according to the Deuteronomist and Psalmist: "Although heaven and the heaven of heavens belong to the LORD your God, the earth with all that is in it" (Deut. 10:14) and "Praise him, you highest heavens, and you waters above the heavens" (Ps. 148:4).

In the third heaven, we find "the throne of grace" (Heb. 4:16) and can receive the mercy of God in time. The Scriptures do not explicate the three heavens any further, but some mystics do.

According to the legends of the Jewish, there are seven heavens.[677] Their seventh heaven is comparable with the third heaven of Christians: "The seventh heaven, on the other hand, contains naught but what is good and beautiful: right, justice, and mercy, the storehouses of life, peace, and blessing, the souls of the pious, the souls and spirits of unborn generations, the dew with which God will revive the dead on the resurrection day, and, above all, the Divine Throne, surrounded by the seraphim, the ofanim, the holy Hayyot, and the ministering angels."[678] This is the highest heaven where God, the seraphim, the holy Hayyot (the living beings in Ezekiel's vision), and the ministering angels reside together. The Throne of God is located there. The ofanim (the wheels of the chariot Ezikiel saw) can be seen there.

THREE HEAVENS FOR MYSTICS

Christian mystics discuss three heavens from their spiritual perspectives. There are three distinctive heavens for Swedenborg: a third or inmost, a second or middle, and a first or outmost heaven. The third or inmost heaven is called celestial, the second or middle heaven is called spiritual, and the outmost or first heaven is called natural. The natural heaven is, however, unlike the natural of the world, but has the spiritual and the celestial within it.[679]

Sundar Singh, once in ecstasy, learned about the three heavens. According to him, the first heaven is the state of bliss on earth. His conversion resulted in such wonderful inward peace and enjoyment of the presence of Christ. The second heaven is an intermediate state. This is the paradise that Christ promised to the thief on the cross (Luke 23:40-43). He was with Christ, but could not see Jesus in paradise. In this second heaven there stay for a time those who are not quite sufficiently advanced in their spiritual state to enter the third heaven. Even though they hear a heavenly music and experience Jesus' influence as if light waves proceed from Him, they miss seeing Him face to face. The third heaven is heaven proper. All righteous people will ultimately reach here. A few are allowed to make short visits there during their earthly life. This is the heaven apostle Paul entered.

When Sundar Singh found himself there, he seemed to have a body with form and shape, but all appeared to be made of light. But when he touched his body, he felt nothing. This is what St. Paul speaks of as a spiritual body: "In Heaven I see not with bodily but with spiritual eyes, and I was told that these spiritual eyes are the same as those that all men will use after permanently leaving the body."[680]

Hell

To describe hell, Jesus uses the metaphor of a harvest field where the reapers collect the weeds first and bind them in bundles to be burned, but gather the wheat into a barn. He explained it: "The Son of Man will send his angels, and they will collect out of his kingdom all causes of sin and all evildoers,[42] and they will throw them into the furnace of fire, where there will be weeping and gnashing of teeth" (Matt. 13:41-42).

In his parable of the fishing net, when it was full, the fishers drew it ashore, sat down, and put the good into baskets but threw out the bad: "So it will be at the end of the age. The angels will come out and separate the evil from the righteous and throw them into the furnace of fire, where there will be weeping and gnashing of teeth" (Matt. 13:48-50). It is a very critical issue for many Christians whether these explanations of the parables are real or are parables. The parables can be both metaphorical and real. "Real" goes beyond "actual." While the Independence Day of America in 1776 was an "actual" event, the independence of America points to reality. It is like the relation between sign and symbol. A sign points to an event whereas a symbol points beyond the event. Parables can be both signs and symbols.

Terms for Hell

HADES

Sometimes, the Greek term Hades (*hạdēs*) is inaccurately translated "hell" in English versions of the NT. It is not necessarily a place of torment for evil persons, but refers to the place of the dead. Even though Hades was the Greek god of the underworld, the name usually refers to his realm where the hardly conscious souls of the dead led a shadowy existence with no memory of their previous life.[681]

Like the old Greek Hades, the old Hebrew biblical concept Sheol *(šĕʾôl)* refers to the place of all the dead where darkness, gloom, and shades prevail over the inevitable existence. Jewish writing in Greek commonly retained the Greek term. Therefore, the Septuagint (LXX) uses the Greek term *Hades* for the Hebrew word *Sheol*. Such Jewish translation of *Sheol* illuminates the ten NT usages of the word *Hades*.[682] Hades or Sheol in most early Jewish literature refers to the place of all the dead[683] and is almost tantamount to death.[684]

God provisionally entrusted the dead to Hades, but at the resurrection, God will claim them back. Death will end and the mouth of Hades will be sealed off or, in another image, Hades and death will be cast into the lake of fire (Rev. 20:14). Despite its close association with death, Hades should not be confused with Gehenna, the place of eternal torment for evildoers after the Day of Judgment.[685]

Sometimes Hades in its final development becomes entirely the place of punishment for the unrighteous, while the righteous at death enters paradise or heaven.[686]

Hades as the place of torment can be seen in Jesus' story of the rich man and Lazarus (Luke 16:19-31). In it, only the rich man goes to Hades where he is tormented in fire, while Lazarus enters "Abraham's bosom" in paradise.[687]

Other NT passages on Hades confirm Jewish usage. Acts 2:27, 31 directly mirror OT usage; Hades is the dwelling place of all the dead before the resurrection.[688] Matthew 11:23 (see also Luke 10:15, cf. Isa. 14:13-15) reflects OT usage.[689] The description in Rev. 20:13 is a traditional apocalyptic one,[690] whereas the personification of Hades, along with death, in this apocalyptic one and in Rev. 6:8, derives from OT usage sustained by later writers (see Ps. 49:14; Isa. 28:15; Hosea 13:14 for both death and Sheol personified).[691]

The gates of Hades (Matt. 16:18) is traditional and the image more immediately echoes the OT (Isa. 38:10; cf. "gates of death" in Job 38:17; Ps. 9:14; 107:18) and later Jewish writings.[692] The gates of Hades hold the dead imprisoned in its territory: "Only God can open them."[693] When Jesus said to Peter, "on this rock I will build my church, and the gates of Hades will not prevail against it" (Matt. 16:18), he must have referred to the power of Hades that holds the dead.[694] Another image is that the risen Christ, who holds the keys of Hades, has the divine power to release the dead from the realm of death: "and the living one. I was dead, and see, I am alive forever and ever; and I have the keys of Death and of Hades" (Rev. 1:18).[695]

GEHENNA

During the OT time, marking the boundary between the inheritance of the tribes of Judah and Benjamin (Josh. 15:8; 18:16, 30), the valley of Hinnom was the place of the idolatrous worship of the Canaanite gods Molech and Baal. This worship involved sacrificing children by passing them through a fire on a high place (*Topheth*) and into the hands of the gods (Jer. 7:31; 19:4-5; 32:35).[696]

INTERTESTAMENTAL PERIOD

Often referred to simply as "the accursed valley" or "abyss," the valley came to represent the place of eschatological judgment of the unrighteous Jews by fire.[697]

By the 1st century CE a figurative understanding of Gehenna emerged as the place of judgment by fire for all wicked everywhere. The judgment of the wicked transpired either as throwing their soul into Gehenna promptly upon death or as throwing their reunited body and soul into Gehenna after the resurrection and last judgment.[698]

The NT uses all of the twelve references to Gehenna as the place of fiery judgment. Eleven references are in the Synoptic Gospels as sayings of Jesus (Matt. 5:22, 29-30; 10:28; 18:9; 23:15, 33; Mark 9:43, 45, 47; Luke 12:5) and one is in James 3:6, which refers to the tongue being itself set on fire by Gehehnna.[699] Jesus warns us to take all precautions not to go into the unquenchable fire of Gehenna (Mark 9:43).

In addition to being the doom and gloom of the wicked (Rev. 20:15; 21:8), Gehenna is the doom and gloom awaiting the devil and his angels (Matt. 25:41; Rev. 20:10), the beast and the false prophet (Rev. 19:20; 20:10), and death and Hades (Rev. 20:13-14).[700]

While Hades is the temporary place of the ungodly between death, resurrection, and final judgment (cf. Rev. 20:13-14) where Hades yields up its dead for judgment and is thrown into the lake of fire at the last judgment), Gehenna is the eternal fiery destination of the wicked after final judgment. Whereas Hades obtains the soul only (Acts 2:27, 31), Gehenna takes both body and soul (Matt. 10:28; cf. Luke 12:5).[701]

TARTARUS (THE DEEPEST DUNGEON OF ETERNAL TORMENT)

Tartarus is the hellish region of ancient Greek mythology. The name originally referred to the deepest region of the world, the lower of the two parts of the underworld. The Greek gods imprisoned their enemies such as the Titans in it. It slowly came to denote the entire underworld.[702]

NT uses the term *Tartarus* to describe the place of punishment of the fallen angels:[703] "if God did not spare the angels when they sinned, but cast them into hell and committed them to chains of deepest darkness to be kept until the judgment" (2 Peter 2:4).

They are cast into *Tartarus* and are chained in the deepest darkness until the Day of Judgment. Similarly, Jesus pronounces the same punishment to the wicked: "Then he will say to those at his left hand, 'You that are accursed, depart from me into the eternal fire prepared for the devil and his angels" (Matt. 25:41). The tormented place for the devil and his angels is *Tartarus*. They suffer from the eternal fire.

Hell and Its Features

Hell is for evildoers, the place of torment with fire, worms, and sulfur, and it is an eternal place.

HELL FOR ALL EVILDOERS

Jesus made it clear that all evildoers will end up in hell:

> The Son of Man will send his angels, and they will collect out of his kingdom all causes of sin and all evildoers, and they will throw them

into the furnace of fire, where there will be weeping and gnashing of teeth. . . . So it will be at the end of the age. The angels will come out and separate the evil from the righteous [50] and throw them into the furnace of fire, where there will be weeping and gnashing of teeth (Matthew 13:41-42, 49-50).

John also tells us that those whose names are not written in the book of life will be thrown into the lake of fire:

Anyone whose name was not found written in the book of life was thrown into the lake of fire (Revelation 20:15).

But as for the cowardly, the faithless, the polluted, the murderers, the fornicators, the sorcerers, the idolaters, and all liars, their place will be in the lake that burns with fire and sulfur, which is the second death" (Revelation 21:8).

Hell of Fire, Worm, Sulfur, and Smoke

Hell is the furnace of eternal fire with the undying worm, torturing sulfur and smoke:

Furnace of fire . . . weeping and gnashing of teeth (Matthew 13:50).

It is better for you to enter the kingdom of God with one eye than to have two eyes and to be thrown into hell, where their worm never dies, and the fire is never quenched (Mark 9:47-48).

They will also drink the wine of God's wrath, poured unmixed into the cup of his anger, and they will be tormented with fire and sulfur in the presence of the holy angels and in the presence of the Lamb (Revelation 14:10).

Hell for Eternity

The devil, false prophet, and evildoers will suffer eternal torment in hell:

"And these will go away into eternal punishment, but the righteous into eternal life" (Matt. 25:46).

And the devil who had deceived them was thrown into the lake of fire and sulfur, where the beast and the false prophet were, and they will be tormented day and night forever and ever (Rev. 20: 10).

And the smoke of their torment goes up forever and ever (Rev. 20: 10).

Eternity and Immortality

According to Strong's Concordance, eternity in Hebrew is *olam*, which means "forever" in short.[704]

Yahweh is the Creator and the eternal God, Lord over the history of all peoples beyond the destiny of Israel. Yahweh remains true to the original creative and redemptive purpose. The metaphysical timelessness of the Platonic ideas cannot be discovered in the Hebrew Bible.[705]

In the post-exilic period, since God's uniqueness was recognized, "'eternity' became more and more a synonym for 'godliness,' soon a somewhat worn symbol for God's world and God's activity. With the increasing development of eschatological concepts in apocalyptic writings eternity (*olam*) becomes the permanent attribute of the life to come (Dan. 12:2: 'everlasting life,' 'everlasting contempt')."[706]

According to Kittel, in the NT eternity (*aiónios*) is used in three ways.

1. It is used of God. As a predicate of God eternity comprises, not only the concept of unlimited time with no beginning or no end, but also of the eternity, which transcends time.
2. In the latter sense it is used also of divine possessions and gifts.
3. The expression *the eternal kingdom or reign* (2 Pet. 1:11) transitions to the use of *eternity* as a term for the object of eschatological expectation: *the promised eternal inheritance*, (Heb. 9:15).[707]

THE MEANING OF ETERNITY

For Paul Tillich, Christianity must refuse the doctrine of natural immortality and must uphold instead the doctrine of eternal life given by God as the power of Being-Itself.[708]

Tillich contends that eternity does not mean timelessness or the endlessness of time. Eternity, which is *olam* in Hebrew and *aiones* in Greek, denotes "the power of embracing all periods of time."[709] Since God created time, God transcends the gap between potentiality and actuality. Moments of time are not unconnected from each other; past and future do not swallow presence; yet the eternal embraces the temporal. Plato's eternity contained time, although it was the time of circular movement.[710]

Tillich uses the only analogy to eternity located in human experience: "that is, the unity of remembered past and anticipated future in an experience present . . . eternity must first be symbolized as an eternal present (*nunc eternum*)."[711]

God created time with the cosmos, but eternity is one of God's attributes. Strictly speaking, eternity is relational time. Eternity is not a measurable time, but is qualitative time with God. It derives from God. So eternal life arrives when we believe in God by accepting Jesus as the Lord: "Very truly, I tell you, anyone who hears my word and believes him who sent me has eternal life, and does not come under judgment, but has passed from death to life" (John 5:24).[712] Using the perfect tense of "pass" (*metabebēken*), this passage states that we have passed from death to life, not after this life, but as soon as we start believing in Jesus.

Eternal life is different from the ancient Greek belief of the immortality of the soul. According to Plato and other ancient Greeks, after this life, everyone will attain the immortality of the soul. In contrast, "eternal life" will arrive in the midst of life, not after life.

Let me illustrate this with the event of Jesus calming the storm in Galilee (Mark 4:35-41). A furious windstorm arose and the waves beat into the boat so that the boat was already being swamped. But he fell asleep in the stern; and they desperately woke him up. He woke up and rebuked the wind and the wind died down with no fear. The fitful sea resumed its tranquility.

The point is this: In the midst of the deadly storm, Jesus was soundly sleeping in peace. His disciples experienced their peace in the midst of the dreadful storm by waking him up. Christians experience Jesus' peace in the midst of our stormy life by waking Jesus up in the midst of their fitful life, not after crossing the fitful sea of life. In Jesus, Christians find eternity now, not later.

This is the difference between the immortality of the soul of the ancient Greeks and the eternal life of Christians. For the Greeks, the immortality of the soul will start after passing through this fitful sea of life; for Christians, eternal life takes place in the midst of the fitful sea of life in Jesus. The Greeks believe this material world is evil and so they became otherworldly while Christians believe we experience the eternal life now even in the midst of sorrows, grief, and the troubles of life. Whereas immortality is the linear concept of time, eternity is the quality of relationship with God in Jesus. We can experience eternal life now and forever by accepting Jesus as Lord (John 3:18) or eternal death now by rejecting Jesus. Eternal life is not the duration of time, but the state of relationship with God in time and beyond.

D. A. Carson claims that eternal life is explicitly defined in a prayer of Jesus: "And this is eternal life, that they may know you, the only true God, and Jesus Christ whom you have sent" (John 17:3). Based on this verse, Carson states that "Eternal life turns on nothing more and nothing less than knowledge of the true God" and that it is "not so much everlasting life as personal knowledge of the Everlasting One."[713]

When we believe in Jesus, we have passed from death to eternal life; there arrives the resurrection life: "Jesus said to her, 'I am the resurrection and the life. Those who believe in me, even though they die, will live, and everyone who lives and believes in me will never die'" (John 11:25-26). Jesus is our eternal life now.

Eternal death is the life separated from God. The heart that accepts Jesus as Lord has enjoyed the light of the eternal life and the heart that rejects Jesus as the Lord has experienced eternal death already:

Indeed, God did not send the Son into the world to condemn the world, but in order that the world might be saved through him. Those who believe in him are not condemned; but those who do not believe are condemned already, because they have not believed in the name of the only Son of God. And this is the judgment, that the light has come into the world, and people loved darkness rather than light because their deeds were evil (John 3:17-19).

If we realize that eternity is not quantitative or endlessness time, but rather qualitative time of our relationship with God in time and beyond, such realization would help us understand the meanings of eternal or everlasting fire and eternal life. In light of the meaning of eternity, we can grasp the eternal judgment of God, which may not be endless torment, but may be the state of our broken relationship with God beyond time.

Eternal life is the abundant life with God in Jesus Christ and eternal death is the state of life estranged from God in Jesus: "For all who do evil hate the light and do not come to the light, so that their deeds may not be exposed. But those who do what is true come to the light, so that it may be clearly seen that their deeds have been done in God" (John 3:20). By loving darkness more than the light of Jesus, people are alienated from Jesus and judged by rejecting the light of Jesus itself. This judgment is self-incurring by choosing the darkness of evil deeds over Jesus' light.

Jesus and Universalism and anti-Universalism

Numerous Christians are Universalists while many other Christians are not. In this section let's explore whether the Scriptures uphold universalism and why and how long hell is going to exist.

For Christian Universalists, hell may exist in the present, but it will eventually be empty and closed down due to the irresistible love of God. God's love and hell cannot coexist for too long. First of all, let us check five types of universalism.

FIVE TYPES OF UNIVERSALISM

There are four different types of universalism in Jürgen Moltmann's theology: True universalism, true particularism, hypothetical universalism, and open universalism.[714] I add one more to them: evangelical universalism.

True Universalism: Calvinist Friedrich Schleiermacher represents this type of universalism. For Schleiermacher, the universalism of salvation is unconditional. God temporally allows disbelief, but God will ultimately save all through God's love. The human being cannot eternally resist God's irresistible grace. Moltmann is rather close to true universalism.[715]

True Particularism: God does not will that all human beings should be helped to find salvation. The universalism of true Particularism is that God's glory should prevail in both the salvation of the elect and the damnation of the sinner. It is exemplified by Augustine's theology of predestination and by the Calvinist doctrine of double predestination.

Open Universalism: Karl Barth fulfills Moltmann's type of Open Universalism. Unlike Calvin who proposes "double predestination," Barth champions God's single election of all human beings in Jesus Christ. His idea of predestination points to an open universalism of salvation. Although Barth does not advocate particularism in principle, he does not defend automatic universalism, either. Believers only expect "an open multiplicity of the elect" and universal salvation in hope.[716]

Hypothetical Universalism: Calvinist Moyse Amyraut developed Calvin's idea of the general proclamation of the gospel further. This universalism declares the hearing of the gospel for everyone, even though God foresees that only a few will be saved. In it, God's intention is universal, but its reality in history is particular.[717]

Evangelical Universalism: A contemporary evangelical universal movement was ignited with the publication of *The Evangelical Universalist* by Gregory MacDonald (alias for Robin Parry) in 2006.[718] The publication torched a forum to talk about evangelical universalism with Gregory MacDonald and Thomas Talbott in 2008.[719]

These evangelical Universalists have declared their manifesto:

The Evangelical Universalists therefore believe 1) in reliance on the Bible alone as the only rule for faith and practice, 2) That salvation is only by grace alone and through faith in Jesus alone and apart from works and 3) the necessity of a personal relationship with Jesus Christ. We believe in the Great Commission, which is the clear command of Lord Jesus that we are to evangelize the world for him, and finally, 4) the belief that ultimately everyone who ever lived will be saved, some by being called and redeemed in this life and the rest by being called and redeemed from hell in the after life.[720]

While this movement aims to promote God's universal love and salvation toward all sentient beings, it concretely intends to reconcile the divided evangelical Christian faith of Calvinists and Arminians through the truth of God's universal love in dialogue.[721]
While Universalists affirm that hell will be empty because of God's love, anti-universalists underscore that God's justice will prevail throughout eternity.

One critical issue is how we understand the term "eternity." Whether hell will be eternal or not is a significant issue for Universalists and non-universalists.

On the one hand, the Bible speaks about neither God's unending punishment of sinners nor the annihilation of them, but speaks of eternal fire and everlasting contempt. On the other, the Bible does not support universal salvation. Here "everlasting" in the Hebrew Bible is the Hebrew translation of eternity (*olam*) and "forever and ever" in the Greek Bible is the Greek translation of eternity (*aiōnas*).

> And they shall go out and look at the dead bodies of the people who have rebelled against me; for their worm shall not die, their fire shall not be quenched, and they shall be an abhorrence to all flesh (Isa. 66:24).
>
> Many of those who sleep in the dust of the earth shall awake, some to everlasting life, and some to shame and everlasting contempt" (Dan. 12:2).
>
> It is better for you to enter life maimed or lame than to have two hands or two feet and to be thrown into the eternal fire . . . the hell of fire" (Matt. 18:8-9).

Then he will say to those on his left, "Depart from me, you cursed, into *the eternal fire* prepared for the devil and his angels." . . . And these will go away into *eternal punishment*, but the righteous into eternal life" (Matt. 25:41-46).

It is better for you to enter the kingdom of God with one eye than to have two eyes and be thrown into hell,[48] where "the worms that eat them do not die, and the fire is not quenched" (Mark 9:47-48).

They will be tormented with fire and sulfur in the presence of the holy angels and in the presence of the Lamb.[11] And the smoke of their torment goes up forever and ever (Rev. 14:10-11).

And the devil who had deceived them was thrown into the lake of fire and sulfur, where the beast and the false prophet were, and they will be tormented day and night forever and ever. . . . Then Death and Hades were thrown into the lake of fire. This is the second death, the lake of fire;[15] and anyone whose name was not found written in the book of life was thrown into the lake of fire (Rev. 20:10, 14-15).

As we discussed before, the eternal torment does not refer to the quantitative time of endlessness, but the qualitative time of relationship with God. We know little about the possibility of the mending of our relationships with God in hell except that Jesus "went and made a proclamation to the spirits in prison,[20] who in former times did not obey, when God waited patiently in the days of Noah, during the building of the ark, in which a few, that is, eight persons, were saved through water" (1 Pet. 3:19-20). Is there any chance for the spirits in prison to change people's hearts in the next life? Otherwise, Jesus would not descend into hell to proclaim the gospel to the imprisoned spirits. That is confirmed later in 1 Peter: "For this is the reason the gospel was proclaimed even to the dead, so that, though they had been judged in the flesh as everyone is judged, they might live in the spirit as God does" (1 Pet. 4:6). Even the unrepentant dead may have a chance to hear the gospel and turn around to God.

We know that we cannot separate space from time in the Einsteinian universe. Time arises from space. Since there is no physical space in the next life, quantitative time (*Chronos*) does not exist there. Subsequently, the endless torment may denote something else than our customary understanding of never-ending duration in heaven. The eternal torment does not mean the endless torment, but the non-measurable duration of torment for the unrepentant in relation to God. If some of the imprisoned spirits had repented after Jesus' proclamation, their eternal torments must have ceased by restoring their right relationships with God.

The position of Universalists on temporary hell, however, has its predicaments. If the Universalists are certain that God will save everyone in the earth, such certainty may invalidate the freedom God has given to each of us. We know that to save all human beings is God's desire: "This is right and is acceptable in the sight of God our Savior, who desires everyone to be saved and to come to the knowledge of the truth" (1 Tim. 2:3-4). The term "desire" *Thélō* is to wish or will, or want what is *best* because someone is *ready* and *willing* to act.[722]

We find several passages in the Bible that express God's willingness to save all, but that does not mean God will override our will. The certainty of universal salvation is not in the Bible. God permits the choices of the beast and others: "And the devil who had deceived them was thrown into the lake of fire and sulfur, where the beast and the false prophet were, and they will be tormented day and night forever and ever" (Rev. 20:10). Universal salvation is God's ardent desire and our hope but is not and should not be the teaching of the church.

My View

Hell may exist forever as long as anyone wants to move away from God. Hell is not the place of the punishment of God, but the space for the unrepentant as a result of their sins. But if we are certain that hell will exist endlessly, we may underestimate the strength of God to save everyone. When God is willing to wait for the returning of God's lost son or daughter, we are not in the position to say to God that such waiting is a waste of time and that God should forget him or her. If we think that such waiting for, or welcoming of, the returning son or daughter is unjust or unfair, we turn out to be the older son in the parable of the lost son in Luke 15. We cannot play God by telling God what God should or should not do. God can transcend every category of human rules we conjure up. God alone is absolute. We should not elevate any beliefs we have produced. We worship God alone. It is sufficient for us to thank God for God's willingness to save the last lost son or daughter of God with God's Mercy. God's Mercy endures forever (Ps. 136:1).

However, even though it is God's will to save everyone, God will not impose God's unilateral will upon us. God will respect the freedom of each of us. God's willingness to save all is different from God's determinism to save all. If we turn God's will to save all into a deterministic universalism, such a belief depicts God as an authoritarian who dictates to us what to do. Universalism does not take God's respect for our freedom seriously. It is a kind of predestination. God is very patient. God may wait for the return of the last forever. God in the Bible does not coerce anybody to subjugate his or her free will to God's. Love and freedom are inseparable. God's love offers us the free will to choose. God is gracious enough to wait for us. What we need to do is to pray and work for the fulfillment of God's purpose for universal salvation, trusting the victory of God's love and truth in the end. Our trust in the fulfillment of God's will is faith. By faith we carry out God's command to fulfill God's desire to save all.

The Bible seems to provide both motifs of universal salvation and limited salvation. Therefore, it would be hasty for us to conclude universal or limited salvation. It is still open as to whether everyone will accept God's invitation to salvation or not. But it is God's will that we do our best to fulfill God's yearning to save all. We are not just hoping that God will save up to the last person, but we also have to be actively involved in such efforts. Jesus says, "And this good news of the kingdom will be proclaimed throughout the world, as a testimony to all the nations; and then the end will come" (Matt. 24:1).

Why do much Fewer People Experience Hell than Heaven?

THE ESTIMATED INCIDENCE of distressing or disturbing NDEs (dNDEs) has ranged from 1% to 15% of all NDEs.[723] There are at least four reasons for the imbalance between heavenly NDEs and disturbing NDEs

First, NDErs repress their disturbing NDEs because of a built-in self-defense mechanism.

Second, people usually feel embarrassed and ashamed and fearful of sharing their hellish NDEs.

Third, NDErs' often have a limited understanding of the world of spirits.

Fourth, seduction and deceptions by evil spirits may cause hell-bound NDErs to think that they are in heaven.

Self-Defense Mechanism

The first reason is that people tend to repress their negative and unpleasant experiences. It is our self-defense mechanism that avoids pain and chooses pleasure. Recollecting negative and distressing experiences gives us pain. So we unconsciously tend to repress our painful events.

Dr. Maurice Rawlings provides a good example. He was skeptical about reported NDE experiences until a 48-year-old mail carrier named Charles McKaig dropped dead in his office. Dr. Rawlings made a pacemaker for McKaig's blocked heart and inserted its wire into the large vein beneath the collarbone that led to the heart. Mckaig began "coming to," but he wound lose consciousness and die whenever Dr. Rawlings interrupted his compression of his chest while reaching for instruments. "Each time he regained heartbeat and respiration, the patient screamed, 'I am in hell'! He was terrified and pleaded with me to help him. I was scared to death. In fact, this episode literally sacred the hell out of me! It terrified me enough to write this book."[724] McKaig flatlined several times, but during lucid moments he urgently pleaded with his terrified look to be resuscitated because every time he lost consciousness and died, he was literally in hell. He finally asked Dr. Rawlings to pray for him. Dr. Rawlings told him that he was a doctor, not a preacher.[725] Since this was a dying patient's request, Dr. Rawlings could not refuse, although he barely knew how to pray. So he led him with the following prayer:

> *Lord Jesus, I ask you to keep me out of hell.*
> *Forgive my sins.*
> *I turn my life over to you.*
> *If I die, I want to go to heaven.*
> *If I live, I'll be 'on the hook' forever.*[726]

Mckaig's condition finally stabilized and was he transported to a hospital. A couple of days later, Dr. Rawlings asked Mckaig about his experience of Hell. He responded, "What hell? I don't recall any hell!"[727]

Even though McKaig could not remember anything about hell, he recalled meeting deceased relatives over there and recollected saying the sinner's prayer with Dr. Rawlings. This event literally scared the 'hell' out of both of them. After his experience, Mckaig became a strong Christian. So did Dr. Rawlings. Mckaig repressed his hellish experience, but Dr. Rawlings remembered that incident well.

Embarrassment and Shame

The second reason may be people's feelings of shame and fear about their distressing NDEs. They are reluctant to share their hellish stories with others.

Their own hellish experience would not help them in building up their good image in the eyes of others. If they share their negative experiences, they also need to explain further why they experienced hell. It is a self-denigrating act. Atwater states, "Most often they indicated feeling too ashamed or fearful or angry to talk about it; furthermore, the possibility of another's judgment or criticism bothered them."[728]

The Mix-up between Heaven and the Intermediate World of Spirits

The third reason is due to NDErs' limited exposure to heaven, the world of spirits, and hell. According to mystics such as Emanuel Swedenborg and Sundar Singh, the dead usually enter the world of spirits first. This is the intermediary place between heaven and hell. From there they slowly choose their own place of comfort either in heaven or in hell. Some of them spend in the world of spirits a rather long time, up to one year.

Some spiritually mature people such as Peter and Paul enter heaven directly whereas some people of sin go to hell directly, too.

Most NDErs do not mention about the world of spirits because they did not stay in the spiritual realm long enough to learn about this particular world. They briefly visited the spiritual realm so that they are unable to tell us about the world of spirits unless their guides tell them. Many NDErs who have visited the world of spirits think that they visited heaven because of its fantastically beautiful, peaceful, and loving environment.

Here is an example of this:

Nancy Rynes' life got turned upside down when she was run over while riding her bike. In her book, *Awakenings from the Light,* Nancy tells us about the traumatic story of her crash and the deep spiritual awakening she had during her near-death experience.[729] She began as a skeptical, agnostic scientist, and wound up an awakened writer, artist, and speaker with a joyous view on life.[730]

While her time in the next life was brief in terms of earthly time, she felt as if weeks or months passed when she was there. She perceived an amazing amount in just a couple of human hours at most.[731] The first wonderful thing that she experienced was the beauty of heaven, both visually and feelingly.

When she arrived there, a landscape of gently pealing hills surrounded her. Flower-filled verdant meadows spread out on the hills around her and huge broadleaved trees in full leaf, trees larger and grander than any here on Earth, surrounded the pastures. A barest sense of a light mist, as if it were a moist summer morning, clung to the tops of the trees. The sky displayed a very light blue, similar to what you might see at the ocean's shore, with translucent clouds and a very bright but somewhat dispersed golden light.[732]

That was the optical. But there is more to Heaven than what she can see with her five senses. Beneath the outward visuals was a well of feeling operated by love, peace, and an abiding Presence that she calls "Spirit or God."[733]

Through the landscape around her, she experiences a profound sensation of peace, "rightness," goodness, and love. The beauty there was Beauty. Beyond the Beauty just pleasing to the eye, there was something profounder to it, more congruent, more welcoming, more influential. "Everything *felt* tied together by love and peace, and the beauty of the scenes around me were the product of this unconditional love."[734]

While the beauty of Heaven impressed her profoundly, the Presence of love completely captured her so that she yearned to stay there forever. She felt a deep sense of that love flow through all things around her: the air, the land below her feet, the trees, the clouds, and herself.

That love was curving around her, running through her, and eventually netting her by the heart. She felt held by such a loving Presence so prevailing, yet so gentle, that she cried again. She had never felt such unconditional love and acceptance in all of her years on the planet.[735]

It felt as if this abode were built from love and harmony on a colossus cosmic scale.

Later her Guide told her that love formed the foundations of Heaven. Although each spirit might perceive the "landscape" differently, all recognized and understood that the love formed the basis for everything in the place. That love and peace seemed to play as glimmering of light beneath the surface, blinking in and out of visual sight. It had colors, vivacity, and texture. It seemed to take the form of what she saw such trees and a meadow, but it was also simultaneously detached from the forms themselves.[736]

Her Guide welcomed and greeted her with an energy-embrace of pure love. Love sprang from her Guide and encircled her. Her Guide didn't touch her with her hands or hug her but simply sent Rynes waves of loving energy as a welcome.[737]

In time, as Rynes grew more relaxed in the presence of the Guide, she began telling Rynes more about this place. In fact, Rynes wasn't in Heaven per se, just in a place to prepare her for what was to come. She calls it "a slice of Heaven."[738] It is the "world of spirits" according to Christian mystics. If we could equate Heaven to a cathedral, she was in the vestibule as we come in the exterior doors, but before we enter the main doors into the nave (the main worship area).[739]

If this was the waiting area, heaven's equivalent of TV's green room, she cannot imagine how amazing the full experience of Heaven would be! A glow of hope sparked in her heart.[740]

It is amazing that Rynes' guide differentiated heaven from its green room. Many NDErs visited this area and considered their NDEs as a visit to heaven. Regarding the clarification of heaven and heaven's waiting area, Rynes' NDE is significant to our understanding of NDE.

The Seduction and Deception of Evil Spirits

The fourth reason may be caused by deceptive evil spirits so that they as angels of light mislead hell-bound NDErs into the delusion that they are in heaven. Satan masquerades as an angel of light (2 Cor 11:14).

Here is one of stories that explain the lure of an evil spirit as an angel: the story of Bob Taylor.

Tracy H. Goza mentioned Bob Taylor's story in her book, *I Heart Heaven*.[741] He was diagnosed with a condition known as Chronic Venous Insufficiency (CVI) in both legs. His condition was so critical that his chance of surviving the first night was one out of one hundred thousand.[742]

After dying on a beach and then at the hospital, Taylor felt himself walking down a slightly curved corridor toward his rest. He felt physically and emotionally exhausted.[743]

He then heard a voice just slightly behind him and to his left. He looked toward the source of the voice and realized that he was unable to see it. "The voice seemed to contain everything you ever wanted to hear from someone. It came across as compassionate, knowing, encouraging, soothing, intellectual, analytical, logical, and more."[744] Then he stopped walking when the voice first says "Congratulations," carrying with it the connotation of "Well done!"[745] Following "Congratulations" was "You made it through."[746] He was relieved that it was over. The voice continued saying, "You know, if you were to go back you will be a vegetable and blind. All you need to do is keep walking and you not only will have made it, but you will be able to rest."[747]

He responded, "But God isn't finished with me."[748] Then he knew the voice was not his friend, but was his enemy. The voice told him again, "All you have to do is keep walking and everything will be all right. Peace and joy await you."[749] In spite of such a good sound, he reaffirmed that God was not finished with him yet.

As soon as he said this, the corridor and the voice disappeared. The revelatory insight from the Lord: "The voice was the enemy (2 Cor 11:14,15); the enemy may know things that you are not yet aware of."[750] The enemy tried to trap Taylor to come to the next life without finishing his task on earth.

This was the case also of Howard Storm whom the demons pretended to lead to a good place, but instead led him to hell. There are deceptions from the enemy in the spiritual realm. This kind of NDEs lured by deceptive evil spirits is infrequent. Demonic spirits, however, crave to mislead people in NDEs to believe that all will go to heaven after this life.

Here is another case. Dr. Jeff Long reports on John L's NDE in which Satan disguised himself into a woman seduced him to destruction. This episode shows the deceiving power and desire of evil spirits that attempt to trap and destroy a dying person in the spiritual realm.

And then there's the hellish NDE of the severely alcoholic John L., who was stabbed in the chest. The knife was plunged deeply into his upper chest, puncturing his left lung and slicing through his pulmonary vein.

John's sister pulled him into her car and began driving to the hospital. Although John tried to stay calm, he soon began coughing up blood and "felt my arms and legs feeling very numb." "I'm not going to die," he said to his sister. "But you'd better hurry up!"

John inserted the middle finger of his right hand into the wound to stem the bleeding and felt his life slip away. "So this is it," he thought over his sister's screams. Then he passed out. Here's the rest of the story in John's own words:

I closed my eyes and prepared myself for whatever was coming. My faith had taught me that there would be bright light and peace, so I guess that's what I waited for. Instead, I focused on the little lights you see whenever you close your eyes real hard. They were moving around really fast, but then they began to slow down and disappear, until there was only one left.

. . . .

Many voices were coming from different sources, but the underlying message was to pay attention. They said, "Remember," and "You have to let them know," "You are being shown," and "Don't forget!" I began to think about my life and wondered whether it would be played back and I would be judged accordingly—as my auntie had always told me would happen. And as I was wondering this, I could see all of the things I did throughout my life just as they happened, but faster—the good, the bad, and the ugly. Everything I was proud of and every dirty little secret. I felt remorse, fear, and shame for my indiscretions and understood clearly that we all must account for everything that we do.

I saw thousands and thousands, if not millions, of people moving about aimlessly below me. Each person emitted strong feelings of foreboding, pain, and fear. "These are the lost," a voice told me. Then, as though it was reading my mind, "This is real." I began to feel afraid, but my fear paled compared with what I felt coming from all the people. "What is waiting for me?" I wondered.

I wanted something or someone to hold on to. I could hear childlike laughing and giggling, but it carried an air of seduction. A form came toward me that was neither male nor female, young nor old, living nor dead. I felt like it was mocking me each time it laughed.

This made me angry, but at the same time I was overcome with a strong desire for this being—which had become a seductive and beautiful female. She came closer and pulled me down with tremendous strength and kissed me hard on my neck and shoulder. Again she laughed, and I could feel pain return to my chest.[751]

I looked down and saw blood everywhere! The being was bathed in it! I felt something grab me and say, "Get out of here! What are you doing here?" I was surrounded by people tugging and pulling on me. "Why are you here?" they asked. The woman was suddenly gone, and in her place was a little girl who sat up and smiled at me. But I still felt like I had done something wrong and was in trouble. Was I evil? I frantically looked around for help, but there wasn't any. The people in this hellish place began pushing me away and yelling at me: "Remember to tell them!"

The next thing I heard was, "He's conscious!" and then endless questions, like "What's your name? What's your social security number?" I was alive![752]

John L's case discloses the demonic seduction and manipulation in the spiritual world to confuse and devastate a lost spirit. This kind of demons is able to trick confused and lost spirits believing that they are heaven-bound.

Bibliography

Alexander, Eben. Proof of Heaven: a Neurosurgeon's Journey Into the Afterlife. New: Simon & Schuster, 2012.

Atwater, P. M. H. The New Children and Near-Death Experiences. Reprint ed. New York: Bear & Company, 2003.

Augustine, City of God against the Pagans, in R. W. Dyson (ed. and trans.), City of God against the Pagans, Cambridge: Cambridge University Press, 1998.

Burpo, Todd, and Lynn Vincent. Heaven Is for Real: A Little Boy's Astounding Story of His Trip to Heaven and Back. Nashville: Thomas Nelson, 2010.

Butterick, George A. Interpreter's Dictionary of the Bible. Vol. 2. Nashville: Abingdon, 1969.

Carson, D. A. The Gospel According to John. Leicester, England: Eerdmans, 1991.

Chan, Francis, and Preston M. Sprinkle. Erasing Hell: What God Said About Eternity and the Things We Made Up. Colorado Springs, CO: David C Cook, 2011.

Crystal McVea and Alex Tresniowski, Waking up in Heaven: A True Story of Brokenness, Heaven, and Life Again. New York: Howard Books, 2013.

Darwin, Charles. The Autobiography of Charles Darwin, 1809-1882. Edited by Nora Barlow. New York: W. W. Norton & Company, 1993.

Davies, Paul. The Mind of God: the Scientific Basis for a Rational World. New York: Simon & Schuster, 1992.

D'Souza, Dinesh. Life After Death: the Evidence. Washinton, DC: Regnery, 2015.

Fenimore, Angie. Beyond the Darkness: My Near-Death Journey to the Edge of Hell. New York: Bantam Books, ©1995.

Fox, Matthew. A Way to God: Thomas Merton's Creation Spirituality Journey. Novato, CA: New World Library, 2016.Freedman, Freedman, David Noel, ed. The Anchor Yale Bible Dictionary. New Haven: Yale University Press, 2008.

Ginzberg, Louis. The Legends of the Jews - Vol. i from the Creation to Jacob. CreateSpace Independent Publishing Platform, 2012

Gowan, Donald E., ed. The Westminster Theological Wordbook of the Bible. Louisville: Westminster John Knox, 2003.

Graden, John J. Near-Death Experiences of Suicide Survivors. publication place: CreateSpace Independent Publishing Platform, 2016. In Kindle.

Happold, F Crossfield. Mysticism: A Study and an Anthology. revised ed. Pelican Books. Harmondsworth, United Kingdom: Penguin Books, 1970.

Herndon, William. Herndon's Lincoln. Springfield, IL: Acheron, 2012.

Hawking, Stephen, and Leonard Mlodinow. The Grand Design. New York: Bantam Books, ©2010.

Housholder, T. L. Near Death Experiences: Power, Love, and a Sound Mind: the Most Exciting and Revealing Near Death Experience:top:100:near Death Experiences:books:ny:times:best:sellers:list:2015(near... Death Experience), 2016.

Joan Hope, "Hope, J. (2016), Get Your Campus Ready for Generation Z," Dean and Provost17, no. 8 (April 2016): 1-7. Accessed August 12, 2016. doi:1710.1002/dap.30174.

Jung, C. G. Memories, Dreams, Reflections. Revised edition. New York: Vintage, 1989.

Kelly, Edward, Emily Williams Kelly, Adam Crabtree, Alan Gauld, Bruce Greyson, and Michael Grosso. Irreducible Mind: Toward a Psychology for the 21st Century. Lanham: Rowman & Littlefield, 2009.

Kittel, Gerhard, and Gerhard Friedrich. Theological Dictionary of the New Testament: An Illustrated Encyclopedia Identifying and Explaining All Proper Names and Significant Terms and Subjects in the Holy Scriptures, Including the Apocrypha, with Attention to Archaeologica. Vol. 2. Grand Rapids: Eerdmans, 1976.

Komp, Diane M. A Window to Heaven: When Children See Life in Death. Grand Rapids, Mich.: Zondervan Pub. House, ©1992.

Kramarik, Akiane, and Foreli Kramarik. Akiane: Her Life, Her Art, Her Poetry. Nashville, Tenn.: W Publishing Group, ©2006. Kindle.

Lawrence, Quigg. Blinded by the Light. Dallas: Thomas Nelson, 1996.

Lewis, C.S. The Problem of Pain. New York: HarperOne, 2015.

Lindley, J. H., Bryan, S., and Conley, B. "Near-Death Experiences in a Pacific Northwest American Population: The Evergreen Study." Journal of Near-Death Studies 1 (1981): 104-124.

Lommel, Pim van. Consciousness Beyond Life: the Science of the Near-Death Experience. Reprint edition. New York: HarperOne, 2011.

Long, Jeffrey, and Paul Perry. Evidence of the Afterlife: the Science of Near-Death Experiences. Reprint ed. New York: HarperOne, 2011.

Long, Jeffrey, and Paul Perry. God and the Afterlife: the Groundbreaking New Evidence for God and Near-Death Experience. New York: HarperOne, 2016.

McVea, Crystal, and Alex Tresniowski. Waking up in Heaven: A True Story of Brokenness, Heaven, and Life Again. New York: Howard, 2013.

Miller, Prana. "2015 Conference Call." International Association For Near Death Studies. December 11, 2015. Accessed October 29, 2016. http://iands.org/groups/group-affiliation-info/group-leader-conference-calls/2015-conf-call-calendar.html?highlight=WyJ1bmNvbmRpdG-lvbmFsIiwibG92ZSIsImxvdmVkIiwibG92aW5nIiwibG92ZXMiLCJsb3ZlbHkiLCJsb3ZlJ3MiLCJsb3ZlJyIsIidsb3ZlJyIsIi.

Miller, J. Steve. Near-Death Experiences as Evidence for the Existence of God and Heaven: a Brief Introduction in Plain Language. Acworth: Wisdom Creek, 2012.

Moltmann, Jürgen. The Coming of God: Christian Eschatology, translated by Margaret Kohl. Minneapolis: Augsburg, 2004.

Moody, Raymond A. Life After Life and Reflections On Life After Life (A Guidepost 2 in 1 Selection). St. Simons Island: Guideposts, 1975.

Moody, Raymond A. Life After Life: The Investigation of a Phenomenon-Survival of Bodily Death. San Francisco: HarperSan, 2001.

Moody, Raymond, and Paul Perry. Paranormal: My Life in Pursuit of the Afterlife. New York: HarperOne, 2013.

Moody, Raymond. Glimpses of Eternity. New York: Guideposts, 2010.

Moody, Raymond A. Reflections On Life After Life. New York: Bantam Books, 1978.

Morse, Melvin, and Paul Perry. Parting Visions: Uses and Meanings of Pre-Death, Psychic, and Spiritual Experiences. New York: Harpercollins, 1996.

Morse, Melvin, and Paul Perry. Transformed by the Light: The Powerful Effect of Near-Death Experiences On People's Lives. New York, NY: Villard Books, 1992.

Neal, Mary C. To Heaven and Back: A Doctor's Extraordinary Account of Her Death, Heaven, Angels, and Life Again. Colorado Springs, Colo.: Waterbrook Press, ©2012.

Parker, Rebecca Jane. Sádhu Sundar Singh, Called of God. London: Fleming H. Revell Company, 1920.

Perera, Mahendra, ed. Making Sense of Near-Death Experiences: a Handbook for Clinicians. London: Jessica Kingsley, 2012.

Plato. The Republic of Plato. 2nd ed. New York: Basic Books, 1991.

R. J. Bonenfant. "A child's encounter with the devil: An unusual near-death experience with both blissful and frightening elements." Journal of Near-Death Studies 20(2) (2001): 87-100.

Rauschenbusch, Walter. A Theology for the Social Gospel. Louisville: Westminster John Knox, 1997.

Rawlings, Maurice. Beyond Death's Door. New York: Bantam, 1985.

Ring, Kenneth, Sharon Cooper, and Charles T. Tart. Mindsight: Near-Death and Out-of-body Experiences in the Blind. Palo Alto: Institute of Transpersonal Psychology, 1999.

Ring, Kenneth. Heading Toward Omega. Amazon Digital Services LLC, 2012.

Ring, Kenneth. Heading Toward Omega: in Search of the Meaning of the Near-Death Experience. New York: Harper Perennial, 1985.

Ritchie, George G. My Life After Dying: Becoming Alive to Universal Love. Norfolk, VA: Hampton Roads, 1991.

Ritchie, George G. Return from Tomorrow. Grand Rapids: Chosen Books, 2007. Kindle edition.

Rommer, Barbara R. Blessing in Disguise: Another Side of the Near-Death Experience. St. Paul, MN: Llewellyn, 2000.

Russell, Bertrand. Why i Am Not a Christian and Other Essays On Religion and Related Subjects. New York: Touchstone, 1967.

Rynes, Nancy. Awakenings from the Light: 12 Life Lessons from a Near Death Experience. North Charleston, South Carolina: CreateSpace Independent Publishing Platform, 2015. Kindle.

Sabom, Michael B. Recollections of Death: a Medical Investigation. New York: Harpercollins, 1982.

Sabom, Michael. Light and Death: One Doctor's Fascinating Account of Near-Death Experiences. Grand Rapids: Zondervan, 1998.

Sartori, Penny. Wisdom of Near Death Experiences: How Understanding Nde's Can Help Us to Live More Fully. London: Watkins, 2014.

Schroeder-Lein, Glenna R. Lincoln and Medicine. Concise Lincoln Library. Carbondale: Southern Illinois University Press, 2012. Accessed July 28, 2016. http://www.myilibrary.com?id=391105&ref=toc.

Seemiller, Corey, and Meghan Grace. Generation z Goes to College. San Francisco: Jossey-Bass, 2016.

Shahar, Shulamith. Growing Old in the Middle Ages: 'winter Clothes Us in Shadow and Pain'. London: Routledge, 1997. Accessed August 14, 2016. http://www.contentreserve.com/titleinfo. asp?id=%7b72114904-41f0-43fd-9a82-cb3063a9a8d9%7d&format=50.

Singh, Sundar. The Christian Witness of Sadhu Sundar Singh: a Collection of His Writings. Edited by T. Dayanandan Francis. Chennai, India: Christian Literature Society, 1989.

Streeter, Burnett Hillman, and A. J. Appasamy. The Sadhu: A Study in Mysticism and Practical Religion. London: MacMillan, 1921.

Streeter, Burnett Hillman, and A. J. Appasamy. The Message of Sadhu Sundar Singh: A Study in Mysticism On Practical Religion. New York: MacMillan, 1921.

Strong, James. The Exhaustive Concordance of the Bible: Showing Every Word of the Text of the Common English Version of the Canonical Books, and Every Occurrence of Each Word in Regular Order, Together with a Key-Word Comparison of Selected Word. New York: Abingdon, 1981.

Strong, James. The New Strong's Expanded Exhaustive Concordance of the Bible. Expanded ed. Peabody, England: Thomas Nelson, 2010.

Swedenborg, Emanuel. A Brief Exposition of the Doctrine of the New Church. Standard. Edited by William Woofenden. West Chester, PA: SWedenborg Foundation, 2009. www.swedenborg.com/wpcontent/uploads/2013/03/swedenborg_foundation_brief_exposition.pdf.

Swedenborg, Emanuel. A Swedenborg Sampler: Selections from Heaven and Hell, Divine Love and Wisdom, Divine Providence, True Christianity, and Secrets of Heaven.

West Chester, PA: Swedenborg Foundation Publishers, 2011.

Swedenborg, Emanuel. Secrets of Heaven: Volume 2.

Portable new century ed. Translated by Lisa Hyatt Cooper. West Chester, Pa.: Swedenborg Foundation,2012.

Swedenborg, Emanuel. Arcana Coelestia [Secrets of Heaven]. Standard. Edited by John Faulkner Potts. Translated by John Clowes. Vol. 7. West Chester: SWEDENBORG FOUNDATION, 2009. Accessed February 25, 2017. http://www.swedenborg.com/wpcontent/uploads/2013/03/swedeborg_foundation_arcana_coelestia_07.pdf.

Swedenborg, Emanuel, and Samuel M. Warren. A Compendium of the Theological Writings of Emanuel Swedenborg. New York: Swedenborg Foundation, 1974.

Swedenborg, Emanuel. Conjugial Love: Delights of Wisdom Relating to Conjugial Love Followed by Pleasures of Insanity Relating to Licentious Love. Edited by Louis H. Tafel. Translated by Samuel Warren. West Chester, PA: Swendenborg Foundation, 2009.

Swedenborg, Emanuel. Divine Love and Wisdom. portable new century ed. Translated by George F. Dole. New Century Edition Ser. West Chester, Pa.: Swedenborg Foundation, 2010.

Swedenborg, Emanuel. Divine Providence. Standard. Translated by William Wunsch. West Chester, PA: Swedenborg Foundation, 2009.

Swedenborg, Emanuel. Heaven and Hell. New York: Swedenborg Foundation, 1984.

Swedenborg, Emanuel. Secrets of Heaven: Volume 2. portable new century ed. Translated by Lisa Hyatt Cooper. West Chester, Pa.: Swedenborg Foundation, 2012. Accessed February 25, 2017. http://site.ebrary.com/id/10528259.

Swedenborg, Emanuel. The Essential Swedenborg: Basic Religious Teachings of Emanuel Swedenborg. Edited by Sigfried T. Synnestvedt. New York: Swedenborg Foundation, 1977.

Swedenborg, Emanuel. Spiritual Diary. AnnieRoseBooks, 2016.

Tafel, Rudolf Leonhard. Documents concerning the life and character of EmanuelSwedenborg. collected, translated, and annotated. London : Swedenborg Society, 1877.

Talbott, Thomas. The Inescapable Love of God. Salem: Universal, 1999.

C. S. Lewis, The Great Divorce. San Francisco: HarperSanFrancisco, 2001.

Tillich, Paul. Systematic Theology, Vol. 1. Chicago: University Of Chicago Press, 1973.

Tracy H. Goza. I Heart Heaven: a Psychotherapist's Biblical Validation for Near-Death Experiences. Grand Rapids: Credo House Publishers, 2015.

Underhill, Evelyn. Practical Mysticism. CreateSpace Independent Publishing Platform, 2013. Kindle.

Weldon, John, and John Ankerberg. The Facts On Life After Death. eBook. ATRI Publishing, 2009.

Wordsworth, R. D, comp. "Abe" Lincoln's anecdotes and stories: A collection of the best stories told by Lincoln, which made him famous as America's best story teller. Boston: Mutual Book, 1908.

Endnotes

1. Ian Sample, "Stephen Hawking: Heaven Is Myth," *The Guardian*, May 15, 2011, accessed November 1, 2013, https://www.theguardian.com/science/2011/may/15/stephen-hawking-interview-there-is-no-heaven.

2. "Stephen Hawking: Life After Death," Channel 4 News, September 22, 2013, accessed November 1, 2013, http://blogs.channel4.com/gurublog/stephen-hawking-life-death/3946.

3. Stephen Hawking and Leonard Mlodinow, *The Grand Design* (New York: Bantam Books, ©2010), 9.

4. Yous Pisoth, "Curiosity.1of 9.did.god.create.the.universe" (video), 01/02/2012, accessed June 10, 2017, http://www.dailymotion.com/video/xndvdy_discovery-ch-curiosity-1of9-did-god-create-the-universe-www-pisothshow-com_shortfilms.

5. Ibid.

6. Rebecca Savastio, "Richard Dawkins 'wonders' What Happens After We Die," Las Vegas Guardian Express, September 25, 2013, accessed November 7, 2013, http://guardianlv.com/2013/09/richard-dawkins-wonders-what-happens-after-we-die/.

7. Rebecca Savastio, "Richard Dawkins 'wonders' What Happens After We Die," Las Vegas Guardian Express, September 25, 2013, accessed November 7, 2013, http://guardianlv.com/2013/09/richard-dawkins-wonders-what-happens-after-we-die/.

8. Ibid.

9. Susan Blackmore, "Who am I?" December 14, 2015, accessed April 9, 2016, http://www.susanblackmore.co.uk/Articles/whoami.htm.

10. Susan J. Blackmore, *Dying to Live*, Reprint ed. (Buffalo: Prometheus, 1993).

11. Ibid., 113-135, 262.

12. Kevin Nelson, *The Spiritual Doorway in the Brain: A Neurologist's Search for the God Experience* (New York: Plume, 2012),125.

13. Nelson, *Spiritual Doorway, 125*.

14. Moody, *Life After Life,* 54.

15. *Oxford English Dictionary*, s.v. "Science," accessed June 29, 2016, http://www.oed.com.sinclair.ohionet.org/view/Entry/172672?redirectedFrom=science#eid.

16. *Cambridge Dictionaries Online*, s.v. "Science," accessed June 29, 2016, http://dictionary.cambridge.org/us/dictionary/english/science.

17. Experiences of NDE that are shared by NDErs' family members or friends.

18. Eben Alexander, professor of Harvard Medical School, died and came back to life. His guide was a young woman during his trip to heaven. Later he found out that he was adopted and that his younger sister died five years before his NDE. The guide was his sister.

19. Pam Reynolds' giant basilar artery aneurysm led her to an extraordinary odyssey which was fully recorded: the blood drained from her head, her heartbeat and breathing stopped, her brain waves flattened, and her body temperature dropped below 60 F. In that condition, she reported all the procedures of the surgery.

20. Raymond Moody and Paul Perry, *Paranormal: My Life in Pursuit of the Afterlife* (New York: HarperOne, 2013), 33.

21. Ibid.

22. Ibid.

23. Raymond Moody, *Life After Life: The Investigation of a Phenomenon-Survival of Bodily Death* (San Francisco: HarperSanFrancisco, 2001), xxvii.

24. Moody, *Paranormal*, 33

25. Raymond Moody, *Glimpses of Eternity*, Book ed. (New York, NY: Guideposts, 2010), 180.

26. Ibid.,183.

27. Ibid., 141.

28. Ibid., 141-172.

29. Ibid., 172.

30. Ibid., 265-274.

31. Ibid., 277.

32. Ibid., 278.

33. Ibid., 13-14; 279.

34. Melvin Morse and Paul Perry, *Parting Visions: Uses and Meanings of Pre-Death, Psychic, and Spiritual Experiences* (New York: HarperCollins, 1996), 45-46.

35. Ibid.

36. Moody, *Glimpses of Eternity*, 206.

37. Ibid., 210.

38. Ibid.

39. Ibid.

40. Moody, *Glimpses of Eternity*, 963.

41. Carl Jung, *Memories, Dreams, Reflections*, rev. ed. (New York: Vintage, 1989), 349-353.

42. Moody, *Glimpses of Eternity*, 1006.

43. Ibid., 988-989.

44. Ibid., 990.

45. Jung, *Memories, Dreams, Reflections*, 364.

46. Moody, *Glimpses of Eternity*, 999.

47. Carl Jung, "On Life After Death," *The Nautis Project* (Publication date): 7, accessed May 30, 2016, http://www.hermetics.org/pdf/C.G._Jung_-_On_Life_After_Death.pdf.

48. Ibid.

49. Ibid.

50. Kenneth Ring, PhD, is Professor Emeritus of Psychology at the University of Connecticut, where Sharon Cooper, MA, was Research Assistant at the time of this study.

51. Kenneth Ring and Sharon Cooper, "Near-Death and Out-of-Body Experiences in the Blind: A Study of Apparent Eyeless Vision," Journal of Near-Death Studies 16 (1997): 101–147. Results of this study were later presented in further detail: Kenneth Ring, Sharon Cooper, and Charles T. Tart, *Mindsight: Near-Death and Out-of-body Experiences in the Blind* (Palo Alto: Institute of Transpersonal Psychology, 1999).

52. Ibid., 101.

53. Rollye James, "Vicki Noratuk On Coast-To-Coast," June 27, 2013, accessed September 24, 2015, http://ndestories.org/vicki-noratuk/.

54. Dr. Cooper was a research assistant to Dr. Ring at that time.

55. Ring et al., *Mindset*, 15; Kevin Williams, "People Born Blind Can See During an NDE," accessed December 12, 2012, http://near-death.com/experiences/evidence03.html.

56. Ibid., 30.

57. Ibid., 16.

58. Ibid.

59. Rollye James, "Vicki Noratuk."

60. Ibid., 101.

61. Jeffrey Long and Paul Perry, *Evidence of the Afterlife: the Science of Near-Death Experiences*, Reprint ed. (New York: HarperOne, 2011), 85-92.

62. Michael B. Sabom, *Recollections of Death: a Medical Investigation* (New York: HarperCollins, 1982), 2.

63. Ibid., 3.

64. J. Steve Miller, *Near-Death Experiences as Evidence for the Existence of God and Heaven: a Brief Introduction in Plain Language* (Acworth: Wisdom Creek Press, 2012), 2207.

65. Sabom, *Recollections of Death*, 2.

66. Ibid., 186.

67. Ibid.

68. Michael Sabom, *Light and Death: One Doctor's Fascinating Account of Near-Death Experiences* (Grand Rapids: Zondervan, 1998).

69. Ibid., 2602-06.

70. Ibid., 471-479.

71. Ibid., 513.

72. Ibid., 520.

73. Ibid., 526.

74. Ibid., 526.

75. Ibid., 534.

76. Ibid.

77. Ibid., 539.

78. Ibid., 552.

79. Ibid., 559.

80. Ibid., 561.

81. Ibid., 563.

82. Ibid., 563-570.

83. Ibid., 574-576.

84. Ibid., 576-582.

85. Ibid., 587.

86. Ibid., 589.

87. Ibid., 593.

88. Ibid.

89. Ibid., 601-604.

90. Ibid., 620.

91. Ibid., 653-659.

92. Ibid., 3108-3112.

93. Pim van Lommel, *Consciousness Beyond Life: the Science of the Near-Death Experience*, Reprint ed. (New York: HarperOne, 2011).

94. Ibid., 11.

95. Ibid.

96. Ibid.

97. Ibid., 23.

98. Pim van Lommel, "Continuity of Consciousness," in the Research of International Association for Near Death Studies, accessed September 25, 2015, https://www.iands.org/research/important-research-articles/43-dr-pim-van-lommel-md-continuity-of-consciousness.html?showall=1.

99. Ibid.

100. Ibid.

101. Ibid.

102. Ibid.

103. Peter Fenwick, Science and Spirituality, in the Research of International Association for Near Death Studies, accessed April 22, 2016, http://iands.org/research/nde-research/important-research-articles/42-dr-peter-fenwick-md-science-and-spirituality.html?showall=1.

104. Mary Neal, "About Dr. Mary Neal," Mary Neal, MD, accessed January 13, 2017, http://drmaryneal.com/about-dr-mary-neal.html.

105. Mary Neal, "A Sneak Peek of Heaven," *Guideposts*, accessed January 14, 2017, https://www.guideposts.org/inspiration/life-after-death/a-sneak-peek-of-heaven.

106. Ibid.

107. Ibid.

108. Mary C. Neal, *To Heaven and Back: A Doctor's Extraordinary Account of Her Death, Heaven, Angels, and Life Again* (Colorado Springs, Colo.: Waterbrook Press, ©2012), 639, Kindle.

109. Neal, "A Sneak Peek of Heaven."

110. Ibid.

111. "Mary Neal Says She Knew About Her Son's Death Years Before It Happened," *Huffington Post*, 02/09/2015, accessed January 16, 2017, http://www.huffingtonpost.com/2015/02/09/dr-mary-neal-in-deep-shift_n_6633758.html.

112. Neal, "A Sneak Peek of Heaven."

113. Ibid.

114. Ibid.

115. Ibid.

116. "What Dr. Mary Neal Saw When She Died Read More," Oprah.com, accessed January 16, 2017, http://www.oprah.com/own-indeepshift/what-dr-mary-neal-saw-when-she-died-video#ixzz4VxrYGy6E.

117. Neal, *To Heaven and Back*, 816.

118. Ibid., 819.

119. Ibid., 826-829.

120. Ibid., 832.

121. Ibid., 839.

122. "Mary Neal Says She Knew About Her Son's Death Years Before It Happened," *Huffington Post*.

123. Neal, *To Heaven and Back*, 1417.

124. Ibid., 1420.

125. Ibid.

126. Ibid., 643.

127. "Mary Neal Says She Knew About Her Son's Death Years Before It Happened," *Huffington Post*.

128. Neal, *To Heaven and Back*, 1705.

129. Eben Alexander III, "My Experience in Coma," *AANS Neurosurgeon* 21, no. 2 (2012): 1, accessed April 21, 2016, http://v1archives.aansneurosurgeon.org/210212/6/1611.

130. Leslie Kaufman, "Readers Join Doctor's Journey to the Afterworld's Gates," *New York Times*, NOV. 25, 2012, 1, accessed April 21, 2016, http://www.nytimes.com/2012/11/26/books/dr-eben-alexanders-tells-of-near-death-in-proof-of-heaven.html?pagewanted=all&_r=1.

131. Eben Alexander, *Proof of Heaven: a Neurosurgeon's Journey Into the Afterlife* (New York: Simon & Schuster, 2012), 19.

132. Ibid., 20.

133. Ibid., 107.

134. Alexander, *Proof of Heaven*, 40.

135. Ibid., 41. In heaven, these three parts are true.

136. Ibid., 46.

137. Kaufman, "Readers Join Doctor's Journey."

138. Eben Alexandar, "Proof of Heaven: A Doctor's Experience with the Afterlife," *Newsweek*, October 8, 2012, 1, accessed April 22, 2016, http://www.newsweek.com/proof-heaven-doctors-experience-afterlife-65327.

139. Ibid.

140. Edward Kelly et al., *Irreducible Mind: Toward a Psychology for the 21st Century* (Lanham:Rowman & Littlefield Publishers, 2009), quoted in Eben Alexander III (2012), "My Experience in Coma". AANS Neurosurgeon 21 (2), accessed August 23, 2014, http://www.ebenalexander.com/my-experience-in-coma/.

141. Eben Alexandar, "Proof of Heaven: A Doctor's Experience with the Afterlife," *Newsweek*, October 8, 2012, accessed August 23, 2014, http://www.newsweek.com/proof-heaven-doctors-experience-afterlife-65327.

142. Alexander, *Proof of Heaven*, 52-53.

143. Ibid., 61-67.

144. Ibid., 165-68.

145. Ibid. 168-69.

146. Ibid., 147.

147. Kelly, *Irreducible Mind*, quoted in Alexander, "My Experience in Coma."

148. Eben Alexander, *The Map of Heaven: How Science, Religion, and Ordinary People Are Proving the Afterlife* (New York: Simon & Schuster, 2014), 151.

149. Ibid., 60.

150. Ibid.,109.

151. Jen Mulson, "Near Death Experiences at Heart of Jeff Olsen's Memoir, Lecture in Colorado Springs," *Gazette*, August 25, 2016, accessed September 13, 2016, http://gazette.com/near-death-experiences-at-heart-of-jeff-olsens-memoir-lecture-in-colorado-springs/article/1558025.

152. Jeff Olsen, *I Knew Their Hearts* (Springville, Utah: Plain Slight Pub., 2012), 413, Kindle.

153. Ibid., 420.

154. Ibid., 429.

155. Ibid.

156. Ibid., 433.

157. Ibid., 437.

158. Ibid., 441.

159. Ibid., 449.

160. Ibid.

161. Mulson, "Near Death Experiences at Heart of Jeff Olsen's Memoir, Lecture in Colorado Springs."

162. Ibid.

163. Jeff Olsen, interviewed by Erica Mckenzie, February 18, 2915.

164. Mulson, "Near Death Experiences at Heart of Jeff Olsen's Memoir, Lecture in Colorado Springs."

165. Ibid.

166. Nancy Rynes, *Awakenings from the Light: 12 Life Lessons from a Near Death Experience* (North Charleston, South Carolina: CreateSpace Independent Publishing Platform, 2015). Kindle.

167. Amy Collette, "Author Nancy Rynes," Unleash Your Inner Author!, July 15, 2015, accessed July 25, 2017, http://www.amycollette.com/podcast/pp05-author-nancy-rynes.

168. Nancy Rynes, "How i Saw and Experienced Heaven," The Spirit Way, March 10, 2014, accessed July 25, 2017, http://thespiritway.blogspot.com/2014/03/how-i-saw-and-experienced-heaven.html.

169. Ibid.

170. Ibid.

171. Ibid.

172. Ibid.

173. Ibid.

174. Nancy Rynes, *Awakenings from the Light*, 526.

175. Ibid., 560.

176. Ibid.

177. Ibid., 564.

178. *The Autobiography of Charles Darwin, 1809-1882*, ed. Nora Barlow (New York: W. W. Norton & Company, 1993), 87.

179. Bertrand Russell, *Why I Am Not a Christian and Other Essays On Religion and Related Subjects* (New York: Touchstone, 1967), 17-18.

180. Augustine, *The City of God* [Book XXI], Ch. 9, Fathers of the Church (New Advent), accessed April 16, 2017, http://www.newadvent.org/fathers/120121.htm.

181. Ibid.

182. Ibid.

183. Rob Bell, *Love Wins: A Book About Heaven, Hell, and the Fate of Every Person Who Ever Lived* (New York, NY: HarperOne, 2011, ©2011), 68.

184. Ibid., 69-70.

185. Ibid., 70.

186. Ibid., viii.

187. Francis Chan and Preston M. Sprinkle, *Erasing Hell: What God Said About Eternity and the Things We Made Up* (Colorado Springs, CO: David C Cook, 2011), 149.

188. James Strong, *The Exhaustive Concordance of the Bible: Showing Every Word of the Text of the Common English Version of the Canonical Books, and Every Occurrence of Each Word in Regular Order, Together with a Key-Word Comparison of Selected Word* (New York: Abingdon, 1981), 33.

189. Emanuel Swedenborg, *Heaven and Hell* (New York: Swedenborg Foundation, 1984), 468-469.

190. Ibid., 453-454.

191. Ibid., 452-453.

192. Ibid., 456.

193. Sundar Singh, *The Christian Witness of Sadhu Sundar Singh: a Collection of His Writings*, ed. T. Dayanandan Francis (Chennai, India: Christian Literature Society, 1989), 266.

194. Ibid.

195. Ibid., 267.

196. Ibid.

197. Ibid.

198. I learned these analogies from Sundar Singh, but cannot find them in his books.

199. Singh, *The Christian Witness,* 254-255.

200. *Jewish Encyclopedia*, s.v. "Sheol," accessed July 12, 2017, http://www.jewishencyclopedia.com/articles/13563-sheol.

201. Kittel, *Theological Dictionary of the New Testament*, s.v. "ἄδης (Hades)," 149.

202. Swedenborg, *Heaven and Hell,* 429.

203. Ibid., 453-54.

204. Ibid.

205. Ibid., 455-456.

206. C. S. Lewis, *The Problem of Pain* (London : Centenary Press, 1940), 72, accessed December, 2, 2015, http://www.pc-freak.net/files/ProblemOfPain.pdf.

207. *The Great Divorce by C. S. Lewis* (San Francisco: HarperSanFrancisco, 2001).

208. Ibid., 69.

209. IANDS, "Distressing Near Death Experiences," accessed on September 4, 2014, http://iands.org/distressing-near-death-experiences.html.

210. Howard Storm, *Descent into Death: A Second Chance at Life* (New York: Doubleday, 2005), 9.

211. Ibid., 11.

212. Ibid., 13.

213. Ibid., 15.

214. Ibid., 16.

215. Ibid., 17.

216. Ibid., 18.

217. Ibid., 19.

218. Ibid.

219. Ibid., 20.

220. Ibid.

221. Ibid.

222. Ibid., 24.

223. Ibid., 25.

224. Ibid.

225. Ibid., 26.

226. Mark Ellis, "Atheist professor's near-death experience in hell left him changed," March 10, 2012, accessed on March 30, 2015, http://blog.godreports.com/2012/03/atheist-professors-near-death-experience-in-hell-left-him-changed/.

227. Ibid.

228. Ibid.

229. Howard Storm, *Descent into Death*, 30.

230. Mark Ellis, "Atheist professor's near-death."

231. Ibid.

232. Ibid.

233. Ibid.

234. Howard Storm, accessed on March 31, 2015, "Saved from Hell: Howard Storm's near-death experience," http://www.neardeathsite.com/storm.php.

235. Ibid.
236. Kevin Williams, "Reverend Howard Storm's Near-Death Experience," accessed April 1, 2015, http://www.near-death.com/storm.html.
237. Ibid.
238. Ibid.
239. Ibid.
240. Ibid.
241. Ibid.
242. Ibid.
243. Ibid.
244. Ibid.
245. Ibid.
246. Ibid.
247. Ibid.
248. Ibid.
249. Ibid.
250. Ibid.
251. George Rodonaia, "George Rodonaia—a Scientist's Afterlife," NDE Accounts, September 16, 2013, accessed June 20, 2016, http://ndeaccounts.com/near-death-experiences-stories/george-rodonaia-a-scientists-afterlife/.
252. Phillip L. Berman, *The Journey Home: What Near-Death Experiences and Mysticism Teach Us About the Gift of Life* (New York: Pocket Books, 1998, 1996), 33–35.
253. Ibid., 33.
254. Maurice Rawlins, "Dr. George Rodonaia," Divine Revelations, accessed June 20, 2016, http://www.divinerevelations.info/documents/rawlings/dr_rawlings_near_death_experiences.htm.
255. Ibid.
256. Ibid.
257. Berman, *The Journey Home*, 34.
258. Ibid., 33–34.
259. Ibid.

260. Ibid.

261. Ibid., 35.

262. Ibid.

263. Ibid.

264. Kevin Williams, "Some People Were Dead for Several Days," Near Death Experiences and the Afterlife, accessed June 20, 2016, http://www.near-death.com/science/evidence/some-people-were-dead-for-several-days.html.

265. Berman, *The Journey Home,* 35–36.

266. Ibid., 36.

267. Williams, "Some People."

268. Berman, *The Journey Home,* 36.

269. Ibid., 37.

270. Nancy Botsford, *A Day in Hell: Death to Life to Hope* (Mustang, OK: Tate Publishing & Enterprises, LLC, 2010), 35.

271. Ibid., 36.

272. Mark Ellis, "Businessman's near-death experience in hell transformed his life," accessed April 1, 2015, http://blog.godreports.com/2013/08/businessmans-near-death-experience-in-hell-transformed-his-life/.

273. Ibid.

274. Ibid.

275. Ibid.

276. Ibid.

277. Ibid.

278. Ibid.

279. Swedenborg, *Heaven and Hell.*

280. John Bunyan, *Visions of Heaven and Hell: Where Will You Spend Eternity?* (Quest Publications, 2013), 36. See, https://www.near-death.com/archives/false/john-bunyan.html.

281. Ibid., 49.

282. Ibid., 51.

283. Ibid., 169.

284. Ibid., 371.

285. Ibid., 385.

286. Ibid., 396.
287. Ibid., 609.
288. Ibid., 612.
289. Ibid., 613.
290. Ibid., 617.
291. Ibid.
292. Ibid., 620.
293. Ibid., 624.
294. Ibid., 627.
295. Ibid., 629.
296. Ibid., 631–643.
297. Ibid., 644.
298. Ibid., 647.
299. Ibid., 648–651.
300. Ibid., 652–654.
301. Ibid., 654–658.
302. Ibid., 659.
303. Thomas Hobbes, *Leviathan*, (London: Andrew Crooks, 1651), 246.
304. "Dying Children Lead Atheist Doc to the Lord," was beneath the headline of "DATELINE—MAY 1997, Boca Raton, Florida," cited in Atwater, *The New Children*, 190.
305. Diane Komp, *A Window to Heaven: When Children See Life in Death*. (Grand Rapids, Mich.: Zondervan Pub. House,1992).
306. Ibid.
307. P. M. H. Atwater, *The New Children and Near-Death Experiences*, Reprint ed. (New York: Bear & Company, 2003), 1549, Kindle.
308. Ibid., 328.
309. Ibid., 340.
310. Melvin Morse and Paul Perry, *Transformed by the Light: The Powerful Effect of Near-Death Experiences On People's Lives* (New York: Villard Books, 1992), 342, Kindle.
311. Ibid., 344.
312. Atwater, *The New Children, 2867*.

313. Ibid.

314. Lori Rose Centi, "Interview: Akiane Speaks of Heaven and Paintings," *Washington Times*, December 31, 2014, accessed August 4, 2016, http://www.washingtontimes.com/news/2014/dec/31/interview-akiane-speaks-heaven-and-paintings/#ixzz3gkAO69zb.

315. Todd Burpo and Lynn Vincent, *Heaven Is for Real: A Little Boy's Astounding Story of His Trip to Heaven and Back* (Nashville: Thomas Nelson, 2010), 142.

316. Ibid., 151.

317. Ibid., 154.

318. "Akiane Kramarik (Child Art Prodigy): Her Story Is Believable, but i Have Concerns…," Singapore Christian, July 4, 2015, accessed October 6, 2016, https://singaporechristian.com/2015/04/07/akiane-kramarik-child-art-prodigy-her-story-is-believable-but-my-only-concern-is/.

319. "Learn the Akiane Kramarik Story: The Child Prodigy and Painter of "Prince of Peace"," Art & Soulworks, 2016, accessed October 6, 2016, https://art-soulworks.com/pages/about-akiane-kramarik.

320. Mark Ellis, "For Child Art Prodigy Akiane, Jesus Is for Real," *God Reports*, January 4, 2012, 1, accessed October 6, 2016, http://blog.godreports.com/2012/01/for-child-art-prodigy-akiane-jesus-is-for-real/.

321. "Akiane Kramarik (Child Art Prodigy)."

322. Ibid.

323. Ibid.

324. Lori Centi, "Interview: Akiane Speaks of Heaven and Paintings," *Washington Times*, December 31, 2014, accessed October 8, 2016, http://www.washingtontimes.com/news/2014/dec/31/interview-akiane-speaks-heaven-and-paintings/.

325. Ibid.

326. Akiane Kramarik and Foreli Kramarik, *Akiane: Her Life, Her Art, Her Poetry* (Nashville, Tenn.: W Publishing Group, ©2006), 599, Kindle.

327. Ibid.

328. Ibid., 605.

329. Ibid., 753.

330. Ibid., 760.

331. Ibid., 764.

332. Ibid.

333. Ibid., 775.

334. Ibid.

335. Ellis, "For Child Art Prodigy Akiane, Jesus Is for Real."

336. Ibid.

337. Ibid.

338. Ibid.

339. Ibid.

340. Ibid., 2615.

341. R. D Wordsworth, comp., *"Abe" Lincoln's anecdotes and stories: A collection of the best stories told by Lincoln, which made him famous as America's best story teller* (Boston: Mutual Book, 1908), 79.

342. Atwater, *The New Children*, 2619.

343. William Herndon, *Herndon's Lincoln* (Springfield, IL: Acheron, 2012), 51.

344. Ibid.

345. Glenna R. Schroeder-Lein, *Lincoln and Medicine*, Concise Lincoln Library (Carbondale: Southern Illinois University Press, 2012), 1, accessed July 28, 2016, http://www.myilibrary.com?id=391105&ref=toc.

346. Atwater, *The New Children*, 2615.

347. Ibid., 2634.

348. Ibid.

349. Ibid.

350. J. Timothy Green, "Did a Near Death Experience Inspire Einstein's Theory of Relativity?" accessed August 4, 2016, http://www.world-of-lucid-dreaming.com/was-einstein-influenced-by-a-near-death-experience.html.

351. Ibid., 2634.

352. J. Timothy Green, "Did a Near Death Experience?"

353. Atwater, *The New Children*, 2649.

354. Ibid.

355. Ibid., 3846-3866.

356. Ibid.

357. http://www.cdc.gov/violenceprevention/pdf/suicide_factsheet-a.pdf. New statistics show one-in-five Canadian teens has seriously thought about taking their own life for last twelve months and girls are twice as likely to have suicidal thoughts as boys. http://www.news1130.com/2016/09/08/alarming-statistics-about-teens-whove-considered-sui.

Some statistics just jump off the page. For example, on average in Ohio, one person dies by suicide every six hours. While the state's suicide rate dropped last year to its lowest point in more than a decade, it still accounted for 10.8 deaths per 100,000 people. Nationwide, more than 41,000 people died by suicide – roughly one death every 13.7 minutes, according to the Centers for Disease Control and Prevention. http://community-common.com/news/2368/run-brings-awareness-to-suicide-problem.

358. kevin Williams, "The Three Classifications of Suicide Near-Death Experiences," Near Death Experiences and the Afterlife, accessed July 15, 2017, http://www.near-death.com/experiences/suicide01.html.

359. George G. Ritchie, *My Life After Dying: Becoming Alive to Universal Love* (Norfolk, Va.: Hampton Roads Pub. Co., 1991), 24.

360. Ibid.

361. George Ritchie, *Return from Tomorrow* (Grand Rapids: Chosen Books, 2007), 728, Kindle.

362. http://www.cdc.gov/violenceprevention/pdf/suicide-datasheet-a.PDF.

363. Ritchie, *Return from Tomorrow,* 692-703.

364. Ibid., 705-713.

365. Raymond A. Moody, *Reflections On Life After Life* (New York: Bantam Books, 1978), 45.

366. Ibid., 45-46.

367. Ibid., 46.

368. Angie Fenimore, *Beyond the Darkness: My Near-Death Journey to the Edge of Hell* (New York: Bantam Books, 1995), 25-37.

369. Ibid., 27.

370. Ibid., 31-37.

371. Ibid., 55-68.

372. Ibid., 1-2.

373. Ibid., 83-89.

374. Ibid., 89-90.

375. Ibid., 92.

376. Ibid.

377. Ibid.

378. Ibid., 94.

379. Ibid., 95.

380. Ibid., 96.

381. Ibid., 96-97.

382. Ibid., 99.

383. Ibid.

384. Ibid., 99-101.

385. Ibid., 102.

386. Ibid., 102-105.

387. Ibid., 112.

388. Ibid., 112-115.

389. Ibid., 121-122.

390. Ibid.

391. Peter R, "Peter r Nde 159," Near Death Experience Research Foundation, accessed June 26, 2017, http://www.nderf.org/Experiences/1peter_r_nde.html.

392. John J. Graden, *Near-Death Experiences of Suicide Survivors* (publication place: CreateSpace Independent Publishing Platform, 2016), 485, Kindle.

393. Ibid., 491.

394. Ibid., 493.

395. Ibid.

396. Ibid.

397. Dr. Gary Kohls, "Brain Altering Drugs," Global Research: Centre for Research on Globalization, August 24, 2016, accessed September 8, 2016, http://www.globalresearch.ca/brain-altering-drugs-the-drug-induced-suicide-of-robin-williams-two-years-later/5542304.

Mahita Gajanan, "Heroin Laced with Elephant Tranquilizer Linked to 8 Overdose Deaths in Ohio," *Time*, Sep; 7, 2016, accessed September 8, 2016, http://time.com/4483018/elephant-sedative-overdose-death-ohio/.

398. Josh Katz, "Drug Deaths in America Are Rising Faster Than Ever," *New York Times*, June 5, 2017, accessed June 29, 2017, https://www.nytimes.com/interactive/2017/06/05/upshot/opioid-epidemic-drug-overdose-deaths-are-rising-faster-than-ever.html?mcubz=2.

399. Leo Shane III and Patricia Kime, "New VA Study Finds 20 Veterans Commit Suicide Each Day," *Military Times*, July 7, 2016, accessed September 8, 2016, http://www.militarytimes.com/story/veterans/2016/07/07/va-suicide-20-daily-research/86788332/. This is a figure that dispels the often quoted, but problematic, "22 a day" estimate yet substantiates the disturbing mental health crisis the number implied.

400. William White, *Swedenborg: His Life and Writings* (London: William White, 1856), 43.

401. Emanuel Swedenborg, *Divine Providence*, Standard., trans. William Wunsch (West Chester, PA: Swedenborg Foundation, 2009), 122.

402. P.M.H. Atwater, "17 Near-Dearth Experience Accounts," IANDS, May 18, 2015, accessed January 7, 2017, http://iands.org/ndes/nde-stories/17-nde-accounts-from-beyond-the-light.html.

403. Evelyn Underhill defines mysticism and mystics in this way: "Mysticism is the art of union with Reality. The mystic is a person who has attained that union in greater or less degree; or who aims at and believes in such attainment." Evelyn Underhill, *Practical Mysticism* (CreateSpace Independent Publishing Platform, 2013), 2, Kindle.

404. Emanuel Swedenborg, *The Essential Swedenborg: Basic Religious Teachings of Emanuel Swedenborg*, ed. Sigfried T. Synnestvedt (New York: Swedenborg Foundation, 1977), 16.

405. Ibid., 17.

406. Ibid., 16.

407. The Tempter brought Swedenborg into conflicting thought that tried to destroy his thought of the Holy Spirit.

408. He does not specify what kind of sound he heard. It must be sacred sound.

409. Rudolf Leonhard Tafel, *Documents concerning the life and character of Emanuel Swedenborg*, collected, translated, and annotated (London : Swedenborg Society, 1877), 158-159.

410. Ibid.

411. Swedenborg, *The Essential Swedenborg*, 13, 25-26.

412. Ibid., 26.

413. Ibid., 27-28.

414. Ibid., 28-29. See the next endnote.

415. Ibid., 29. A friend of mine raised this question to me: "Also, while not doubting the reality of Swedenborg's encounters with the dead - isn't this forbidden by scripture?"

    The following is my tentative understanding: The Bible (OT) does not allow us to contact low-level spirits in hell or Sheol in order to do sorcery, fortune telling, or oracles: "When you come into the land that the LORD your God is giving you, you must not learn to imitate the abhorrent practices of those nations. No one shall be found among you who makes a son or daughter pass through fire, or who practices divination, or is a soothsayer, or an augur, or a sorcerer, or one who casts spells, or who consults ghosts or spirits, or who seeks oracles from the dead. For whoever does these things is abhorrent to the LORD" (DEUT 18:9-12).

    In the New Testament, Jesus allows his disciples to meet dead saints (e.g., Peter, James, and John met Moses and Elijah: Matt 17:1-8). Also John in his spirit saw "the twenty-four elders fall before the one who is seated on the throne and worship the one who lives forever and ever; they cast their crowns before the throne," singing praises to the Lord (Rev 4:10) and John reported it to us.

    It seems that the Bible is more concerned about our imitating of the pagan practices of soothsaying, augury, sorcery, or witchcraft than our encountering of good angels or saints for noble purposes.

416. Ibid., 33-34.

417. Swedenborg, *Heaven and Hell*, 346.

418. Ibid., 349. There are many hells in accordance with different types of hellish people.

419. Ibid., 355.

420. Ibid., 453.

421. Swedenborg, *The Essential Swedenborg,* 106.

422. Swedenborg, *Heaven and Hell,* 398.

423. Ibid., 400.

424. Ibid., 399.

425. Ibid., 356.

426. Ibid., 403. When he says "a year," it confuses us. By it, he could mean an earthly year or a symbolic expression of heavenly duration such as the "thousand years" in the book of Revelation (Rev. 20:7).

427. Ibid., 409.

428. Ibid., 418.

429. Swedenborg, *The Essential Swedenborg,* 107-109.

430. George G. Ritchie, *My Life After Dying: Becoming Alive to Universal Love* (Norfolk, VA: Hampton Roads, 1991), 23.

431. Ibid.

432. Ibid.

433. Ibid., 24.

434. Swedenborg, *Heaven and Hell,* 363.

435. Ibid., 364.

436. Ibid., 380.

437. IANDS, "There Is No Hell. We All Go Home.," International Association For Near Death Studies, April 25, 2015, accessed August 16, 2016, http://iands.org/ndes/nde-stories/858-there-is-no-hell-we-all-go-home.html.

438. Jeffrey Long and Paul Perry, *God and the Afterlife: the Groundbreaking New Evidence for God and Near-Death Experience* (New York: HarperOne, 2016), 1568, Kindle.

439. Ibid.

440. Ibid., *God and the Afterlife,* 1547.

441. Swedenborg, *Heaven and Hell,* 456.

442. Ibid., 432.

443. Ibid., 28.

444. Ibid.

445. Ibid.

446. Swedenborg, *The Essential Swedenborg,* 160-161.

447. Ibid., 161. The italics are mine.

448. Ibid., 164. The italics are mine.

449. Emanuel Swedenborg, *A Brief Exposition of the Doctrine of the New Church,* Standard., ed. William Woofenden (West Chester, PA: Swedenborg Foundation, 2009), 223, www.swedenborg.com/wp-content/uploads/2013/03/swedenborg_foundation_brief_exposition.pdf.

450. Swedenborg, *The Essential Swedenborg,* 161. The italics are mine.

451. Swedenborg believes that the doctrine of the Trinity started with the Incarnation of Jesus, the truly Divine and the truly Human.

452. Swedenborg, *Heaven and Hell,* 29.

453. Ibid.

454. Long and Perry, *God and the Afterlife,* 673.

455. Ibid.

456. Swedenborg, *Heaven and Hell,* 427.

457. Ibid., 427-28.

458. Ibid., 428.

459. Ibid., 429.

460. Ibid., 429.

461. Ibid., 430.

462. Ibid., 431.

463. Swedenborg, *Heaven and Hell,* 32.

464. Ibid.

465. Ibid., 33.

466. Ibid., 33-34.

467. Swedenborg, *The Essential Swedenborg,* 140.

468. Emanuel Swedenborg, *Conjugal Love: Delights of Wisdom Relating to Conjugal Love Followed by Pleasures of Insanity Relating to Licentious Love,* ed. Louis H. Tafel, trans. Samuel Warren (West Chester, PA: Swedenborg Foundation, 2009), 134.

469. Swedenborg, *The Essential Swedenborg,* 141.

470. Ibid. 120.

471. Ibid., 45.

472. Ibid., 43.

473. Ibid., 30, 43.

474. Ibid., 36-37.

475. Ibid., 81.

476. Ibid., 94.

477. Ibid., 80.

478. Ibid., 81.

479. In the allegory of the cave, Plato likens people to prisoners chained in a cave, unable to who are behind the prisoners, hold up puppets that cast shadows on the wall of the cave. What the prisoners see and hear are shadows and echoes cast by objects that they do not see. They would be mistaken the shadows as the real things. Plato, *The Republic of Plato*, 2nd ed. (New York: Basic Books, 1991), 514a–520a.

480. Swedenborg, *The Essential Swedenborg,* 86.

481. Ibid., 95.

482. Emanuel Swedenborg, *A Swedenborg Sampler: Selections from Heaven and Hell, Divine Love and Wisdom, Divine Providence, True Christianity, Secrets of Heaven*, trans. Morgan Beard et al. (West Chester, Pa.: Swedenborg Foundation Press, ©2011), 153. Kindle 1192-1194.

483. Ibid., 157.

484. Ibid., 427.

485. "Kairos," *Greek Dictionary of the New Testament in The Exhaustive Concordance of the Bible: Showing Every Word of the Text of the Common English Version of the Canonical Books, and Every Occurrence of Each Word in Regular Order, Together with a Key-Word Comparison of Selected Word.* Ed. James Strong, (New York: Abingdon, 1981), 39. It means an opportune time, a "moment" or a "season" such as "harvest time."

486. "Ibid., 78. It points to a specific amount of time, such as a day or an hour.

487. http://people.bu.edu/wwildman/bce/tillich.htm

488. Swedenborg, *Heaven and Hell*, 129.

489. Ibid., 129.

490. Ibid., 130-131.

491. Ibid. Consequently, anything that is temporal for us changes into an idea of state for the angel. Spring and morning change into an idea of love and wisdom the way they are for angels in their first state; summer and noon change into an idea of love and wisdom as they are in the second state; autumn and evening, as they are in the third state; and night and winter into a concept of the kind of state that is characteristic in hell. This is why similar things are meant by these times in the Word. To understand the heavenly states further, please go to page 124

492. Ibid.

493. Ibid., 41-46, 50-51.

494. Swedenborg, *The Essential Swedenborg,* 113.

495. Ibid., 145.

496. Ibid., 160.

497. Swedenborg, *Heaven and Hell*, 157.

498. Ibid., 157.

499. Ibid., 158.

500. Ibid., 159.

501. Ibid., 29.

502. Ibid., 250.

503. Ibid., 256.

504. Nick Pisa, "The Pope Ends State of Limbo After 800 Years," *Telegraph*, April 23, 2007, accessed August 15, 2016, http://www.telegraph.co.uk/news/worldnews/1549439/The-Pope-ends-state-of-limbo-after-800-years.html.

505. Swedenborg, *Heaven and Hell*, 306.

506. Ibid., 307.

507. Ibid., 315.

508. Ibid., 319-320.

509. Ibid., 316.

510. Ibid., 320.

511. Ibid., 321.

512. Matthew Fox, *A Way to God: Thomas Merton's Creation Spirituality Journey* (Novato, CA: New World Library, 2016), 165-166.

513. Shulamith Shahar, *Growing Old in the Middle Ages: 'winter Clothes Us in Shadow and Pain'* (London: Routledge, 1997), 68, accessed August 14, 2016, http://www.contentreserve.com/titleinfo.asp?id={72114904-41f0-43fd-9a82-cb3063a9a8d9}&format=50.

514. Emanuel Swedenborg, *Divine Love and Wisdom*, portable new century ed., trans. George F. Dole New Century Edition Ser. (West Chester, Pa.: Swedenborg Foundation, 2010), N335.

515. Swedenborg, *Heaven and Hell*, 446.

516. Ibid., 449.

517. Ibid., 449-450.

518. IANDS, "There Is No Hell."

519. Swedenborg, *Heaven and Hell*, 459-60.

520. Ibid., 460-61.

521. Ibid., 462.

522. Ibid.

523. Ibid., 462-63.

524. Ibid., 464.

525. Ibid., 465.

526. Ibid., 471.

527. Ibid., 473.

528. Ibid., 474.

529. Ibid., 477.

530. Ibid., 483.

531. Ibid.

532. Ibid., 484.

533. Ibid.

534. All the communities of hell according to the types and species of their evils. Further, there is a corresponding community of hell underneath every community of heaven, and this opposing correspondence yields

an equilibrium. These genii constantly attack heaven and trying to destroy it. See Swedenborg, *Heaven and Hell,* 499.

535. Ibid., 484-85.

536. Swedenborg, *Heaven and Hell,* 215.

537. Emanuel Swedenborg, *Spiritual Diary* (publication place: @AnnieRose-Books, 2016), 3525.

538. Emanuel Swedenborg and Samuel M. Warren, *A Compendium of the Theological Writings of Emanuel Swedenborg* (New York: Swedenborg Foundation, 1974), 611.

539. Ibid., 612.

540. Ibid., 615.

541. Emanuel Swedenborg, *Divine Providence,* portable new century ed., trans. George F. Dole New Century Edition (West Chester, Pa.: Swedenborg Foundation, ©2010), 321.3.

542. Ibid.

543. Swedenborg, *A Swedenborg Sampler: Selections from Heaven and Hell, Divine Love and Wisdom, Divine Providence, True Christianity, Secrets of Heaven,* trans. Morgan Beard et al. (West Chester, Pa.: Swedenborg Foundation Press, 2011), 2583.

544. Ibid., 308.

545. Swedenborg, *Divine Love and Wisdom: Portable: the Portable New Century Edition (New Century Edition),* Portable ed. (West Chester, Pa.: Swedenborg Foundation Publishers, 2010), 152.

546. Swedenborg, *Secrets of Heaven: Volume 2,* portable new century ed., trans. Lisa Hyatt Cooper (West Chester, Pa.: Swedenborg Foundation, 2012), 1226.

547. Swedenborg, *A Swedenborg Sampler,* 1282.

548. Swedenborg, *The Essential Swedenborg,* 167.

549. Swedenborg, *Secrets of Heaven:* Volume 5, portable new century ed., trans. John Clowes, rev. and ed. John Faulkner Potts, (West Chester, Pa.: Swedenborg Foundation, 2009), 4227:4.

550. Swedenborg, *Secrets of Heaven:* Volume 11, 10299.

551. B. H. Streeter and A. J. Appasamy, *The Sadhu: A Study in Mysticism and Practical Religion* (London: MacMillan & Co., 1921), 2-4.

552. Ibid., 5.

553. Ibid., 5-6.

554. Ibid., 2.

555. Ibid., 6.

556. Ibid., 6-7.

557. Rebecca Jane Parker, *Sádhu Sundar Singh, Called of God* (London: Fleming H. Revell Company, 1920), 23-24.

558. Ibid., 26-29.

559. Ibid., 93.

560. Ibid., 93-94.

561. Ibid., 64-66.

562. Ibid., 67-68.

563. Sundar Singh, *The Christian Witness of Sadhu Sundar Singh: A Collection of His Writings*, ed. T. Dayanandan Francis (Chennai, India: The Christian Literature Society Press, 1989), 27-28.

564. Ibid., 28.

565. Ibid., 241.

566. Toward the end of his life, he received a home from his converted father.

567. Ibid., 3.

568. Ibid., 16.

569. Kathryn Linskoog, "Links in a Golden Chain," The Golden Key, accessed January 3, 2017, http://www.george-macdonald.com/articles/sundar_singh.html, and Dibin Samuel, "Mahatma Gandhi and Christianity," *Christian Today*, August 14 2008, 1, accessed January 3, 2017, http://www.christiantoday.co.in/article/mahatma.gandhi.and.christianity/2837.htm.

570. Streeter and Appasamy, *The Sadhu*, 54.

571. Ibid.

572. Ibid., 54-55. According to the authors, elsewhere, the Sadhu does not conceive the Spirit as impersonal.

573. Ibid., 237.

574. Singh, *Sadhu Sundar Singh*, 249.

575. Ibid.

576. Ibid., 254-255.

577. Ibid., 255.

578. Ibid., 255-256.

579. Ibid., 251-252.

580. Ibid., 256-257.

581. Streeter and Appasamy, *The Sadhu*, 126.

582. Ibid., 126-127.

583. Ibid., 127.

584. Ibid., 127-128.

585. Singh, *Sadhu Sundar Singh*, 265.

586. Ibid., 265-266.

587. Ibid., 270.

588. Ibid., 270-271.

589. Ibid., 271.

590. Ibid., 267-268.

591. Ibid., 268.

592. Ibid.

593. Ibid., 268-269.

594. Ibid., 269.

595. Ibid.

596. Ibid., 271-272.

597. Ibid., 272.

598. Ibid., 272-273.

599. Ibid., 260.

600. Ibid., 280.

601. Ibid.

602. Ibid., 281.

603. Ibid., 274.

604. Ibid.

605. Ibid., 275.

606. Ibid.
607. Ibid., 275-276.
608. Ibid., 276.
609. Ibid.
610. Ibid.
611. Ibid.
612. Ibid.
613. Ibid., 276-277.
614. Ibid., 125.
615. Ibid.
616. Ibid.
617. Ibid.
618. Ibid.
619. Ibid., 284.
620. Ibid.
621. Ibid.
622. Ibid., 277.
623. Ibid.
624. Ibid., 278.
625. Ibid.
626. Ibid., 279.
627. Ibid.
628. Ibid.
629. Ibid., 279-280.
630. Ibid., 282.
631. Ibid.
632. Ibid., 282-283.
633. Ibid., 283.
634. Ibid.
635. Ibid., 287.
636. Ibid., 632.
637. Sundar Singh, "A Message On Prayer," Who is This Jesus?, accessed June 22, 2017, https://sites.google.com/site/whoisthisjesus/prayer.

638. Singh, *Sadhu Sundar Singh*, 4.

639. Ibid., 3-4.

640. Kenneth Ring, *Heading Toward Omega* (Amazon Digital Services LLC, 2012), 2350, Kindle. He says, "Each of these elements is supported by the data from one or more items of the RBI (Religious Belief Inventory) and LCQ (Life Changes Questionnaire) as well as from the spoken or written comments of Omega NDErs (his Omega sample of NDErs)."

641. Ibid., 2378.

642. Long, *God and the Afterlife*, 2730.

643. The Editors of Encyclopedia Britannica, "Brahman: Hindu Concept," *Encyclopedia Britannica*, accessed August 20, 2016, https://www.britannica.com/topic/brahman-Hindu-concept.

644. The closest one is the eighth manifestation of Brahman out of twelve. The eighth manifestation is Trimurthis. In it, Brahman became incarnate into three gods: Brahma (creator), Vishnu (preserver), and Shiva (destroyer). Jayaram V., "The 12 Manifestations of Brahman," Hinduwebsite.com, accessed August 20, 2016, http://www.hinduwebsite.com/buzz/the-twelve-manifestations-of-brahman.asp.

645. Atwater, *The New Children and Near-Death Experiences*, 1185.

646. *Catholic Encyclopedia*, "Purgatory," accessed August 11, 2016, http://www.newadvent.org/cathen/p.htm.

647. Ibid., 492.

648. Streeter and Appasamy, *The Sadhu*, 116.

649. Howard Storm, e-mail to Andrew Park, August 31, 2016.

650. Dinesh D'Souza, *Life After Death: the Evidence* (Washinton, DC: Regnery, 2015).

651. T. L. Housholder, *Near Death Experiences: Power, Love, and a Sound Mind: the Most Exciting and Revealing Near Death Experience* (T. L. Housholder), 544.

652. Ibid., 546.

653. Ibid., 548.

654. Anonymous, "Never Wanted to Leave the Presence," IANDS, April 25, 2015, accessed October 29, 2016, http://iands.org/ndes/nde-stories/

iands-nde-accounts/736-never-wanted-to-leave-the-presence.html?tm
pl=component&print=1&page=.

655. Prana Miller, "2015 Conference Call," International Association For
Near Death Studies, December 11, 2015, accessed October 29, 2016,
http://iands.org/groups/group-affiliation-info/group-leader-con-
ference-calls/2015-conf-call-calendar.html?highlight=WyJ1bmNvb-
mRpdGlvbmFsIiwibG92ZSIsImxvdmVkIiwibG92aW5nIiwibG92ZX-
MiLCJsb3ZlbHkiLCJsb3ZlJ3MiLCJsb3ZlJyIsIidsb3ZlJyIsIi.

656. (with reference to chaos theory) the phenomenon whereby a minute
localized change in a complex system can have large effects elsewhere.
Oxford Living Dictionaries, "Butterfly Effect," accessed December 12,
2016, https://en.oxforddictionaries.com/definition/butterfly_effect.

657. Jeffrey Long and Paul Perry, *God and the Afterlife: the Groundbreaking
New Evidence for God and Near-Death Experience* (New York: HarperOne,
2016), 2716, Kindle.

658. J. Steve Miller, *Near-Death Experiences as Evidence for the Existence of God
and Heaven: a Brief Introduction in Plain Language* (Acworth: Wisdom
Creek Press, 2012), 1490–1694, Kindle.

659. Bruce Greyson, *Consciousness Independent of the Brain*, November 9, 2014,
Platos Cave, accessed October 29, 2016, https://www.youtube.com/
watch?v=en-3Bz1RMig.

660. Ibid.

661. Singh, *Sadhu Sundar Singh*, 249.

662. Ibid.

663. Swedenborg, *The Essential Swedenborg*, 140.

664. Ibid., 141.

665. They believe that in the end everyone will be saved because God is love.

666. Emanuel Swedenborg, *Heaven and Hell* (New York: Swedenborg
Foundation, 1984), 474.

667. "Gordon Allen Before His NDE," *Gordon Allen*, http://gordonallen.org/
index.php?option=com_k2&view=item&id=25:gordon-allen-before-
his-nde&Itemid=54.

668. "Gordon Allen," accessed August 6, 2016, http://www.gordonallen.org/.
669. "8064. shamayim," Brown-Driver-Briggs Hebrew and English Lexicon, Unabridged, Electronic Database, http://biblehub.com/hebrew/8064.htm.
670. Gerhard Kittel and Gerhard Friedrich, *Theological Dictionary of the New Testament (Volume I)* (Grand Rapids, MI: Wm. B. Eerdmans Publishing Co., 1964), 686.
671. James Orr. "Heavens, New (and Earth, New)," *International Standard Bible Encyclopedia,* http://www.studylight.org/encyclopedias/isb/view.cgi?n=4191&search=Heavens%20New%20and%20Earth%20New#Heavens New and Earth New.
672. "Paliggenesia," Lexicon: Strong, accessed January 9, 2016, https://www.blueletterbible.org/lang/lexicon/lexicon.cfm?t=kjv&strongs=g3824.
673. Orr, "Heavens."
674. Ibid.
675. George A. Butterick. *Interpreter's Dictionary of the Bible,* vol. 2, (Nashville: Abingdon, 1969), 552.
676. Kittel and Friedrich, *Theological Dictionary*, 543-535.
677. Louis Ginzberg, *The Legends of the Jews - Vol. I from the Creation to Jacob* (CreateSpace Independent Publishing Platform, 2012), 195, Kindle.
678. Ibid., 204-205. The rest of the Jewish heavens are: "The first, the one visible to man, has no function except that of covering up the light during the night time; therefore it disappears every morning. The planets are fastened to the second of the heavens; in the third the manna is made for the pious in the hereafter; the fourth contains the celestial Jerusalem together with the Temple, in which Michael ministers as high priest, and offers the souls of the pious as sacrifices. In the fifth heaven, the angel hosts reside, and sing the praise of God, though only during the night, for by day it is the task of Israel on earth to give glory to God on high. The sixth heaven is an uncanny spot; there originate most of the trials and visitations ordained for the earth and its inhabitants. Snow lies heaped up there and hail; there are lofts full of noxious dew, magazines stocked with storms, and cellars holding reserves of

smoke. Doors of fire separate these celestial chambers, which are under the supervision of the archangel Metatron. Their pernicious contents defiled the heavens until David's time. The pious king prayed God to purge His exalted dwelling of whatever was pregnant with evil; it was not becoming that such things should exist near the Merciful One. Only then they were removed to the earth."

679. Swedenborg, *Heaven and Hell*, 29, 31.

680. Burnett Hillman Streeter and A. J. Appasamy, *The Message of Sadhu Sundar Singh: A Study in Mysticism On Practical Religion* (New York: MacMillan, 1921), 116-17.

681. RICHARD BAUCKHAM, "Hades, Hell," Anchor. I couldn't find this source with the information provided.

682. Ibid.

683. Ibid.; 2 Macc. 6:23; *1 En.* 102:5; 103:7; *Sib. Or.* 1:81-84; *Ps.-Phoc.*112-113; *2 Bar.* 23:4; *T. Ab.* A 8:9; 19:7.

684. Ibid.; Wis. 1:12-16; 16:13; *S. Sol.* 16:2; Rev. 6:8; 20:13.

685. Ibid.

686. Ibid.

687. Ibid.

688. Acts 2:27: "For you will not abandon my soul to Hades, or let your Holy One experience corruption"; Acts 2:31: "Foreseeing this, David spoke of the resurrection of the Messiah, saying, 'He was not abandoned to Hades, nor did his flesh experience corruption.'"

689. Matt. 11:23: "And you, Capernaum, will you be exalted to heaven? No, you will be brought down to Hades. For if the deeds of power done in you had been done in Sodom, it would have remained until this day."

690. *1 En.* 51:3; *4 Ezra* 4:42; 7:32; *2 Bar.* 42:8; 50:2; *Ps.-Philo* 3:10; 33:3.

691. Ibid. Rev. 20:13: And the sea gave up the dead that were in it, Death and Hades gave up the dead that were in them, and all were judged according to what they had done"; Rev. 6:8: "I looked and there was a pale green horse! Its rider's name was Death, and Hades followed with him; they were given authority over a fourth of the earth, to kill with sword, famine, and pestilence, and by the wild animals of the earth."

692. Wis. 16:13; 3 Macc. 5:51; *So. Sol.* 8:6; cf. *Ap. Pet.* 4:3.

693. Ibid. cf. Wis. 16:13; *Ap. Pet.* 4:3, which probably reflects a Jewish description of resurrection; Ps. 107:16 may have been interpreted in this way. Ps. 107:16: "For he shatters the doors of bronze, and cuts in two the bars of iron."

694. Ibid. Matt. 16:18: "And I tell you, you are Peter, and on this rock I will build my church, and the gates of Hades will not prevail against it."

695. Ibid.

696. Ibid.

697. Ibid.; *1 En.* 26–27; 54:1-6; 56:1-4; 90:24-27.

698. Ibid.; 2 Esdr. 7:26-38; *4 Ezra* 7:26-38; *Ascen. Is.* 4:14-18; cf. *Sib. Or.* 4.179-91.

699. Ibid.

700. Ibid.

701. Ibid.

702. The Editors of Encyclopaedia Britanica, "Tartarus," *Encyclopaedia Britanica*, accessed on July 14, 2015, http://www.britannica.com/topic/Tartarus; "5020. *tartaroó*," http://biblehub.com/greek/5020.htm.

703. Orr, "Hell," http://www.studylight.org/encyclopedias/isb/view.cgi?n=4232.

704. "5769. *olam*," http://biblehub.com/hebrew/5769.htm.

705. E. Jenni, "Time," in *The Interpreter's Dictionary of the Bible: An Illustrated Encyclopedia Identifying and Explaining All Proper Names and Significant Terms and Subjects in the Holy Scriptures, Including the Apocrypha, with Attention to Archaeologica*, ed. George Arthur Buttrick (Nashville: Abingdon, 1976), 4:647.

706. Ibid.

707. Kittel and Friedrich, *Theological Dictionary*, 208-209.

708. Paul Tillich, *Systematic Theology, Vol. 1* (Chicago: University Of Chicago Press, 1973), 188.

709. Ibid., 275.

710. Ibid.

711. Ibid., 275.

712. Raymond E. Brown contends that the synoptic gospels count eternal life as something received at the final judgment, or a future age (Mark 10:30, Matthew 18:8-9) but the Gospel of John understands eternal life as a present possibility, as in John 5:24. Cited in Donald E. Gowan, ed., *The Westminster Theological Wordbook of the Bible* (Louisville: Westminster John Knox, 2003), 115-116.

713. D. A. Carson, *The Gospel According to John* (Leicester, England.: Eerdmans, 1991), 556.

714. Jürgen Moltmann, *The Coming of God: Christian Eschatology*. Trans. Margaret Kohl (Minneapolis: Augsburg, 2004), 246-249.

715. Ibid., 248. Although following Barth's line, Moltmann surpasses Barth by positioning the ultimate salvation of all, including Satan and the fallen angels: "In the divine Judgment all sinners, the wicked and the violent, the murderers and the children of Satan, the Devil and the fallen angels will be liberated and saved from their deadly perdition through transformation into their true created being, because God remains true to himself, and does not give up what he has once created and affirmed, or allow it to be lost," Ibid., 255. Therefore, his position is close to True Universalism.

716. Ibid., 249.

717. Ibid., 248.

718. Robin Parry, "Theological Scribbles: Robin Parry Scribbles the Odd Thought On Various Theological Issues and Books.," Theological Scribbles, accessed August 29, 2009, http://theologicalscribbles. blogspot.com/2009/08/i-am-evangelical-universalist.html.

719. Thomas Talbott is professor Emeritus of Philosophy at Willamette University in Salem, Oregon and the author of *The Inescapable Love of God* (Salem: Universal, 1999).

720. William Brennan, "The Evangelical Universalist Association," *The Evangelical Univeralist Association*, accessed November 14, 2015, http:// www.biblicaluniversalism.org/EUA.html.

721. Ibid.

722. "2309. *theló*," http://biblehub.com/greek/2309.htm.

723. Bonenfant, R. J. (2001). "A child's encounter with the devil: An unusual near-death experience with both blissful and frightening elements ". Journal of Near-Death Studies 20(2), pp. 87-100.

724. Maurice Rawlings, *Beyond Death's Door* (NY: Bantam, 1985), 3.

725. Ibid., 4.

726. Ibid.

727. Ibid., 5.

728. P.M.H. Atwater, "Near Death Experiences in Hell," Mind Power News, accessed August 8, 2016, http://www.mindpowernews.com/NearDeathInHell.htm.

729. Nancy Rynes, *Awakenings from the Light: 12 Life Lessons from a Near Death Experience* (North Charleston, South Carolina: CreateSpace Independent Publishing Platform, 2015). Kindle Edition.

730. http://www.amycollette.com/podcast/pp05-author-nancy-rynes.

731. http://thespiritway.blogspot.com/2014/03/how-i-saw-and-experienced-heaven.html.

732. Ibid.

733. Ibid.

734. Ibid.

735. Ibid.

736. Ibid.

737. Nancy Rynes, *Awakenings from the Light*, 526. Kindle.

738. Ibid., 560.

739. Ibid.

740. Ibid., 564.

741. Tracy H. Goza Ph.D., *I Heart Heaven: a Psychotherapist's Biblical Validation for Near-Death Experiences* (Grand Rapids, MI: Credo House Publishers, 2015), 1.

742. Bob Taylor, "A Wake-Up Call to the Church," http://www.wor.org/Books/w/A_Wake-up_Call_to_the_Church.htm accessed April 1, 2016

743. Goza, *I Heart Heaven*, 573.

744. Bob Taylor, "A Wake-Up Call to the Church."

745. Ibid.
746. Ibid.
747. Ibid.
748. Ibid.
749. Ibid.
750. Ibid.
751. Jeffrey Long and Paul Perry, *God and the Afterlife: The Groundbreaking New Evidence for God and Near-Death Experience* (New York, NY: HarperOne, 2016), 2353.
752. Long and Perry, *God and the Afterlife*, 2353-2354.

Made in the USA
Coppell, TX
28 July 2020